Migrant Lives

Migrant Lives

edited by

Radhika Chopra

PENGUIN ENTERPRISE

An imprint of Penguin Random House

PENGUIN ENTERPRISE

USA | Canada | UK | Ireland | Australia
New Zealand | India | South Africa | China

Penguin Enterprise is a part of the Penguin Random House group of companies whose addresses can be found at global.penguinrandomhouse.com

Published by Penguin Random House India Pvt. Ltd.
4th Floor, Capital Tower 1, MG Road,
Gurugram 122 002, Haryana, India

Penguin Random House India

First published in Penguin Enterprise by Penguin Random House India 2022.
Penguin Enterprise is the custom-publishing imprint of Penguin Random House India.

10 9 8 7 6 5 4 3 2 1

The views and opinions expressed in this book are the authors' own. The facts are as reported by them which have been verified to the extent possible. The publishers are not in any way liable for the same. The stories in this book are based on research and interviews, however some names and identifying details have been changed to protect the privacy of the people involved.

ISBN 978-06-70093-58-8

Typeset by Raghav Khattar
Printed at Thomson Press India Ltd, New Delhi

www.penguin.co.in

Contents

Acknowledgements

The research for this book was made possible by the grant awarded by the Indian Council of Social Science Research (ICSSR) and the Economic and Social Research Council (ESRC), UK, under the Joint Collaborative Research Programme on Urban Transformation in India [ES/R006997/1 and ICSSR-ESRC Call I/ UTI/JRP-3/2018.IC]. Both Principal Investigators, Prof. Radhika Chopra and Dr Jeevan Sharma of the Project "*From the Margins: Exploring Low Income Migrant Workers Access to Basic Services*" would like to acknowledge the generous grant that enabled collaborative research between the University of Delhi and the University of Edinburgh. The project team included partners from the North-East Network (India), and the University of Essex (UK), and project research fellows.

All the members of the project team would like to thank the organizations, in Guwahati and Jalandhar, who shared their knowledge and expertise with us. We are very grateful for their help. We are deeply indebted to our respondents in the field. This book would not have been possible without their engagement with the research and their patience with the researchers.

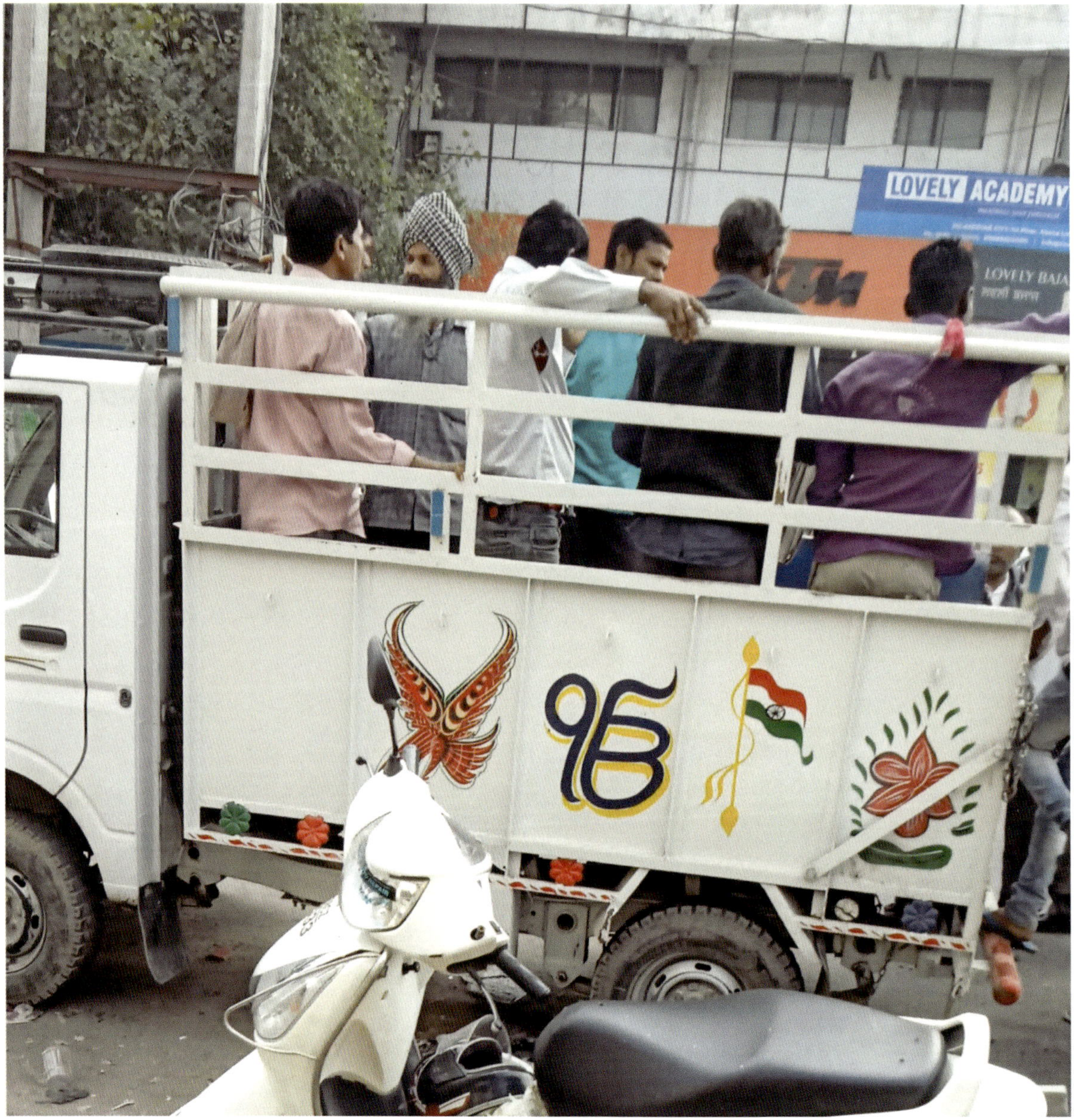
LOVELY ACADEMY
LOVELY BAJA

Introduction

Migrant lives are rarely photographed. In the immediate aftermath of the total lockdown in India in 2020, photographs and television images of thousands and thousands of migrants walking down highways hoping to reach their village-homes, shocked viewers. The 2020 photographs were a window into a world of people we don't usually see. Visual reportage of one of the largest reverse migrations in history, brought Indians in general, and middle-class urban Indians in particular, in touch with migrants. The dramatic newspaper photographs and televised images were a kind of contact zone between two categories of people – those who live securely in cities and others whose lives and livelihoods are perpetually precarious.

Non-resident Indians are extensively chronicled and celebrated in literature and cinema. By contrast, the almost total absence of a visual record of internal migrants severely affects them. Despite the fact that their labour is essential to running our cities, internal migrants are habitually overlooked, literally and metaphorically, by just about everyone, including policy makers and urban citizens. A UNESCO (2013; p.4) study observed that internal migrants are a neglected segment of India's population. It needed a pandemic for Indian city dwellers to realize the vacuum in their knowledge about internal migrants.

What impels people to migrate? For many, it's the lack of livelihood in their places of origin. Figures on poverty in India tell us that roughly 34 per cent of rural Indians live below the poverty line. By the last Census count, over 56 per cent of urban male migrants moved to cities in search of employment. 45 million Indians, nearly 38 per cent of the total population, moved outside their district of birth in search of employment and economic opportunities. For many Indians, migration is not a choice but a compulsion, an index of poverty crossed with extreme need.

A range of surveys and statistics (Census figures, NSSO data, village level surveys) suggest that moving to find work is a clear, identifiable pattern in internal migration. Classically, rural migrants moved to cities in search of work, but small town to metropolis is an increasingly significant pattern. Rural-to-rural movement is a predominant pattern in seasonal migration. Rural migrants remain within the confines of the informal, non-documented economy "making them some of the most vulnerable working groups, which further exclude them from social security benefits and even basic rights at the workplace" (Rajan et al, 2020; p.1023).

A major segment of internal migrants, almost 62 per cent, don't go far, and usually move within their own districts. Poorer households of the marginalized, especially those of the Scheduled Tribes and Scheduled Castes, are over-represented in short-term migration flows (Abbas and Varma, 2014). When the poor migrate, they leave for very short durations, and migrate nearer home where employment opportunities are sparse (Abbas and Varma, 2014; p.2; Coffey et al., 2015; Rajan et al., 2020). The poor simply cannot afford to move, though move they must.

A majority among all internal migrants work in the informal sector. Unprotected and unrecognized, they are unable to access social security programmes like the public distribution of foodgrains under the Public Distribution System, housing or health insurance, which require identity papers and residential proof as a precondition to register in these schemes. Living away from their place of origin and their electoral constituencies, a large number of internal migrants, unable to vote, remain politically voiceless. Though critical to urban development, urban policies and programmes ignore the fact of migration and the political personhood of migrants.

Studies of cross-border migration have theorized that without political recognition, migration almost always involves loss of rights and security (Nail, 2015). This is as true for internal migrants as it is for cross-border, transnational migrants. Every possible piece of evidence and data tells us that people who migrate *within* the boundaries of a single nation state are acutely and adversely affected by movement. We were made witness to the brutal consequences of neglect by the 2020 media images of migrants on the highways. Visual reports brought the loss of rights and the lack of care to the surface.

Seeing the Migrant

The 2020 images of walking migrants raise a fundamental question – why were migrants walking back home? In 'normal' circumstances, migrants do not return home *en masse*. In the normal course of events, the largest number who return home are men from the older age group – those above the age of sixty. Younger male internal migrants cannot afford to return, until age goes against them (Dhar and Bhagat, 2020). Migrants from poorer sections rarely return. There is a clear pattern to reverse migration. The 2020 mass reverse migration of whole families, of the young and the old, women, men and children, wasn't normal.

That's the thing about photographs. They bring neglected issues to the surface. Photographs create a contact zone, a kind of social space for people divided by extreme hierarchies (Pratt, 1991). Photographs enable us to see differences between us but also raise the question: from whose perspective were the 2020 photographs being seen? Even a cursory look at the photographs makes clear that the walking migrants didn't really have a choice of how they wanted to be viewed. The photographs are from 'our' point of view, evidence of the power to show, the power to view and the power to point at what needs to be seen, even to decide what can be overlooked or taken seriously. That power lies not with migrants in the image, but with experts and crews equipped with cameras, lighting, mikes, the multiple paraphernalia and technologies of photography. And then there's you and me, the viewers of these expertly taken photographs. We are the experts who make sense of other lives.

Despite the obvious power imbalances between photographers and walking migrants, Mary Louise Pratt's view of the photograph as a contact zone (1991) does allow us to think through photographs. For a moment, the photograph as contact zone shifts the balance toward the migrant 'in' the image to ask a slightly modified question. Given that cameras are usually in the hands of someone else, is there any space within the frame for migrant subjects to show themselves in ways they want to be seen? Perhaps that wasn't possible in the images published in newspapers, of emaciated bodies with meagre bundles and thin children walking down highways.

But we might consider other ways of taking photographs where we are able to see the point Pratt was making. The photographs in *Migrant Lives* are not reportage. The images emerged from research done as part of a collaborative project "*From the Margins: Exploring Low Income Migrant Workers Access to Basic Services*" between the University of Delhi and the University of Edinburgh, funded by the ESRC and the ICSSR that emphasized urban transformations. The photographs were taken over a period of two years, from 2018, through the course of field-based research in two cities which have significant migrant populations – Jalandhar in Punjab and Guwahati in Assam. The intention of the visual ethnography was to translate the statistics and enumerations into a visual language, to illuminate the conditions of precariousness endured by those left behind by economic change and urban transformations. Tightly focused fieldwork was necessary to make precarity visually evident and translate the everyday contexts of precarity into images. The photographs of *Migrant Lives* begin with two questions: Can insecurity be communicated? What is the visual language to elucidate the conditions of precarity? The images included in *Migrant Lives* are taken both by ethnographers and by migrants to spell out and communicate what migrants felt was significant about their worlds. The visual documents of this book are a two-way process of exchange between migrants and researchers, both trying to illuminate migrant lives.

Unlike the distant view of newspaper and televised images, the photographs of living, loving and working in the city in *Migrant Lives* are not perspectives from 'afar'. The photographs are a nascent beginning toward creating reciprocity between migrants and anthropologists through the image as contact zone. An important thread of the visual story is the fact that if we look, we can see the complexities of insecurity. Without overt statement, everyday dimensions of precarity and how it is lived can be – and are – communicated, made visually apparent, by those in the photograph, in front of the camera.

Unlike professional photographers, the intention of an anthropologist isn't to be a photographer. In fact, anthropologists are a bit apologetic about their field photographs and don't think they're good enough to publish. Despite the hesitation, fieldwork photographs are significant in one important respect. Most images are examined and analyzed *after* the fieldwork is over. This post-facto aspect of fieldwork photographs produces a very interesting perspective on the image. It shows two sets of 'intentions' in the frame. On one hand, the intention to capture a 'typical' instance of migrant life. On the other, to treat the camera lens like a 'microphone' into which, or through which, migrants 'speak'. Speaking visually is apparent in direct looks, gestures toward the camera, or sometimes continuing to work despite the inquisitive presence of the camera. Not stopping 'for' the camera conveys the absolute control work has on migrant lives – to stop is to suggest the leisure to stop and pose. Precarity doesn't allow the luxury of pause.

Migrant Lives – The Broader Picture

Looking at the photographs together, it is hard to ignore the disenfranchisement of internal migrants. We associate transnational immigrants with the loss of citizenship and the loss of rights that are inherent to mobility. But what we see in the photographs of *Migrant Lives* are people who move *within* the borders of India. The images are of internal migrants – citizens all – being unmade as the undocumented, unrecognized 'half citizens' during moments of crisis like the pandemic, or displaced by infrastructural development, or when they move – as so many do – to escape extreme poverty.

Migrants without whose labour cities could not function are the army of labour whose lives are perpetually precarious, always on the brink of job loss. Rendering a population surplus to requirements that can be called up whenever needed is the very condition of urban transformations. The photographs of the unprecedented reverse migration of 2020 starkly show us an entire urban population ruthlessly disenfranchised into unemployable or semi-employed "hands" (Marx, 1976; p. 786). Without migration, from the rural to the city, from city to city, from country to country (what Marx calls the 'floating population'), urban transformation would not happen. A population routinely declared surplus by mobility is the pivot upon which urban transformation turns.

The literature on migration lays bare the conditions which underwrite migration. Informed by this literature, *Migrant Lives* asks: Who is this person in the photograph? The images in this book are not tamed by written text; they are a visual account of migrant lives, as migrants and ethnographers saw them. Speaking through photographs, migrants convey their point of view in visual languages and invite us to consider their lives.

References

Abbas, Rameez and Divya Varma. *Internal Labor Migration in India Raises Integration Challenges for Migrants*, 2014 (migrationpolicy.org (https://www.migrationpolicy.org)

Bhagat, R. B. *Migrants' (denied) right to the city, in urban policies and the right to the City in India: Rights, responsibilities and citizenship* (pp. 48–57). UNECSO and Centre de Sciences Humaines., 2011, (pp, 48-57)

2011, Office of the Registrar General & Census Commissioner, Government of India, 2011.

Coffey, Diane John Papp and Dean Spears. Short-Term Labor Migration from Rural North India: Evidence from New Survey Data, *Population Research and Policy Review*, Vol. 34, No. 3 June 2015, (pp. 361-380)

Dhar, Bidita and R. B. Bhagat. Return migration in India: internal and international dimensions, *Migration and Development*, 2020. (DOI: 10.1080/21632324.2020.1809263)

Mahapatro, Sandhya Rani. Internal Migration: Emerging Patterns. *Handbook of internal migration in India*, ed. S.I. Rajan and M. Sumeetha, 2020, 80–92

Marx, Karl. 1976 [1867]. *Capital: A Critique of Political Economy Vol. 1*. Translated by Ben Fowkes. London: Penguin: New Left Review.

Nail, Thomas, *The figure of the migrant*, Stanford: Stanford University Press, 2015

Nail, Thomas, *The Political Centrality of the Migrant* 2018 .(https://www.e-ir.info/2018/08/17/the-political-centrality-of-the-migrant)

Neetha, N. Making of Female Breadwinners: Migration and social networking of women Domestics in Delhi. *Economic and Political Weekly* 39: 1681–1688, 2004.

Parida, J.K., and S. Madheswaran. Unexplored facets of female migration. *Handbook of internal migration in India*, ed. S.I. Rajan and M. Sumeetha. New Delhi: Sage Publications. 2020.

Pratt, Mary Louise. Arts of the Contact Zone. *Profession*, 1991, 33-40. Accessed 12 March 2021. (http://www.jstor.org/stable/25595469).

Rajan, S.I., and P. Neetha (eds.). 2018. *Migration, Gender and Care Economy*. Abingdon: Routledge.

Rajan, S. Irudaya , P. Sivakumar, Aditya Srinivasan. The COVID 19 Pandemic and Internal Labour Migration in India: A 'Crisis of Mobility', *The Indian Journal of Labour Economics*, 2020, 63:1021–1039 (https://doi.org/10.1007/s41027-020-00293-8)

UNESCO *Social inclusion of internal migrants in India*, June 2013 (https://unesdoc.unesco.org/ark:/48223/pf0000223702)

Getting to Work

Commuting

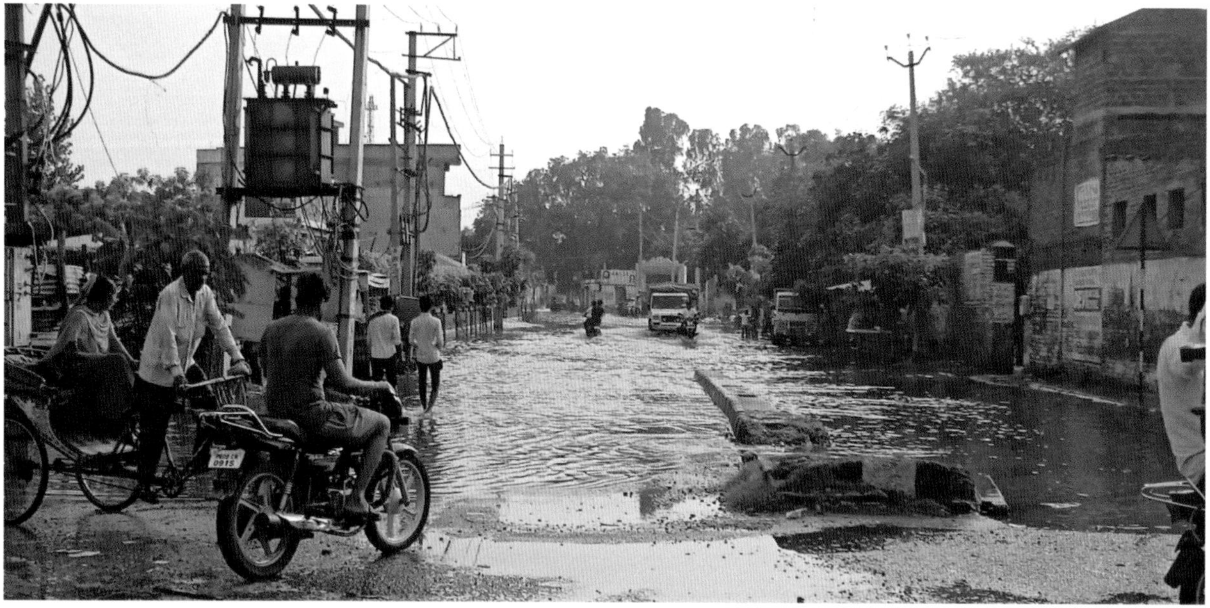

Once they arrive in a city, migrants need to move constantly; to find work and then, to get to work. Travelling to work is vital to livelihoods and earnings. Travel is labour intensive and often risky. In many cities, industrial zones and factories are on the outskirts of city limits, with irregular transport facilities. It requires agility and endurance to get to work, reflecting the insecurity entangled with earning a livelihood. Every possible way to get to work is used. Small vans packed to the gills, hanging precariously on rickety auto *rikshas*, or waiting for 'locals', the trains that run between cities or suburbs bringing in labour and workers are ways of commuting. As soon as they can afford it, migrants invest in bicycles and motorbikes to get to work. Many just have to walk to work.

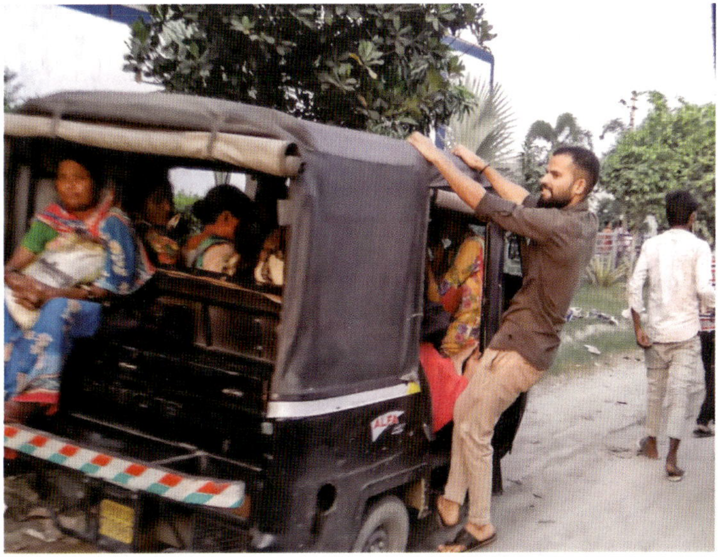

Hazardous travel is part of daily travel routines.

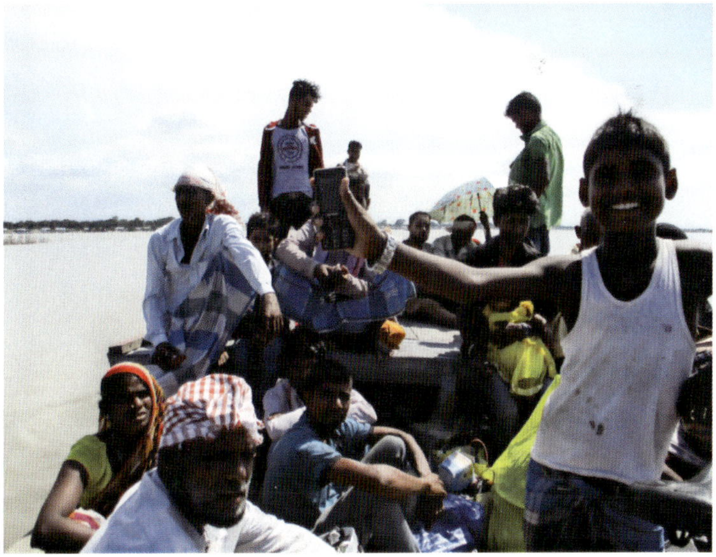

Commuting by boat.

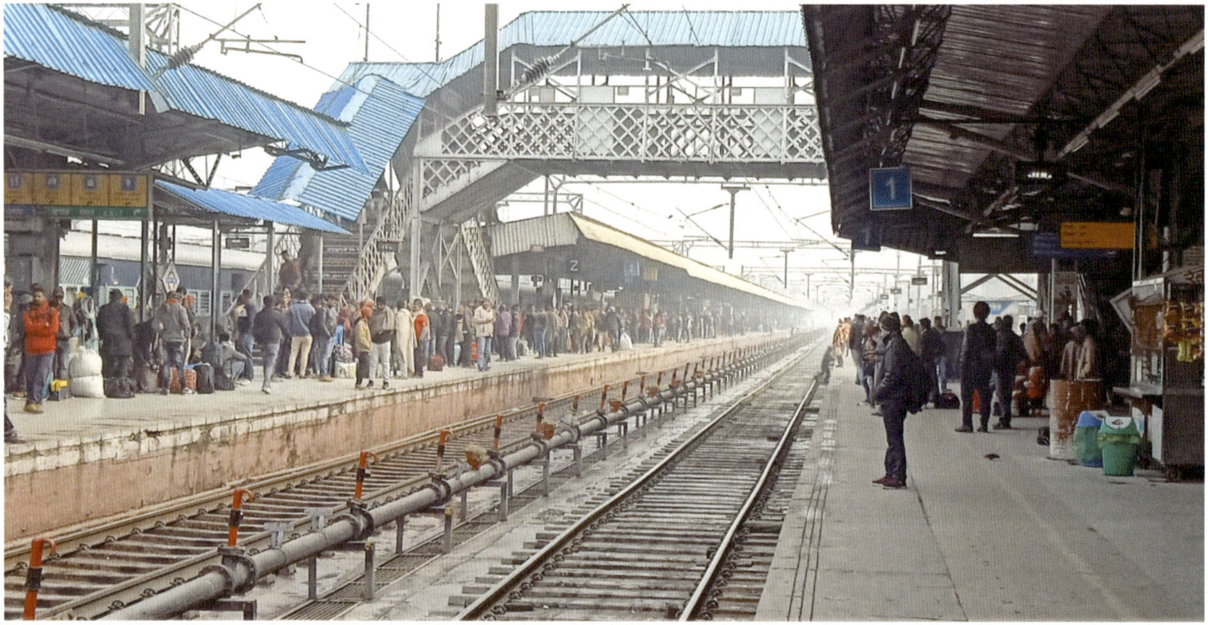

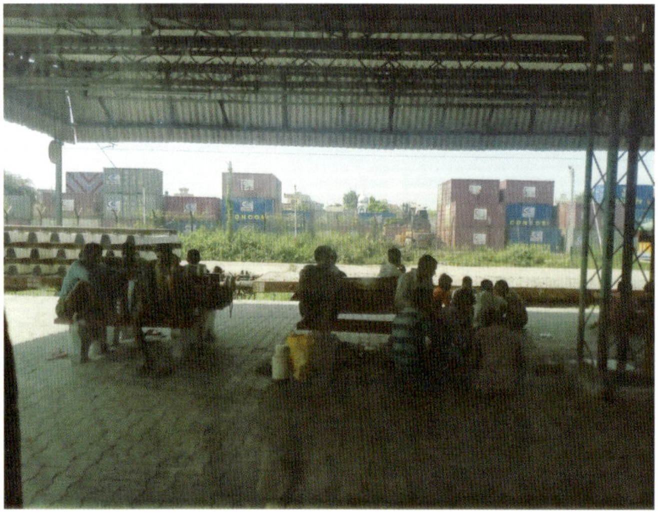

The 'local' suburban train links working class neighbourhoods with urban industrial zones.

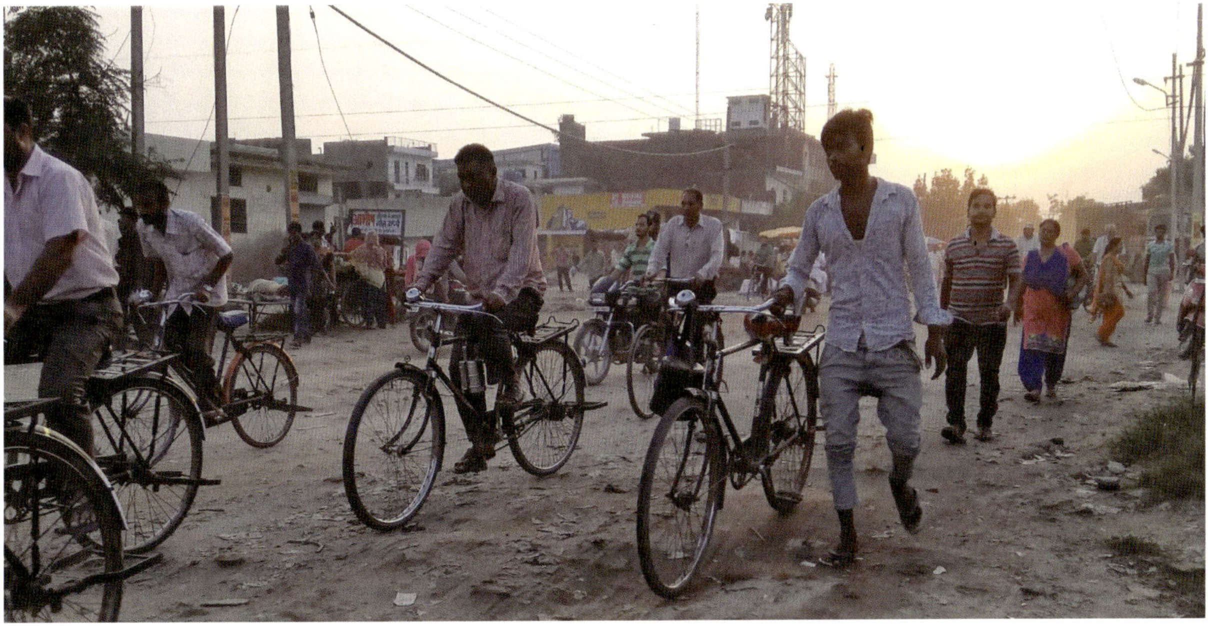

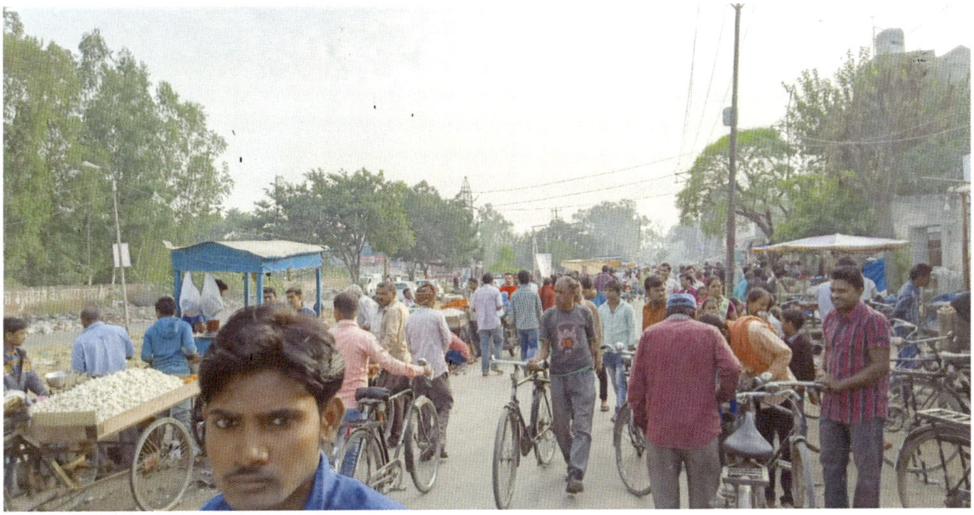

Cycles, dependable and widely used.

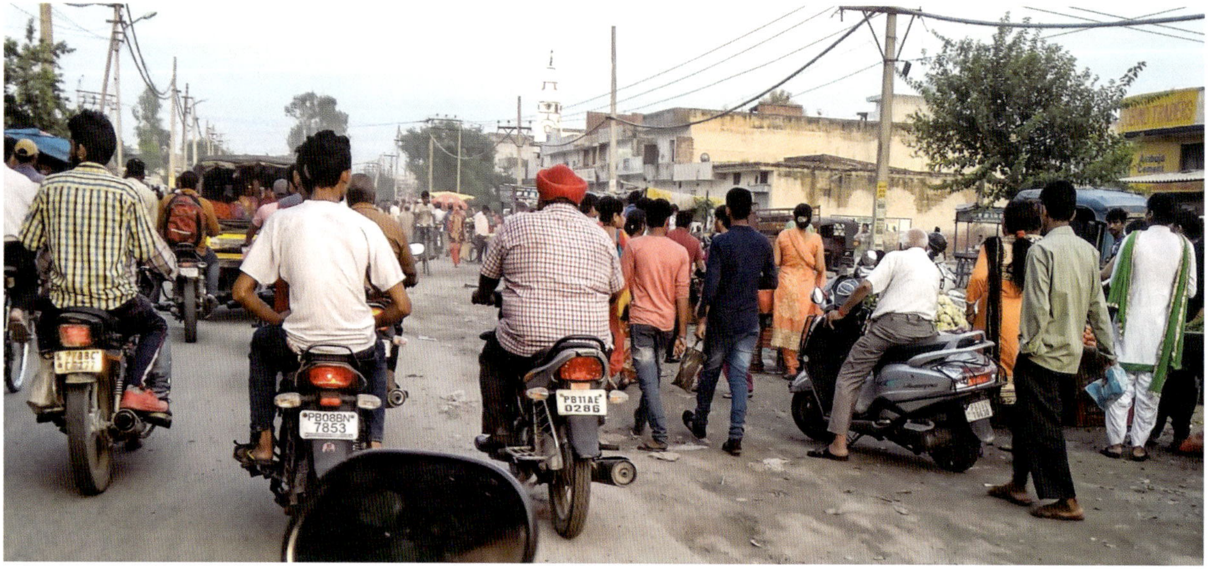

Motorbikes are prized possessions.

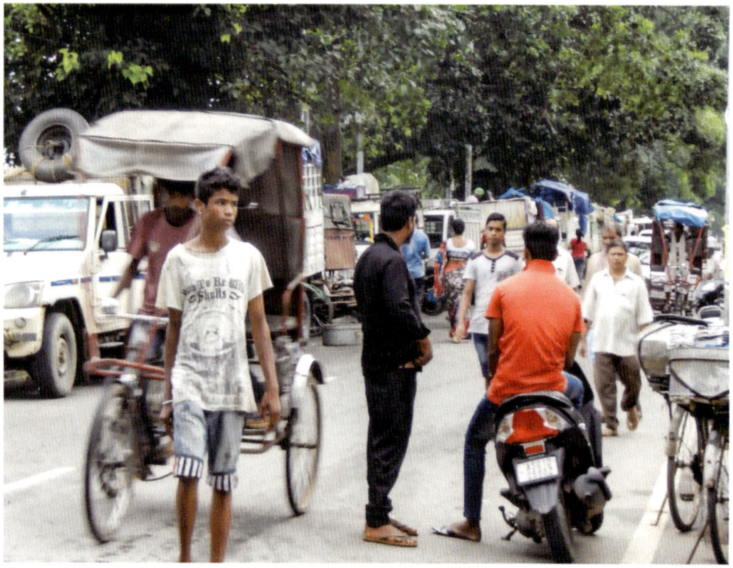

Rikshas, vans, mobikes.
Taking migrants to work.

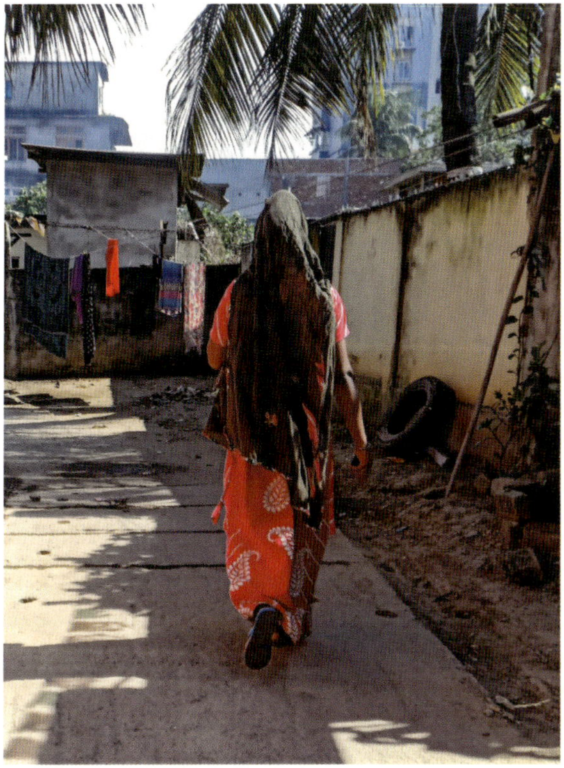

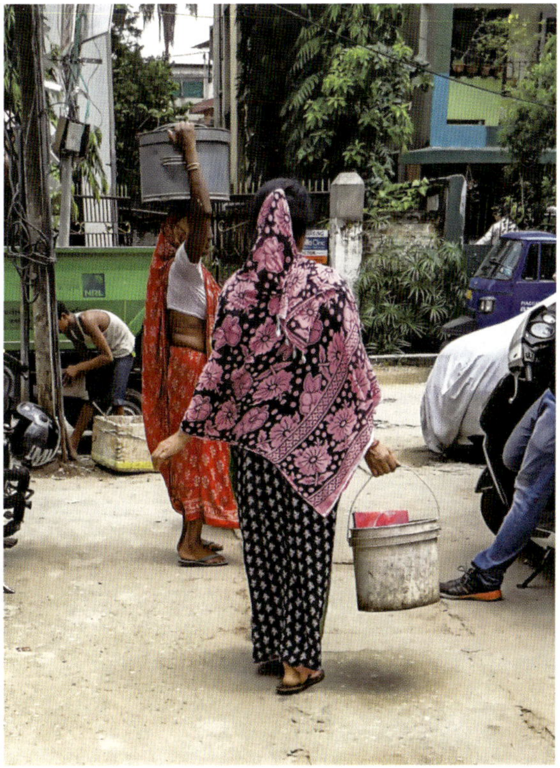

Walking to work.

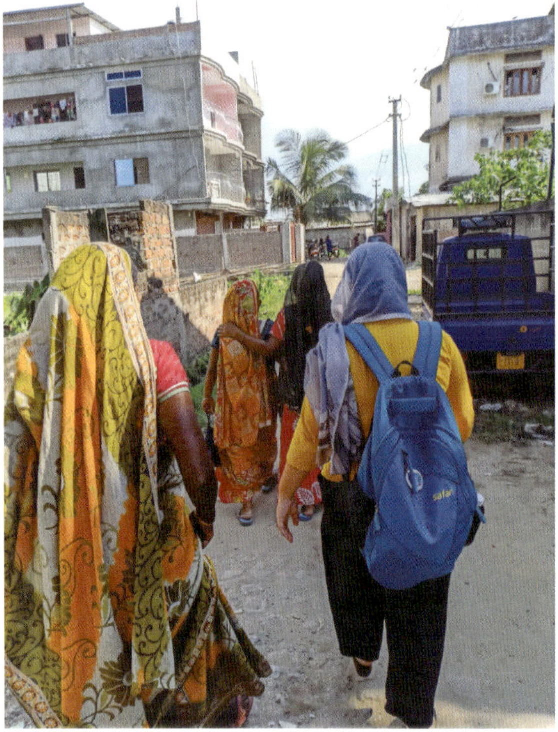

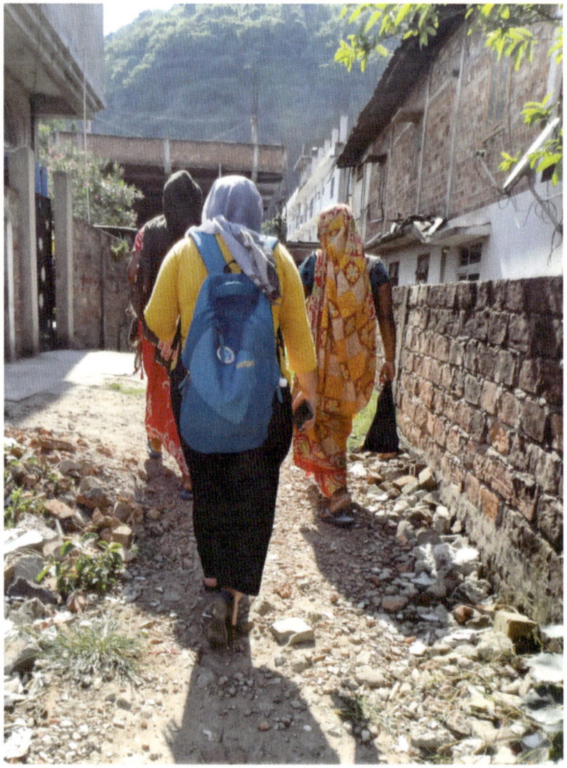

Migrant women are economically active. Many work as domestic labour in middle class homes which are not located near migrant settlements. Women travel to work in whatever erratic and risky transport is available. Many walk quite far to get to work.

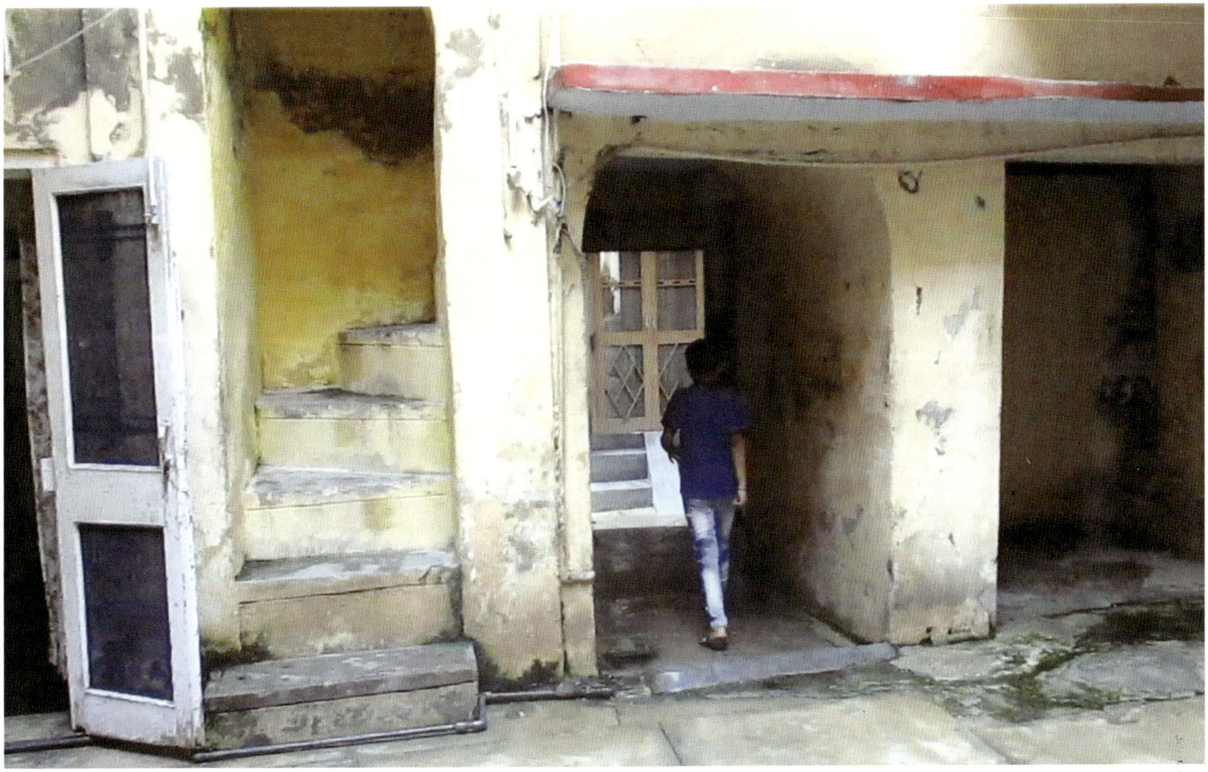

To work.

Getting to Work

Pick-up Points

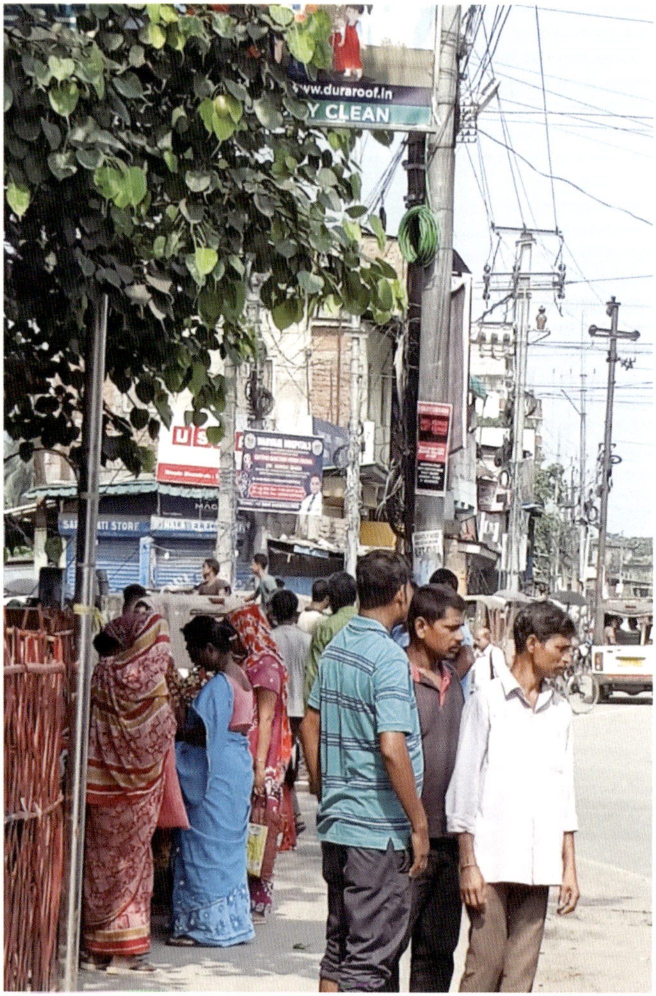

Waiting by the side of the road…

To map a city, migrants have two points of reference: space to live and the place of work. Finding work is a major anxiety. For a majority of manual labour migrants, the place of work is perpetually shifting. A migrant worker might begin her or his day without knowing which part of the city will be the work place for the day.

An urban labour *chowk* or *naka*, is basically an intersection or a junction of the city at which labour is 'bought' and 'sold'. A labour *chowk* is a critical geographic point in space mediating between the absolute need to find work and the uncertainty of where work can be found. Early in the morning, small groups of workers congregate with their tools and implements, their *aujar*, waiting by the side of the road to be 'selected' and 'picked up' by contractors and employers. Some labour *chowks* are named – Focal Point and Doaba Chowk in Jalandhar, for example, are known throughout the city. Specific intersections are familiar to contractors, owners of small business establishments and workshops and MSME managers. Tempos and trucks park near labour *chowks* to take migrant workers to the work site for the day. Transactions in labour are a visible part of everyday urban landscapes.

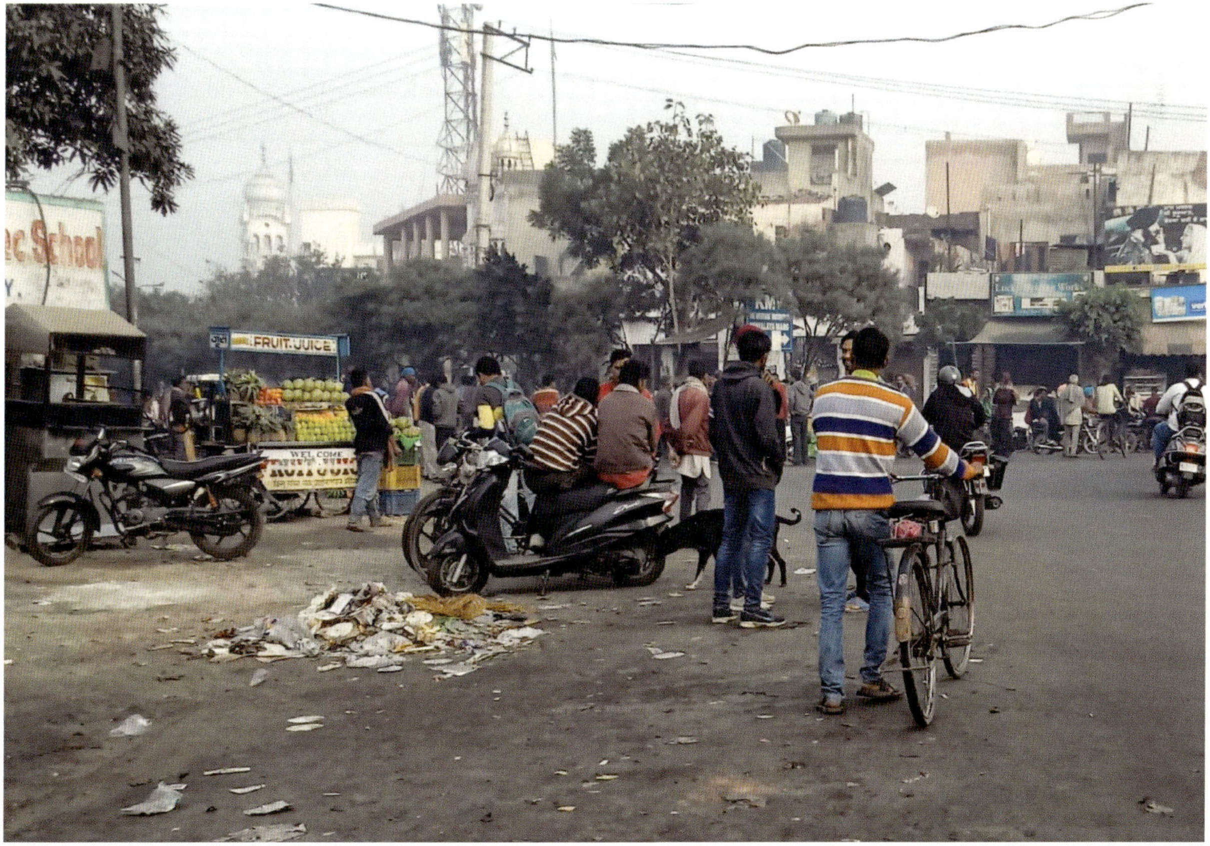

Doaba Chowk, Jalandhar City.

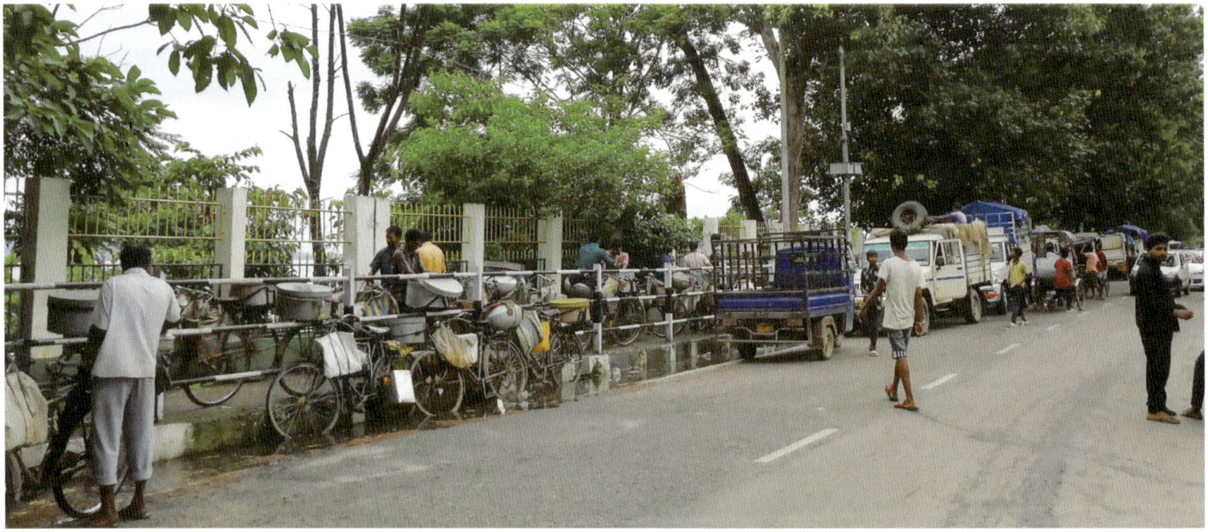

Labour Point Guwahati.

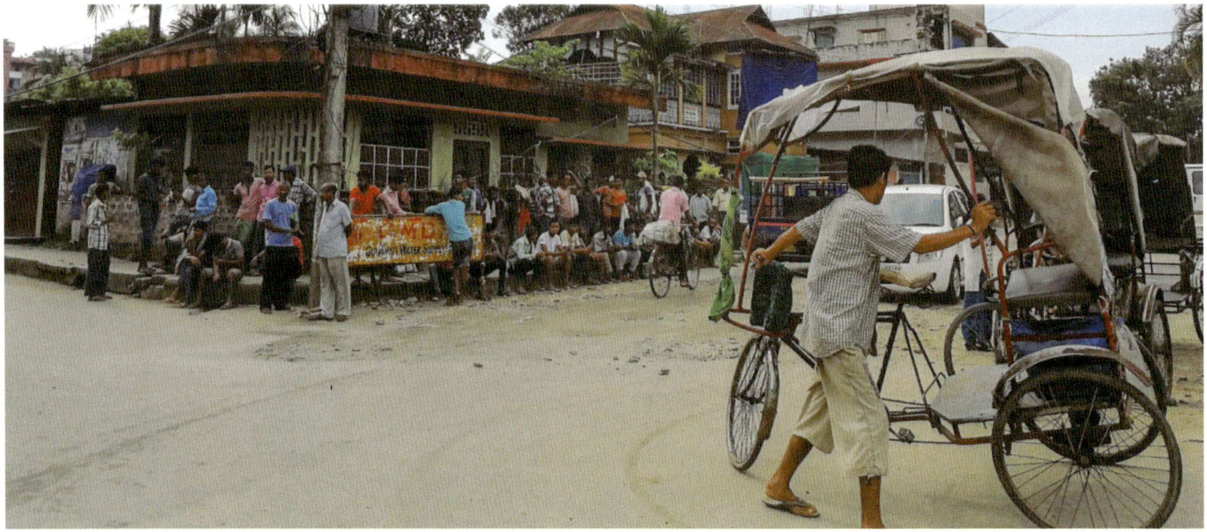

Street corner labour *chowk*.

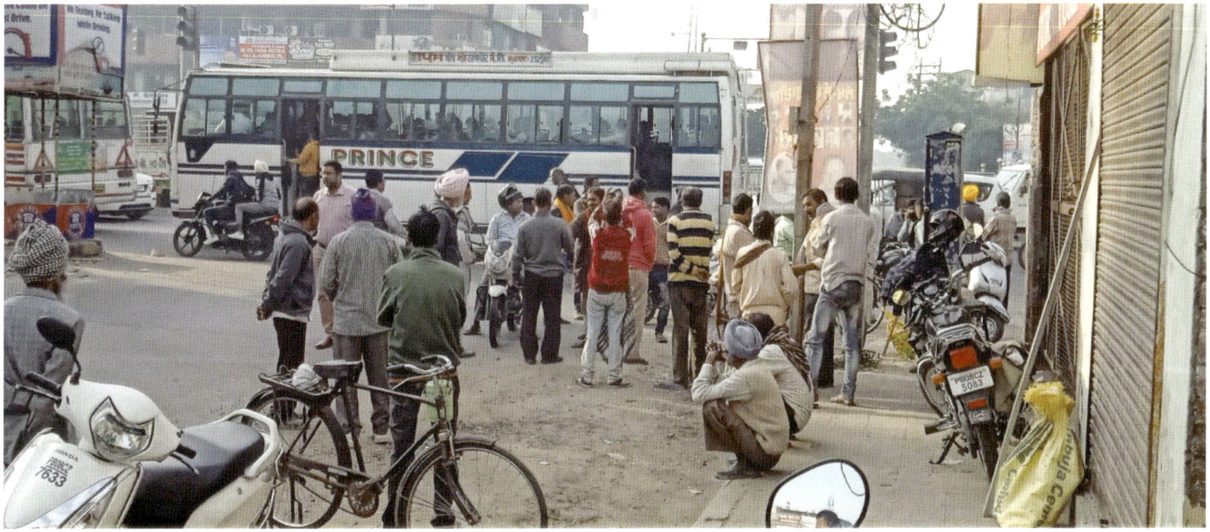

Nakodar Chowk, Jalandhar, November 2018.

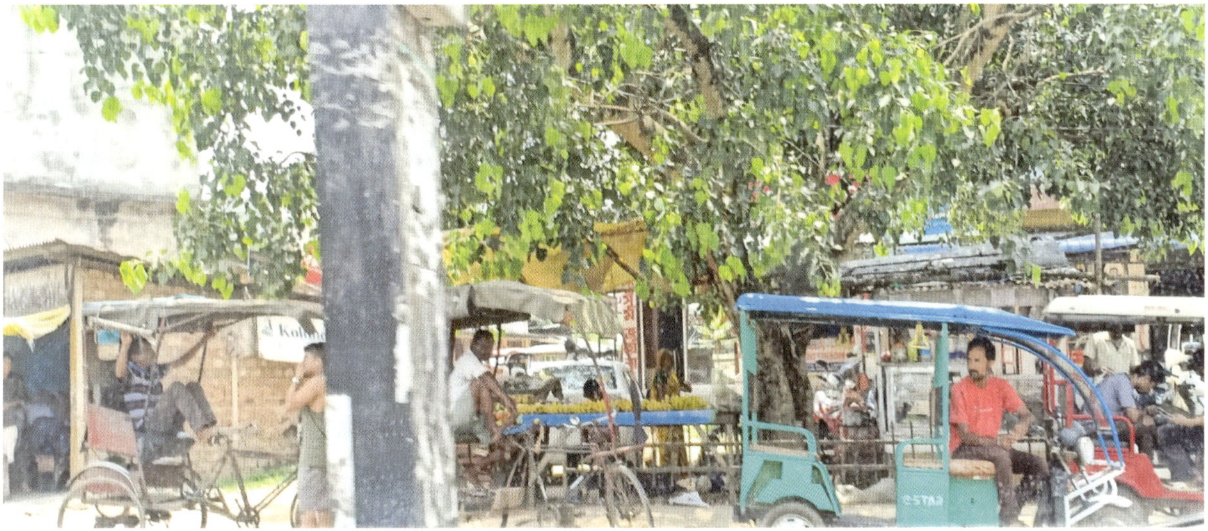

Waiting to carry labour to work.

Working in the City
Ferrying Loads

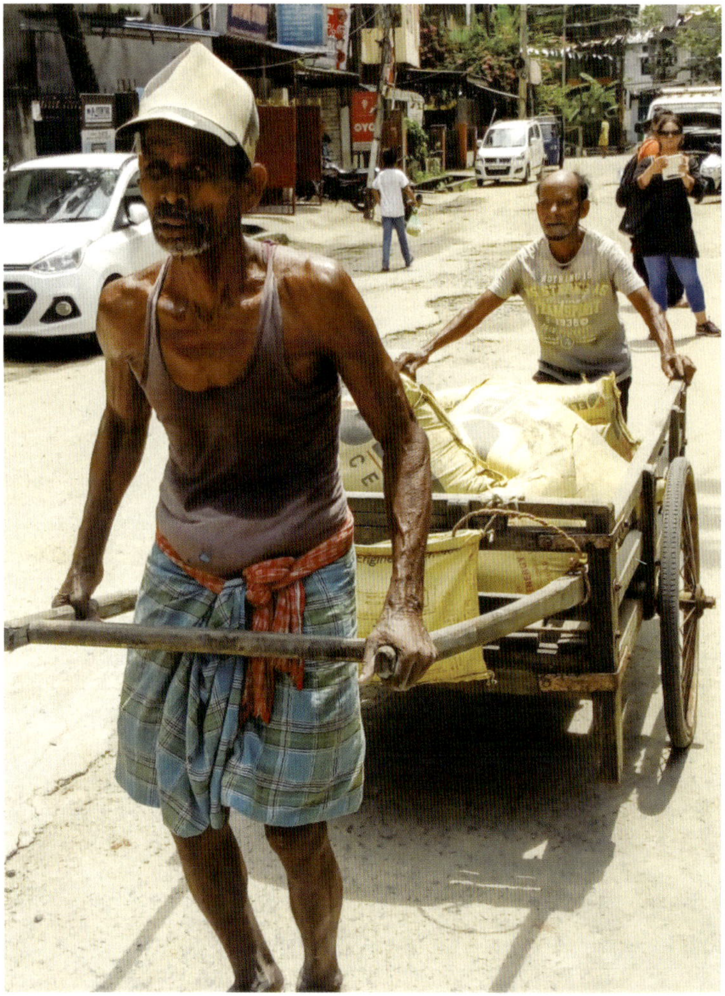

Weary of roamin' on,
Yearning to see the dawn,
Counting the hours till I can lay down my load...

["Waiting at the End of the Road" Lyrics, Irving Berlin, 1929] https://www.lyrics.com/lyric/18360427 Accessed 10 June 2021.

Cities depend on the movement of goods and material. Migrants pulling loaded carts or carrying head loads, dealing with unwieldy lengths of bamboo, are a common sight on urban landscapes. Cities run on the backs and shoulders of migrant bodies.

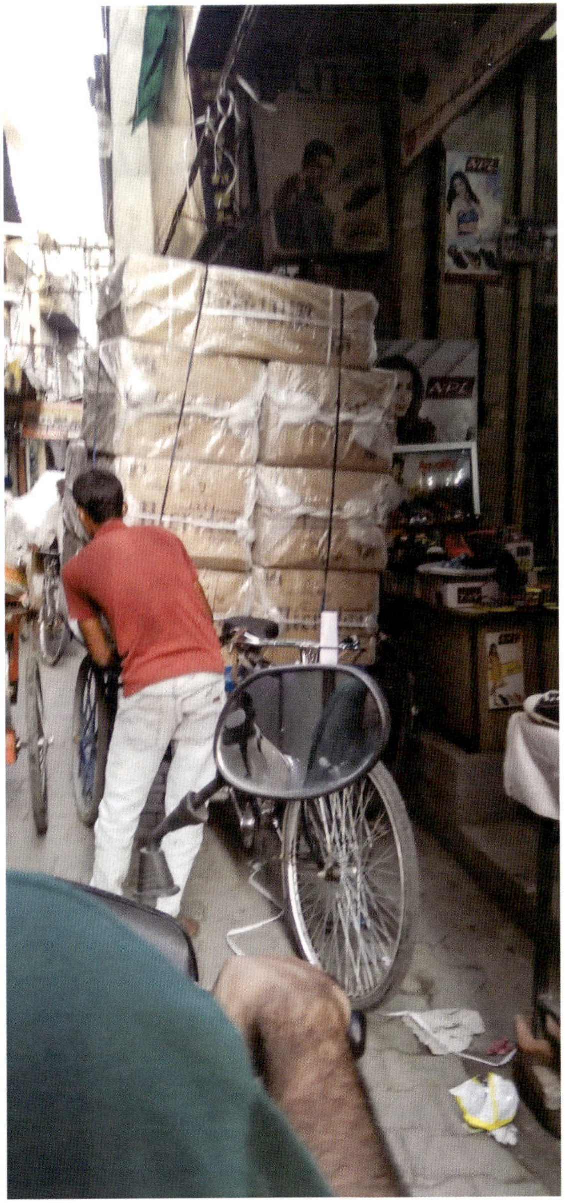

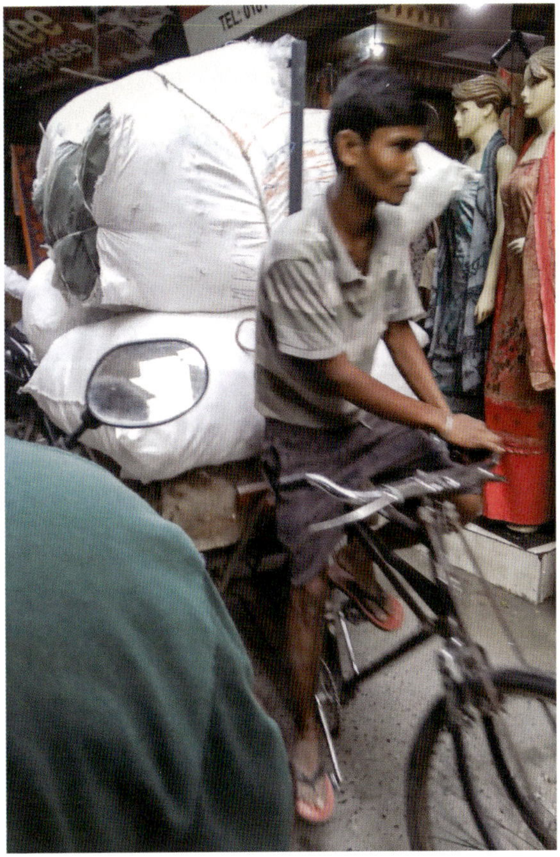

In narrow bazaar lanes, migrant labour load and carry goods in *rikshas* and *rehris*.

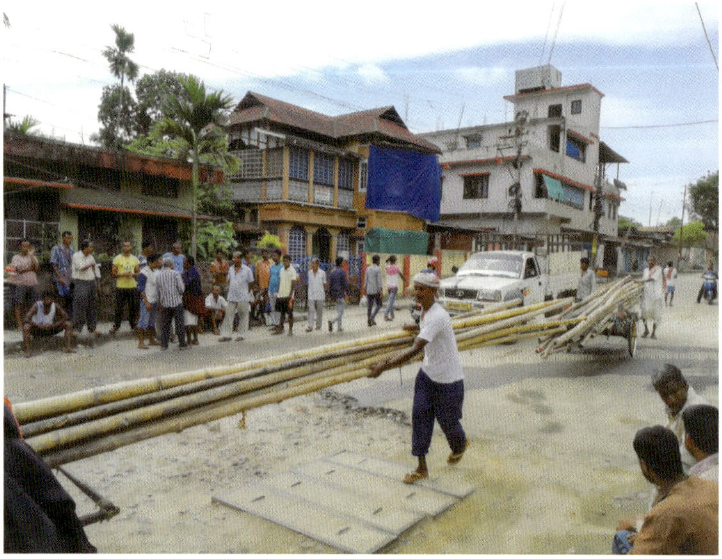

Long lengths of unwieldly bamboo are manoeuvred through the streets of Guwahati to construction sites across the city.

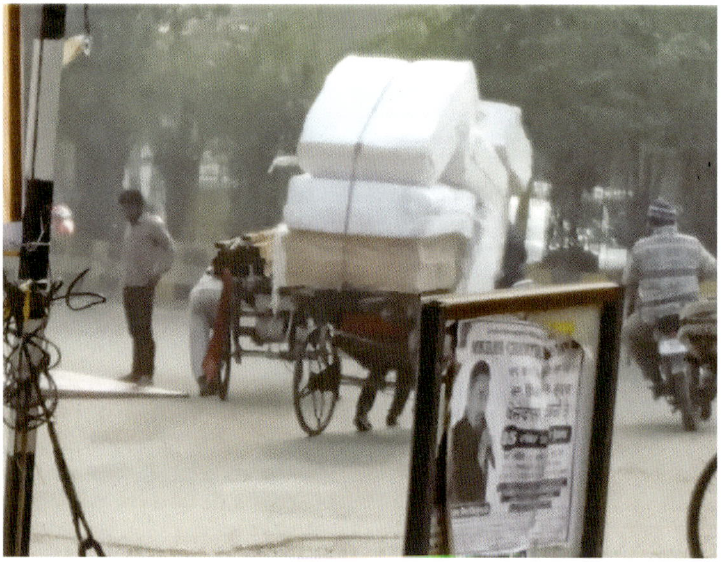

A migrant worker near Patel Chowk, Jalandhar, pulls a *rehri* piled high with goods.

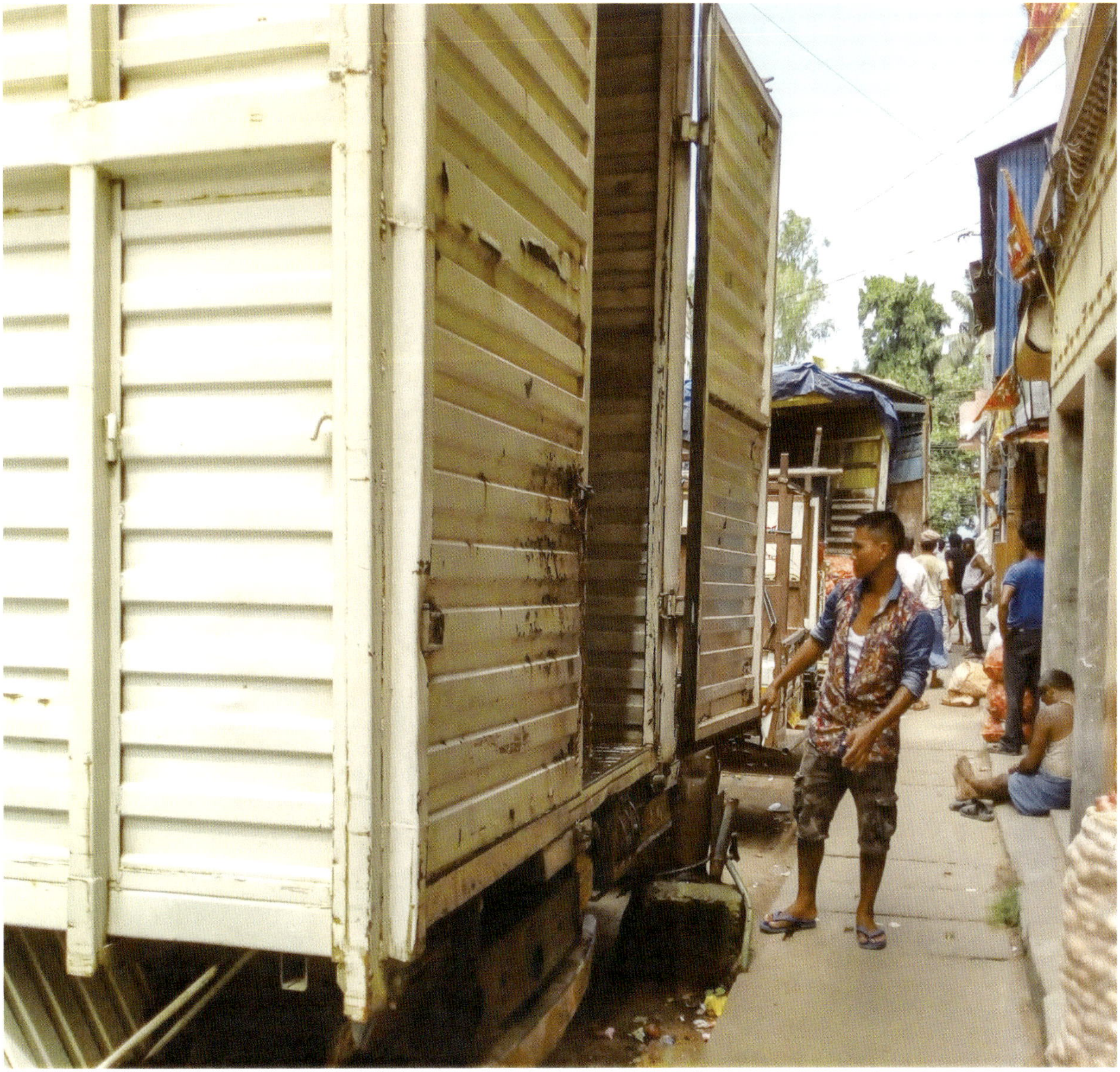

Loaders at work at a warehouse.

Working in the City

The Cart – *Rehri*

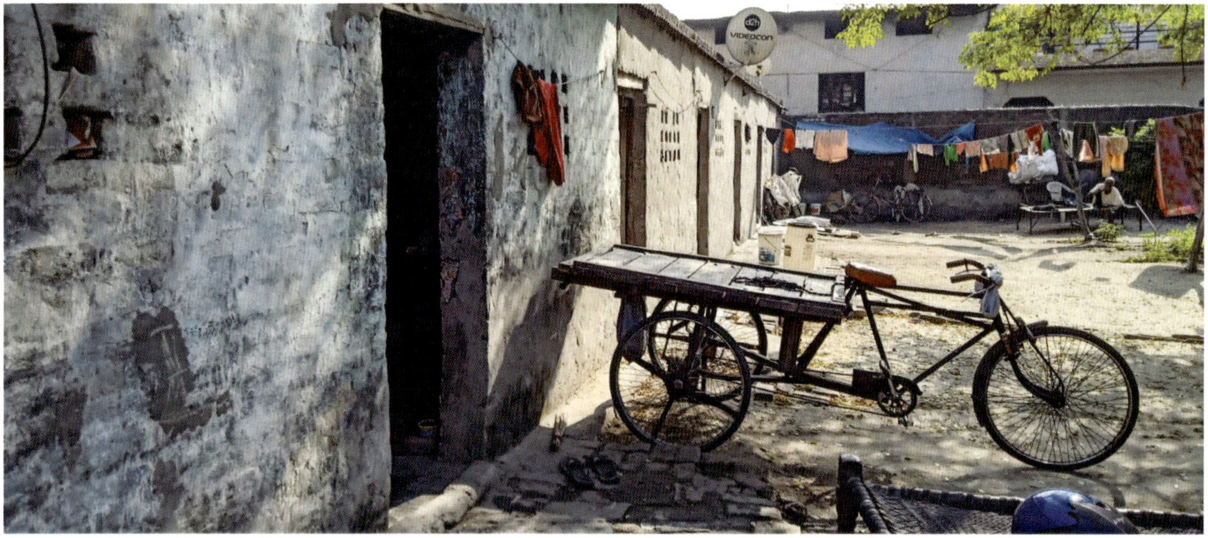

The *rehri* – the wheeled cart – is one of the most common and ubiquitous modes to ferry goods and carry loads. For migrants, a *rehri* is a prized possession. It signals the presence of a longer-term migrant who has tangible assets. It's a fungible asset, used to ferry a variety of loads, or transform into a mobile *dukan*-shop or even a surface for an occasional nap. A *rehri*, parked right outside shacks and doorways of small dwelling where migrants live, is a loaded sign. It conveys an investment in the city, the fact that some money has been made. It signals a daily route or a regular 'spot' at a city junction. A place to park it, a home with family. The *rehri* gives the owner a 'face', evoking familiarity with the city and its 'officials' who must grant its right of existence or overlook its transgressions. Together with a bicycle, a *rehri* signals the small measure of success a migrant can achieve, to create a stake in the city.

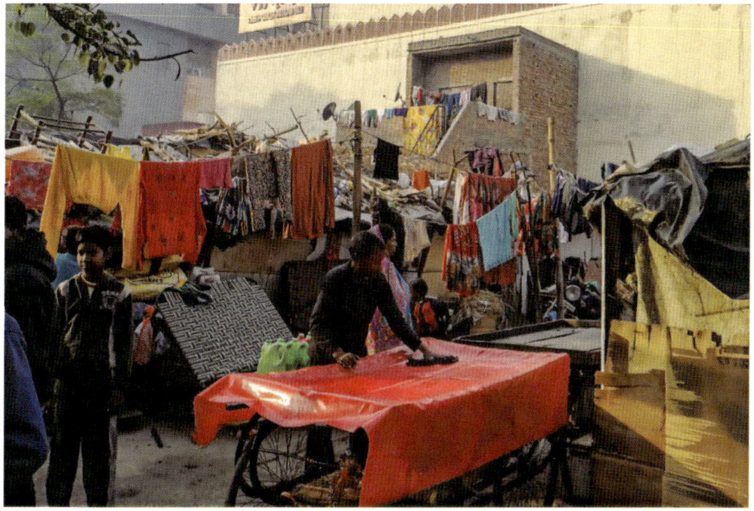

A *rehri* lives with its migrant owner, in the midst of a migrant settlement.

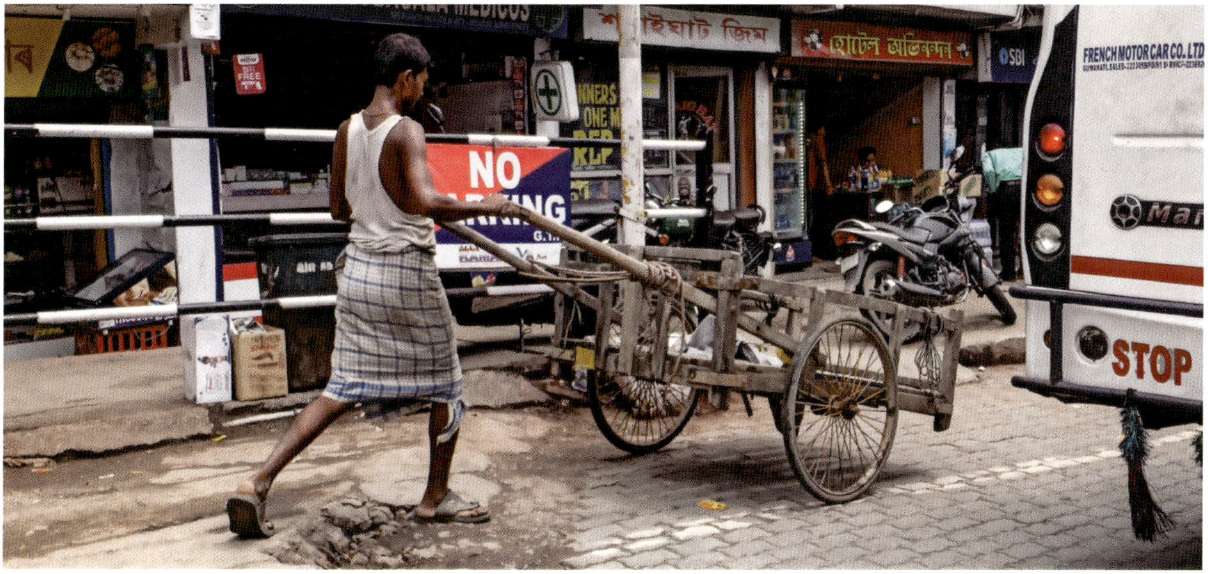

A migrant worker runs along with his *rehri* past shops in Guwahati.

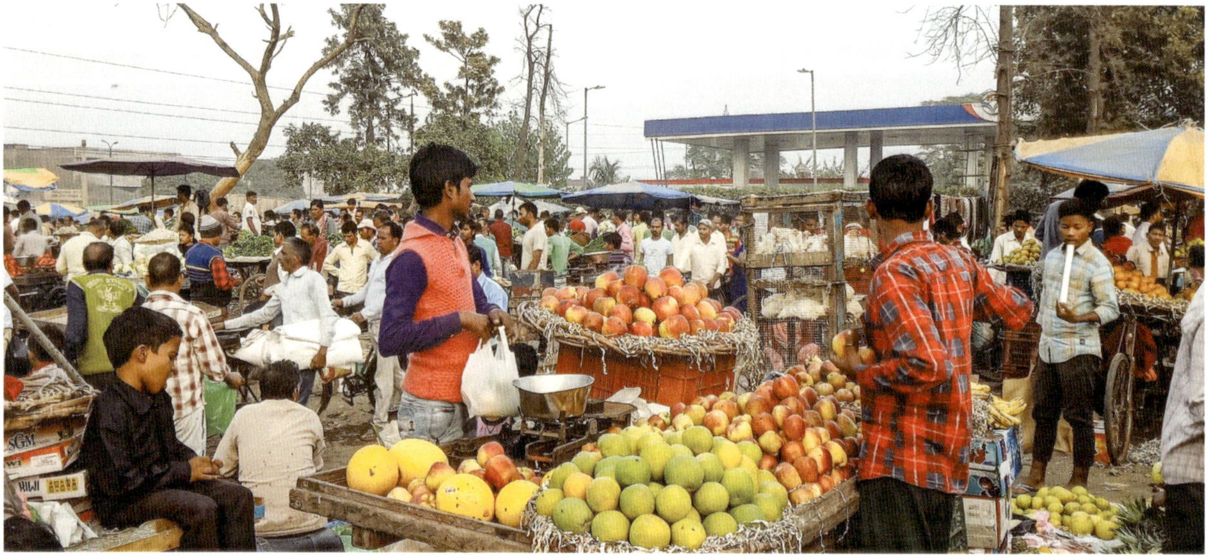

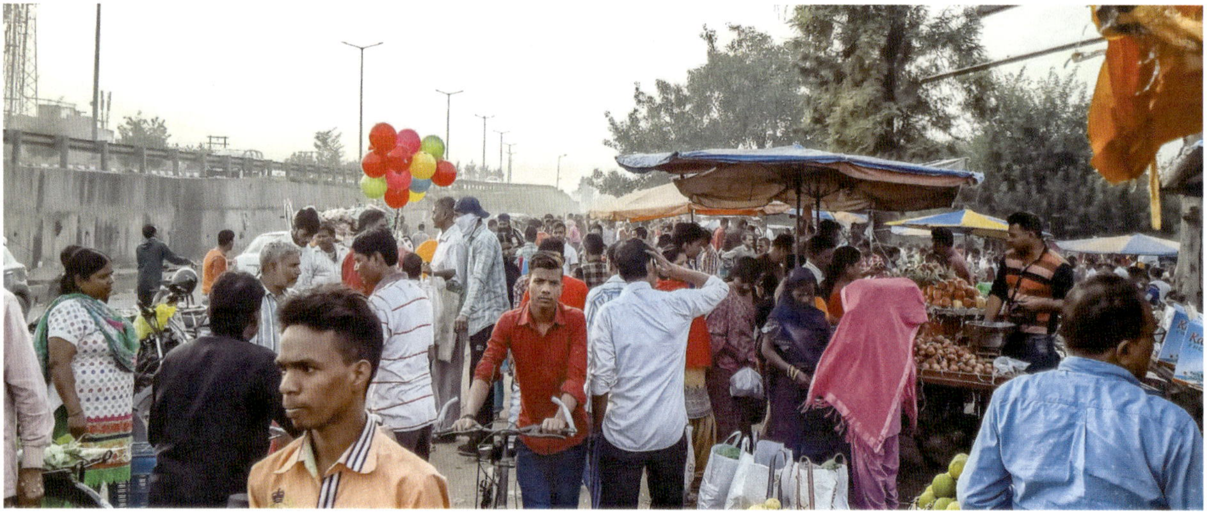

By migrants, for migrants, *rehri bazaars* at Focal Point, Jalandhar.

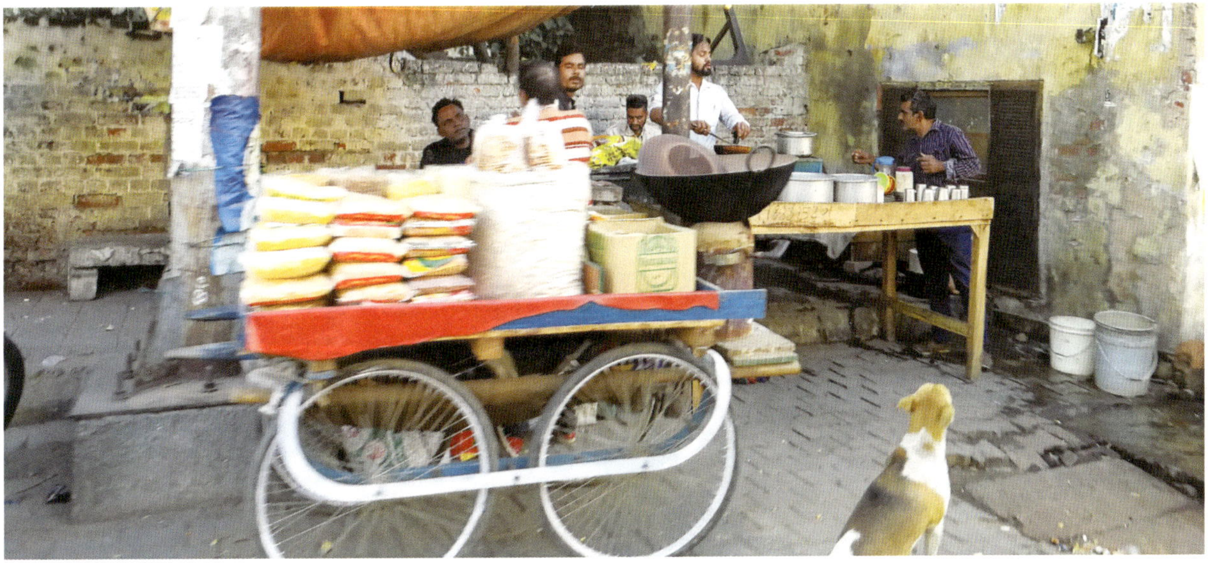

Dukan on a *rehri*, a small investment in the city.

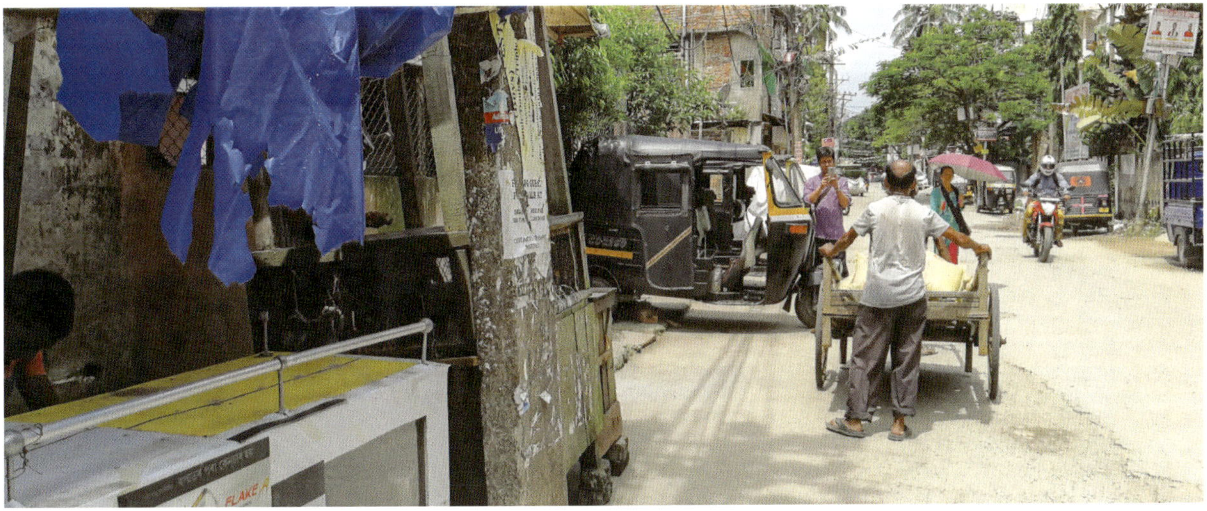

Wheeling daily goods on a *rehri* through neighbourhood streets.

Working in the City

Street Vendors

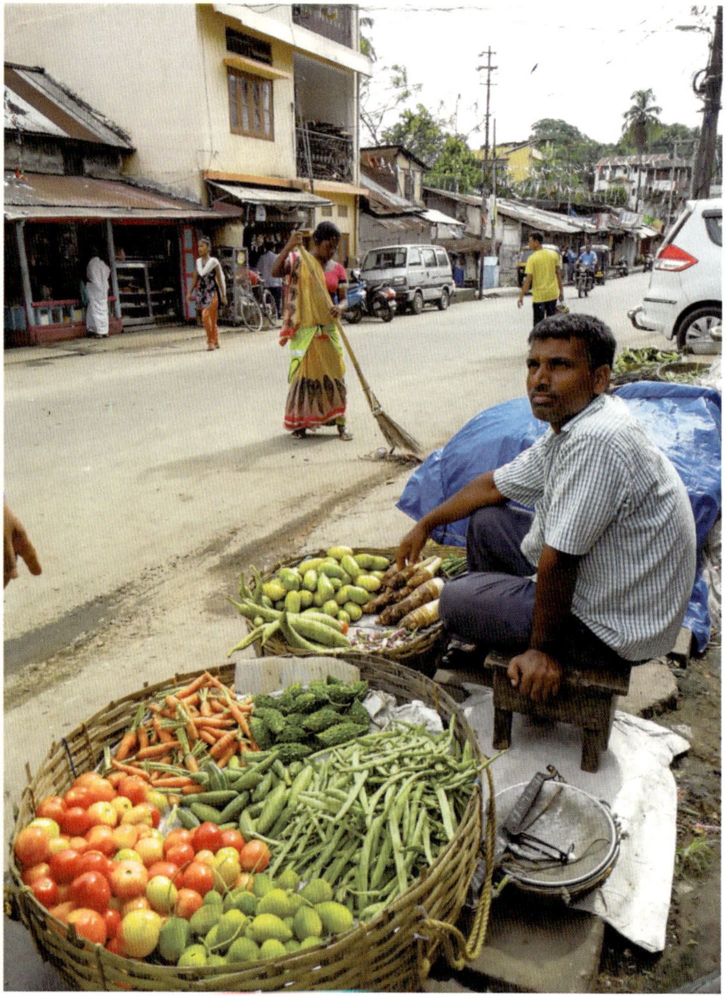

Migrants who have been in the city for a length of time start small, informal, often transient, street-side stalls and pavement shops or *dukans*. Everything from baskets of daily vegetables to fresh fish are taken door-to-door to sell. Often unauthorized, street vending enables migrants to begin earning just a little extra and create some networks in the city.

Short rows of plastic sheets are positioned along routes between home and work, located at key places where migrants live, occupying small niches, sharing street-space with other urban services like bus stops and garbage dumps. Their meagre goods signal the presence of low-income migrants. Pavement *dukans* carry little to sell, and display small amounts. The portable basket and the migrant kitchen share an understanding of the nature of small-scale living and the extreme scarcity of storage space. Everything is freshly bought in small, meagre or miniscule quantities, easily transported in a paper bag or a twist of newspaper.

Tattered tarpaulins are sources of knowledge of migrant lives. Pavement *dukans* are more than merely economic enterprises. Street side *dukans* are useful signposts for newly arrived migrants who spatially orient themselves in unfamiliar urban space by *dukans* located at street corners.

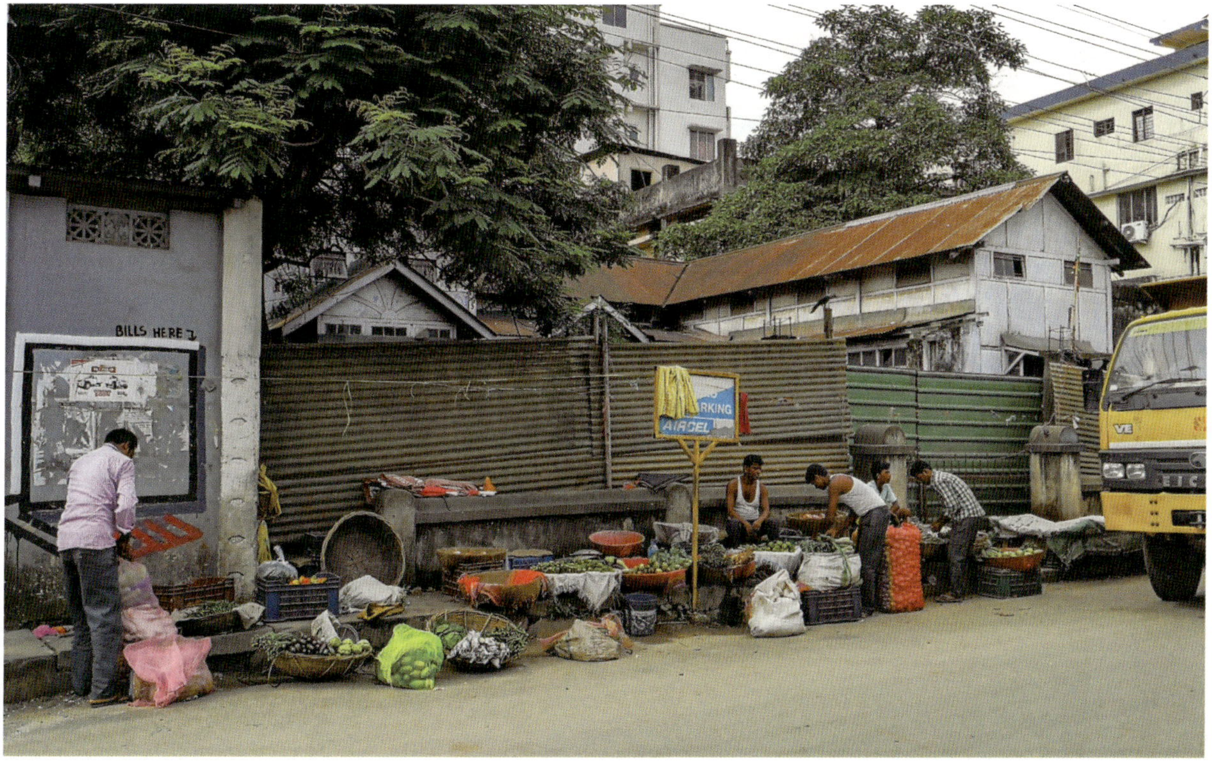

Pavement basket-*dukans*.

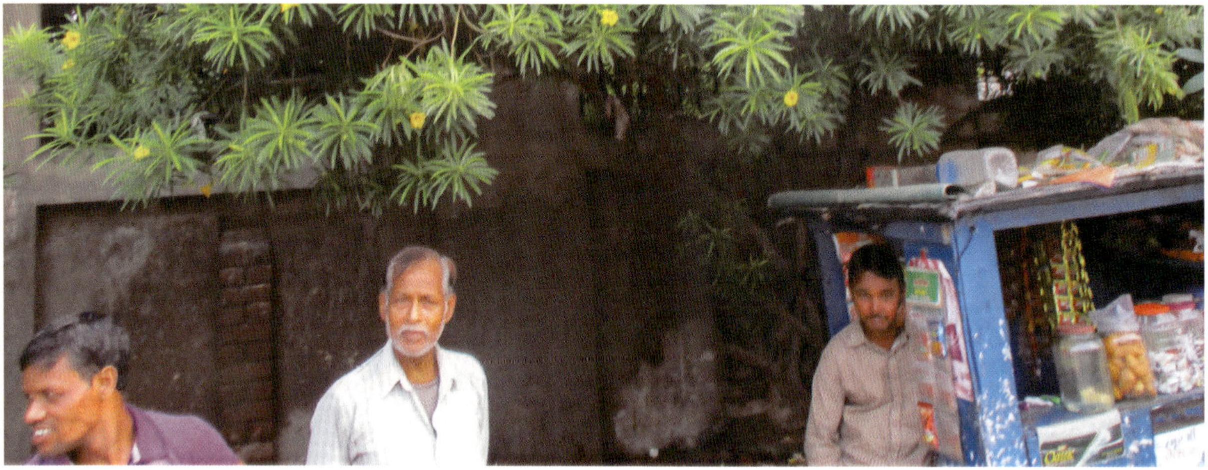

Selling instant energy at the factory gate: tobacco, sweet rolls, biscuits.

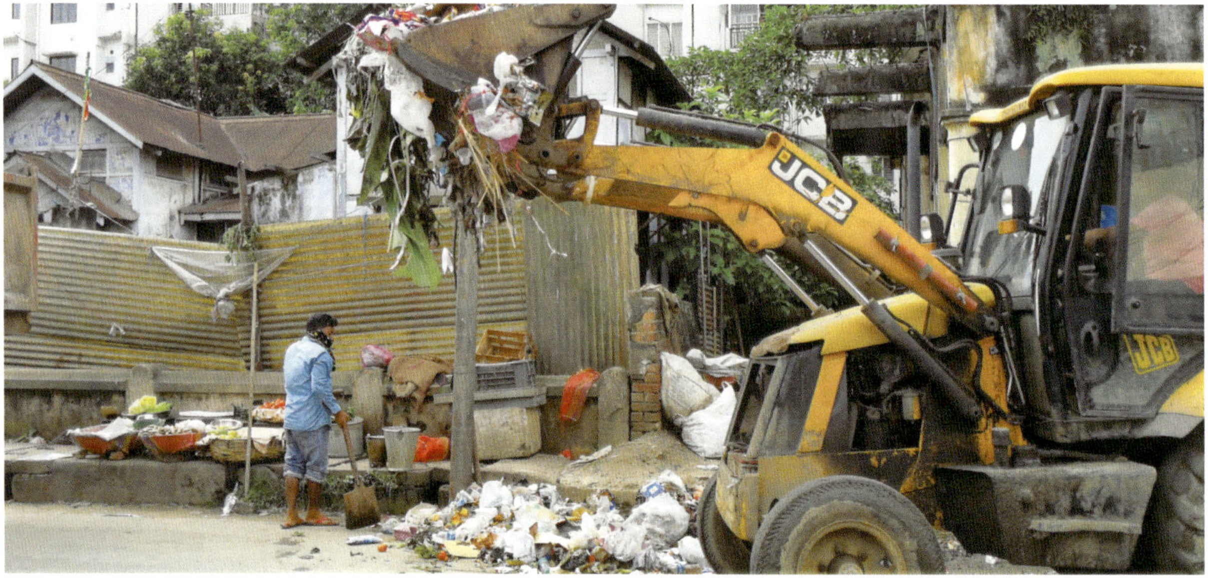

Pavement *dukan* in the gap between a garbage dump and a narrow lane.

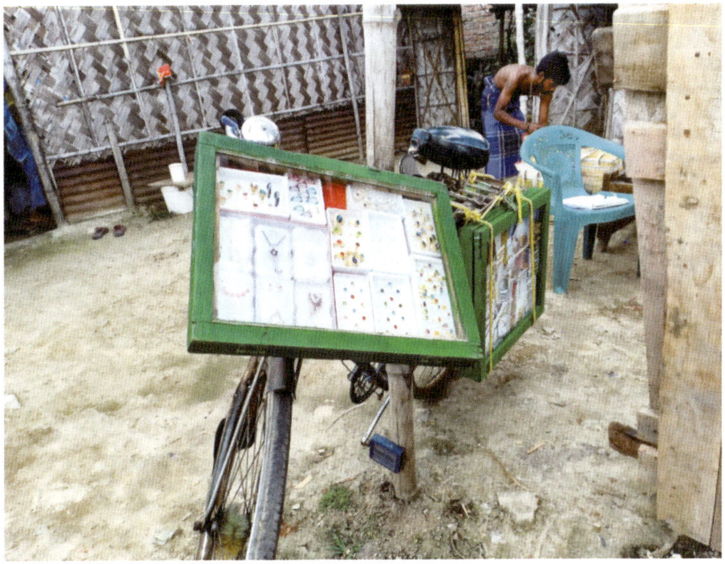

Cycle *dukan*.

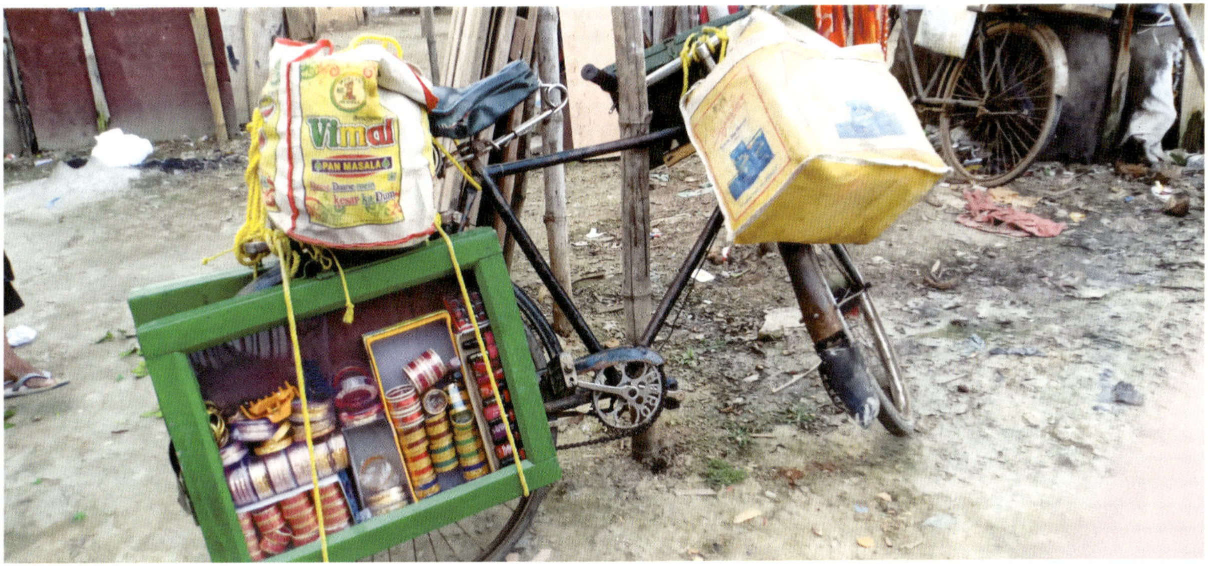

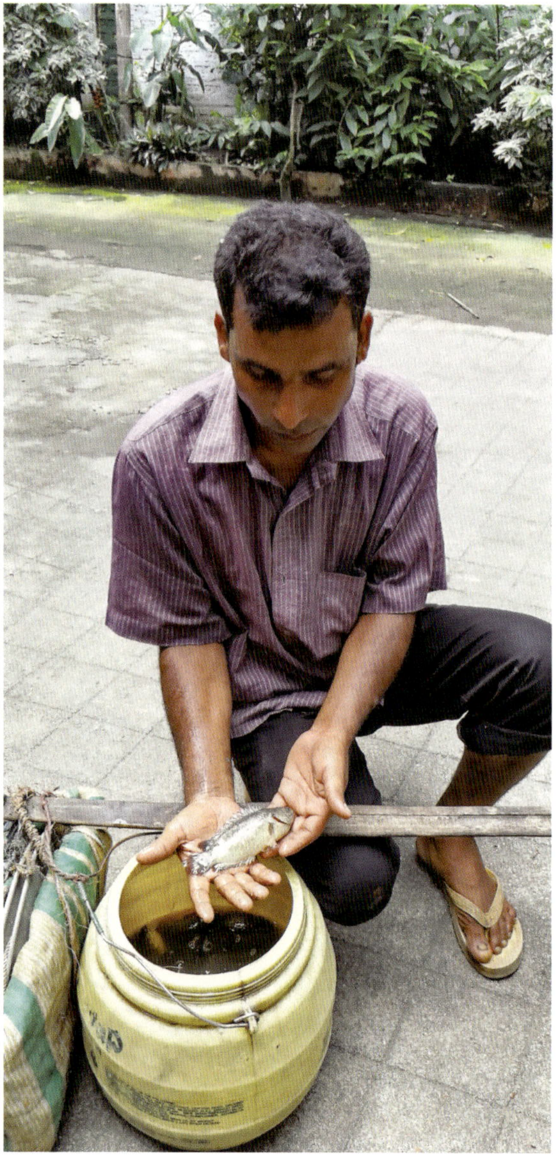

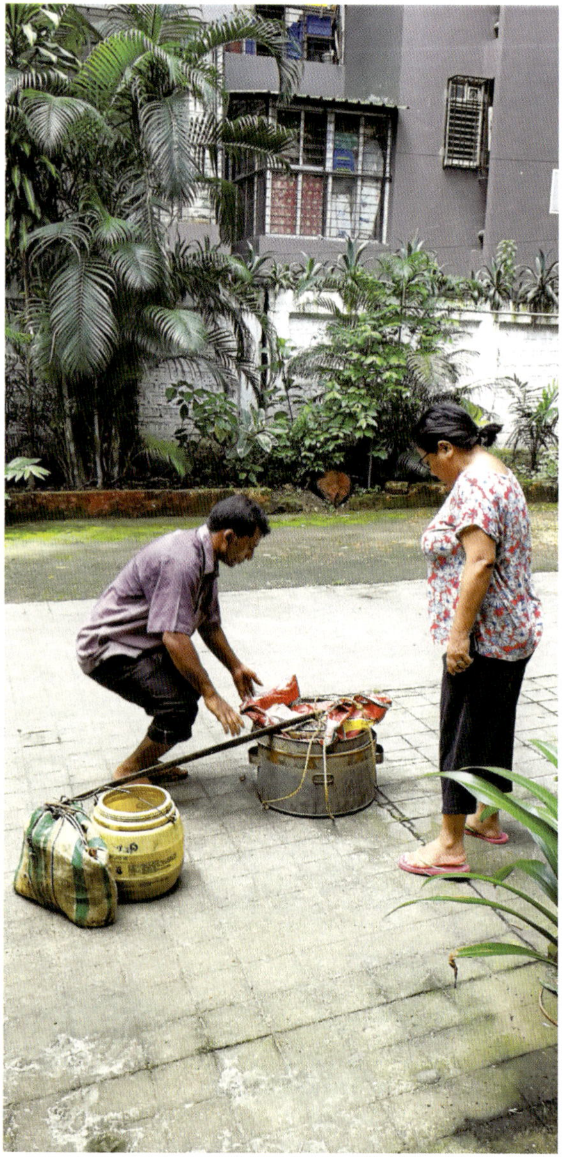

Fresh fish vendors go from door-to-door.

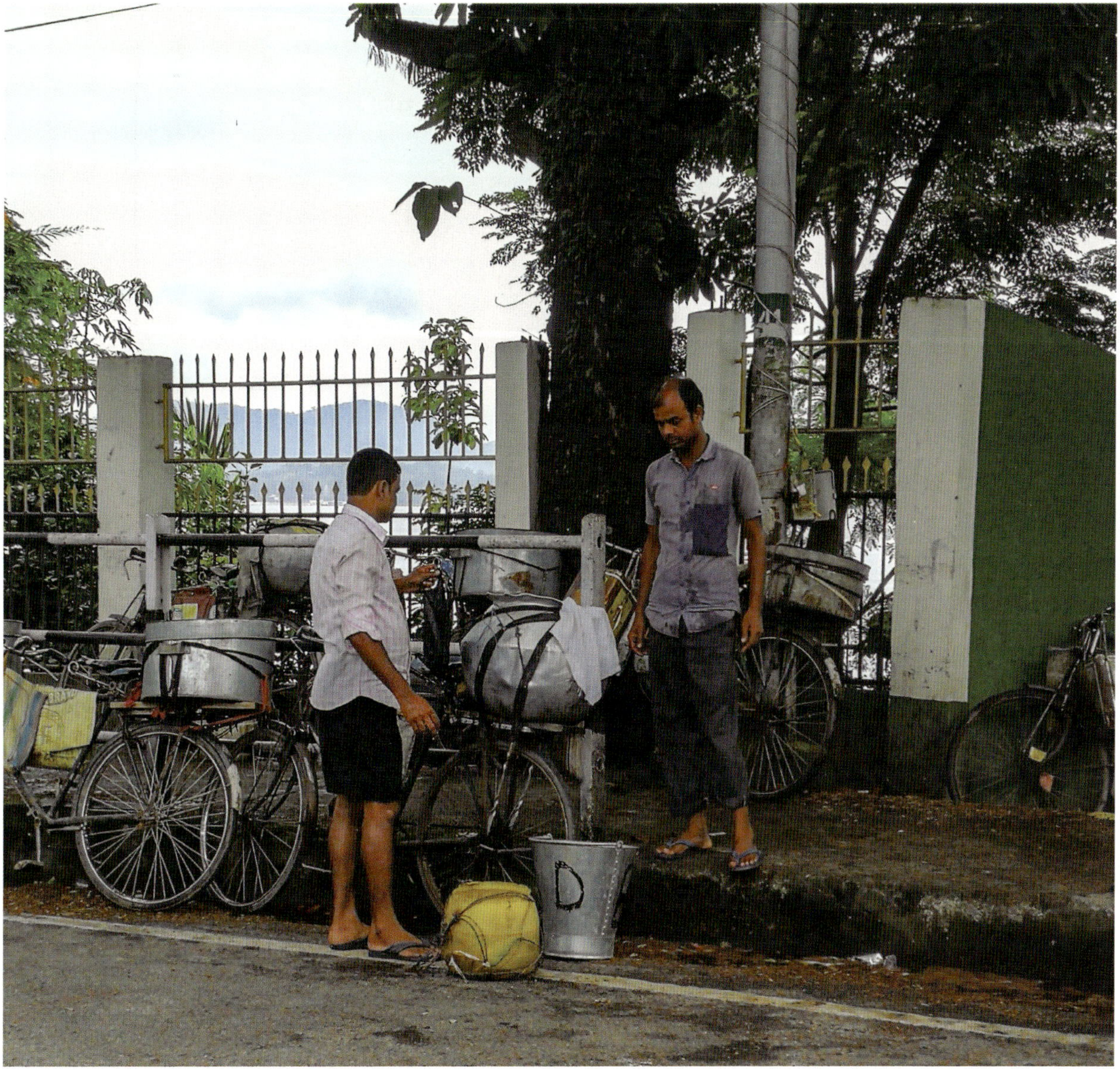

Cycle borne fish sellers.

Working in the City
Aujar – Implements

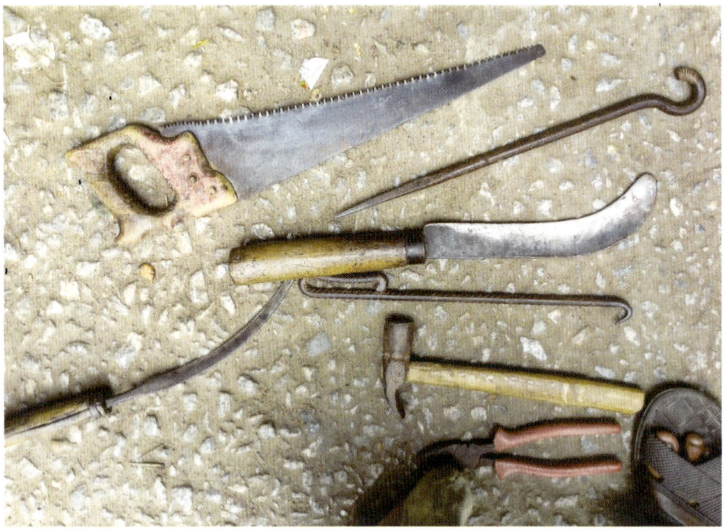

A simple piece of equipment, or implement, the *aujar* defines the worker. Migrants carry their *aujar* with them wherever they seek work. At labour *chowks* and pick up points, skilled workers – masons or carpenters – or manual workers, like diggers – *beldar*, carry their *aujar* as badges of identity. The *aujar* defines skill, work and worker. Potential employers identify the worker by the *aujar* carried almost casually, or laid out next to the worker. Though some are carried in small bundles or bags, an unwieldly part like a handle or a hammer head often sticks out, signaling skill.

Skilled workers are not the only people who carry *aujar*. Daily wage workers at labour *chowks* also carry a number of manual multipurpose tools, wrapped up in polypropylene sacks or carried in bags.

Contractors are a necessary fixture in the lives of skilled and unskilled migrant labour. Transactions with contractors are not random. Many contractors who come to hire daily wage labour have their fixed and favoured labourers, and will hire them almost exclusively, transporting them to worksites in their pickup trucks or *tempos*. Though getting work is a daily transaction, familiarity between contractors and labour is an important part of the employment process.

Extract from fieldnotes, October 2019

> In the course of interviews with migrant labour, Anurag was beckoned by a *mistri*, a mason, carrying a triangular trowel, and a corner trowel, with the words *ye mistri ka bhi thoda jankari le lo* – find out at least a little about this *mistri*. The mason was dressed very differently from other workers, in clean clothes and cap. He carried a wooden handled triangular trowel, to shape corners, and a T-shaped rod, used for levelling. Anurag introduced myself to him and asked where he was from. The *mistri* said that he was from Siwan in Bihar. He gets ₹ 600-650 per day. He does about 32-33 days of daily waged work per month, putting in extra hours as overtime. He doesn't work with a contractor, coming instead to the labour *chowk* to be 'found' by potential employers. Some employers enter into a contract with him for an extended period of time, sometimes as much as ten days. When that happens, he doesn't need to turn up at the labour *chowk* with his *aujar*, but goes straight to the site of work. The mason slipped away when a contractor arrived. Anurag moved away while the negotiations began. He began talking to the another group of labour who were negotiating with a contractor.

End of fieldwork extract.

Extract from fieldwork, Lal Ganesh Labour Chowk, Guwahati, July 2021

> Jeevan arrived at a labour *chowk* named 'Lal Ganesh' in Guwahati, at 6 am. Several Muslim men were gathered there, waiting to be hired as workers for a daily rate. Some carried polypropylene sacks with a few tools. Jeevan asked them about these, and they showed him the tools inside the bags. They explained that they

carry their own tools. The variety of tools they carried signaled the range of work they do as handymen.

One migrant worker's bag contained a handsaw used for cutting wooden objects, different sized sickles used for cutting grass, bushes or small branches of trees, a hammer to drive nails or to shape metals or break bricks, pliers for pulling nails or for fitting nuts and bolts, as well as handmade multipurpose iron tools, used for pulling ropes, shuttering wires or for tying wire. The array of tools reveal the assortment of work required for construction jobs, and the range of skills needed to get different types of masonry or construction jobs done. The bag did not include safety gloves or protective gear.

End of fieldwork extract

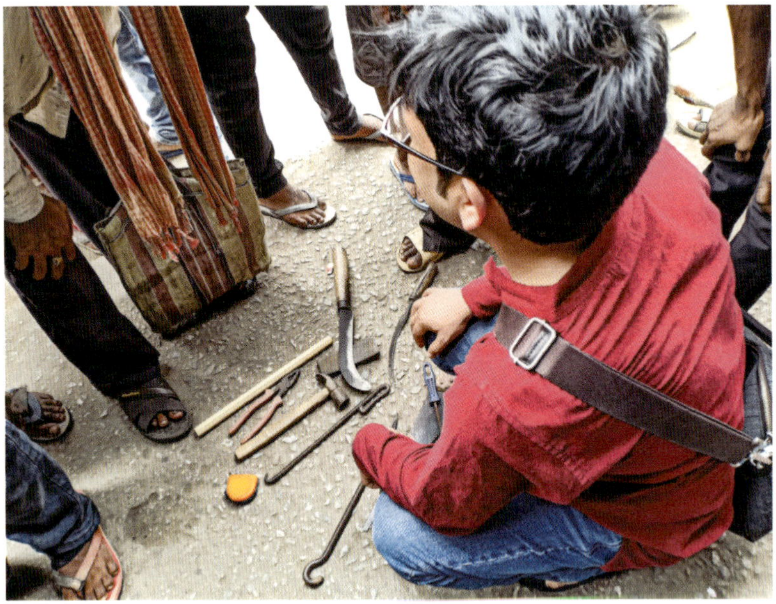

Mistri explaining *aujar* to Jeevan, in Lal Ganesh Labour Chowk, while other workers look on.

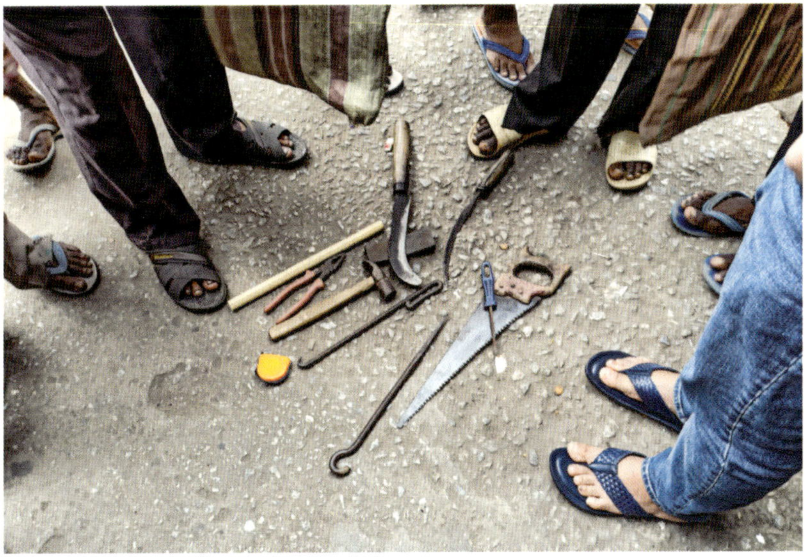

Aujar laid out and explained.

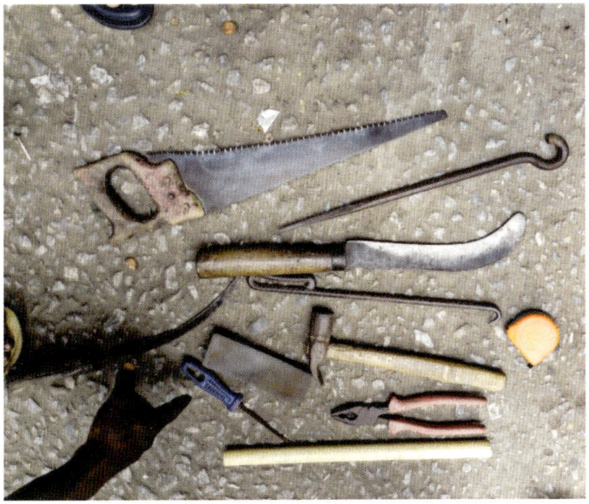

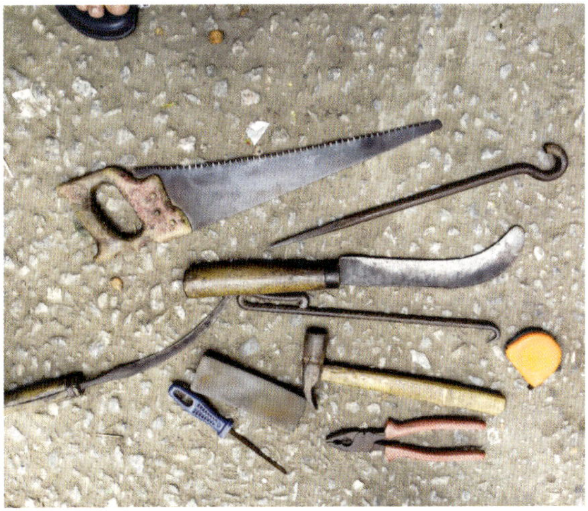

A worker shows his tools, and points towards a sharpening tool.
The orange coloured measuring tape is an essential inclusion among the tools.

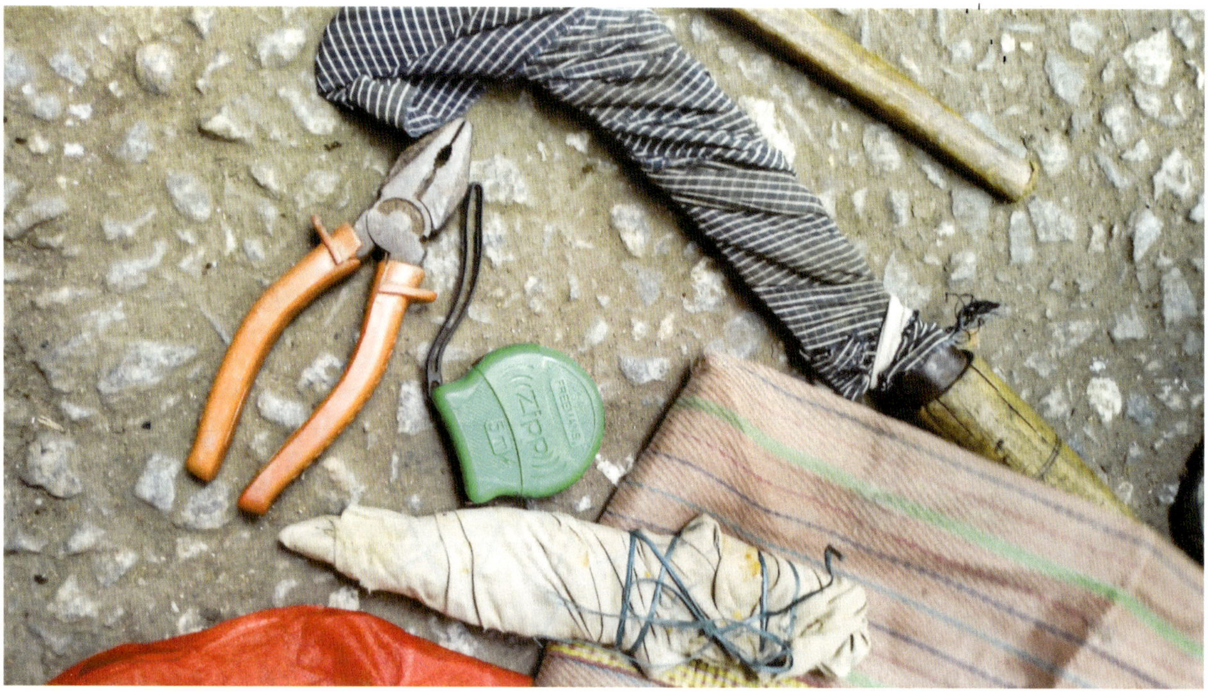

The sharp tools, the sickle and a chisel, are wrapped securely in cloth to prevent any accidental injury while the worker carries them or stores them in the thin bag.

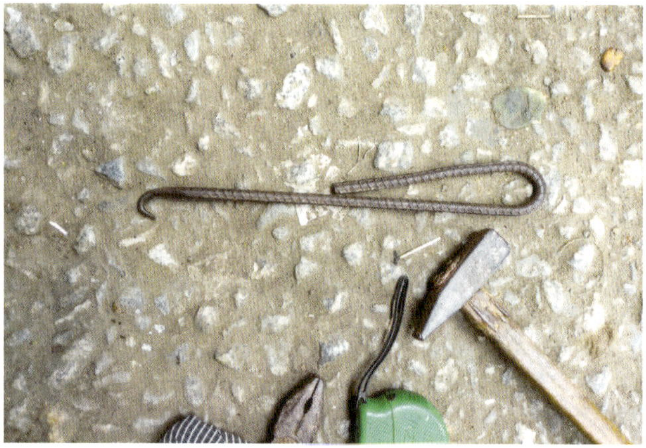

The handmade tool, made from iron rod, is used for shuttering. When shuttering is manually held together with wire, this tool is used to fold the steel wires and bind it tightly.

Working in the City

A Working Day of a Domestic Worker in Guwahati

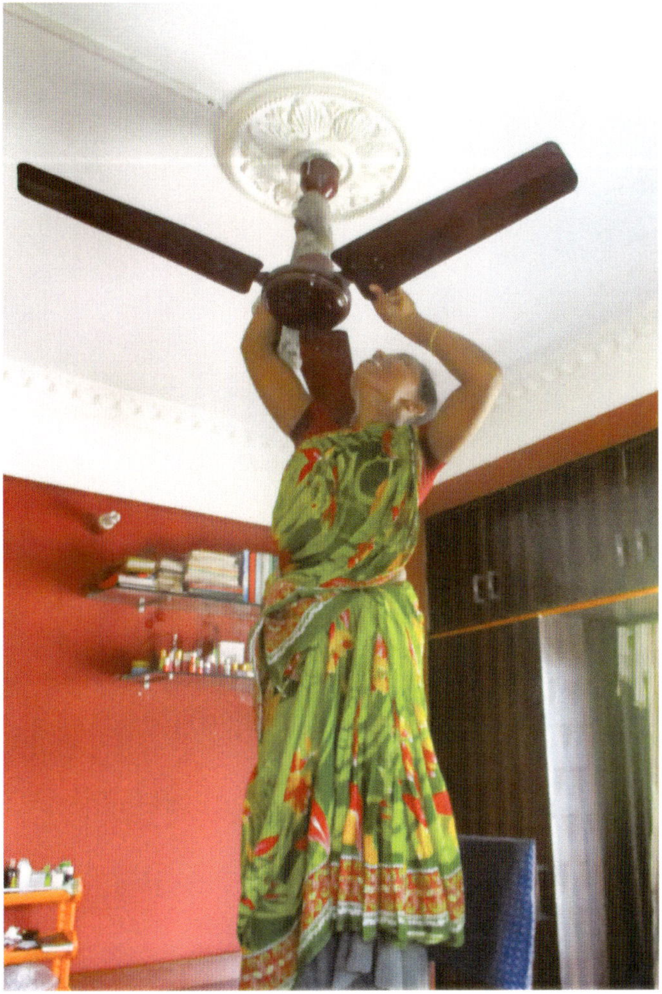

Photographs are a 'contact zone' (Pratt 1992), which enable glimpses of mismatched lives.

The biographies of domestic workers are shaped by their movement between two domesticities. Photographs of a day in the life of a migrant domestic worker show us how the labour of migrant women sustain the lives and homes of middle-class employers.

The migrant domestic worker 'shuttles' between two homes and domestic spaces. In the span of a working day, juxtaposed with a middle-class employer's home, the migrant woman's home comes into view. Both domestic spaces – her own and her employer's home – are transformed by the work she does in both places. Polished mirrors, clean fans, dusted tables; the employer's home gleams with the worker's labour. The worker's home displays its own aesthetic. Walls decorated with calendar art, small corners transformed into small domestic shrines, scrubbed and cleaned cooking utensils neatly aligned, conveying a sense of domestic order.

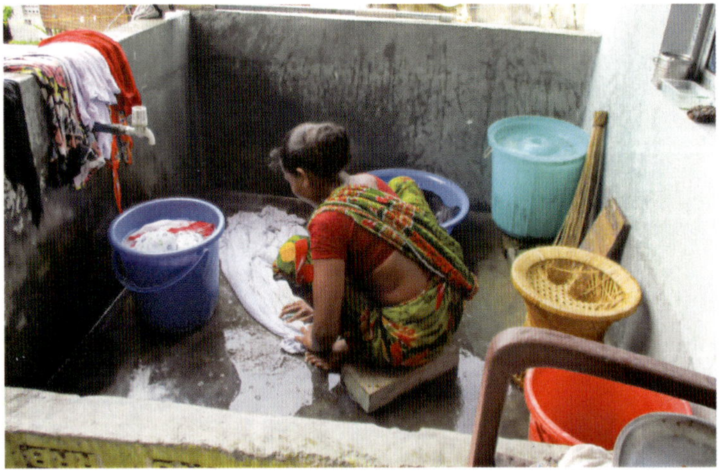

Scrubbing her employer's clothes is a daily chore for the migrant domestic worker.

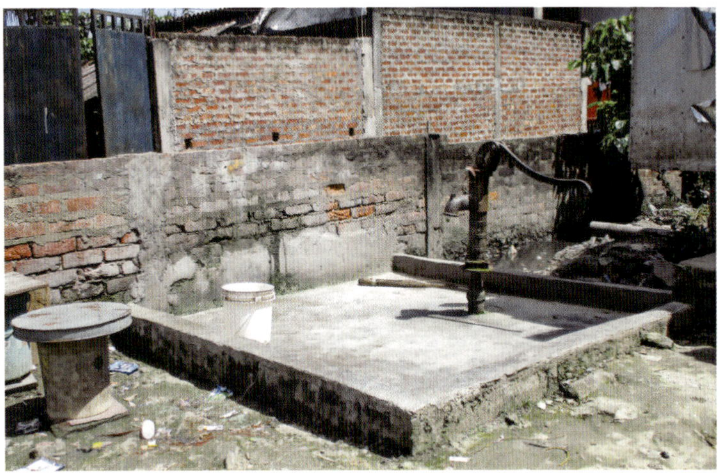

Her own clothes are washed at the community hand pump in the *basti* – working class settlement – where she lives.

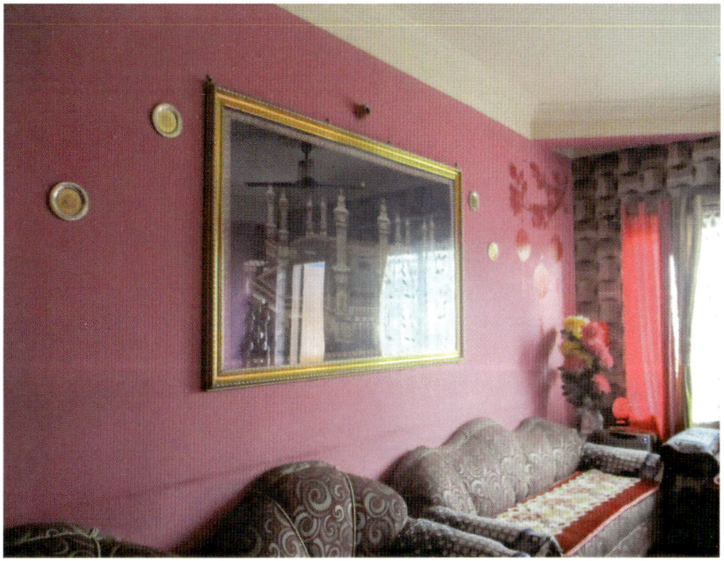

Scrubbed, swept and dusted, her employer's home gleams.

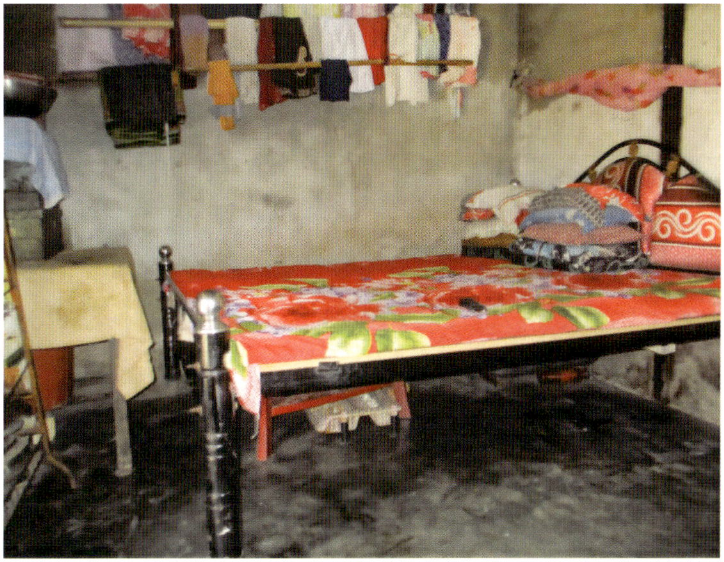

Clothes hang neatly on bare bamboo poles in a worker's home.

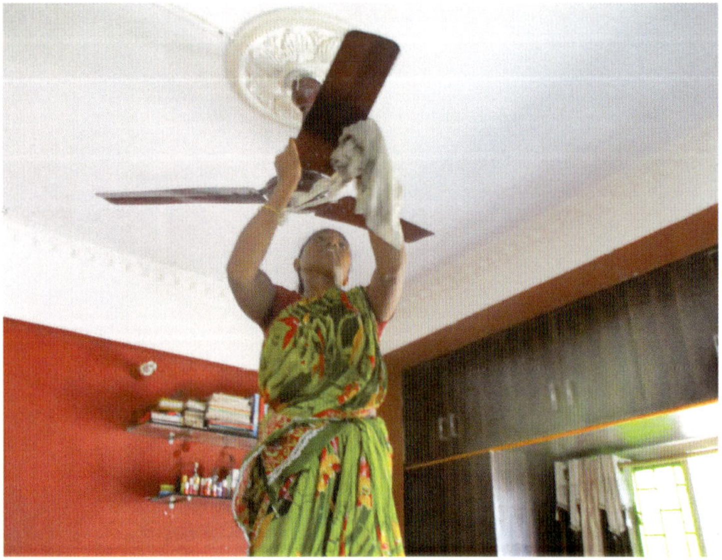

Cleaning inaccessible corners.

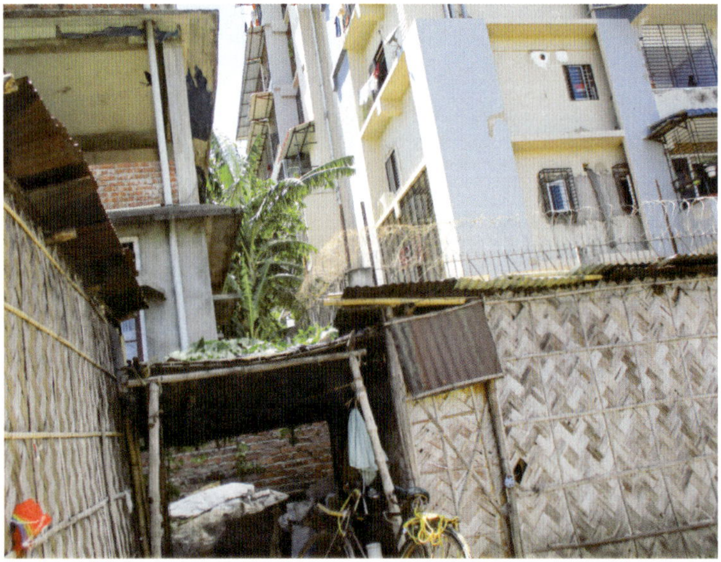

In the lee of an apartment block, woven bamboo walls offer shelter to migrant workers.

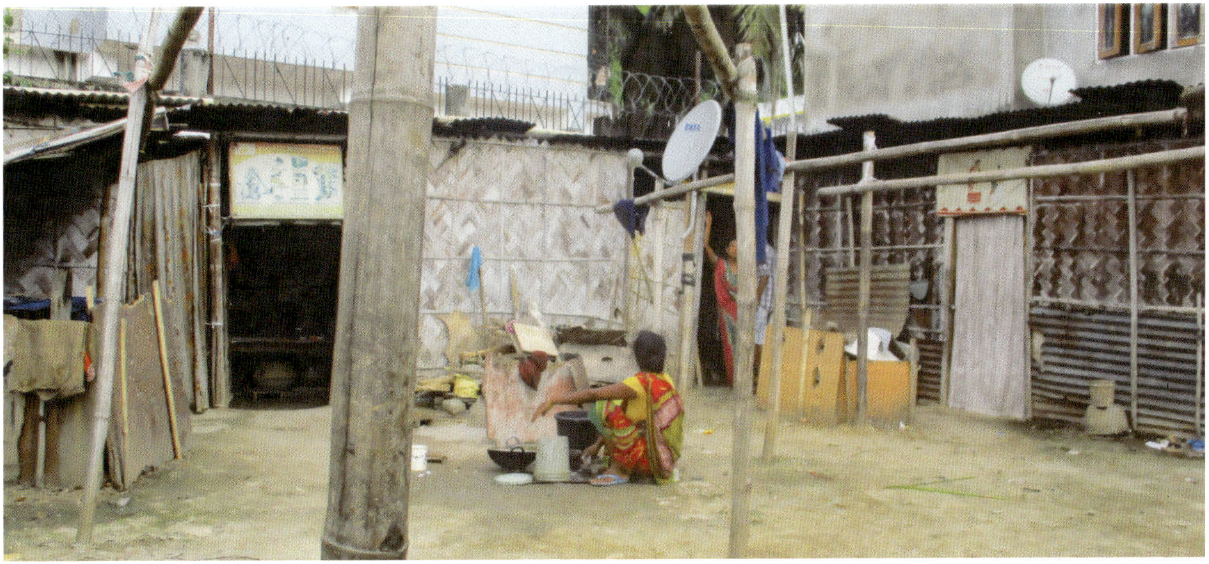

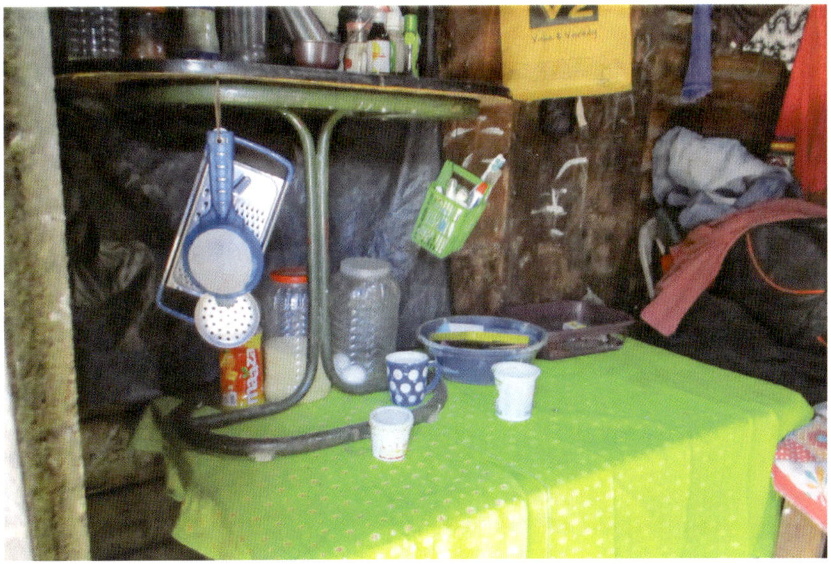

Outside/inside; double-sited kitchen of the migrant's bamboo home.

Worlds of Work

Guwahati Fish Market

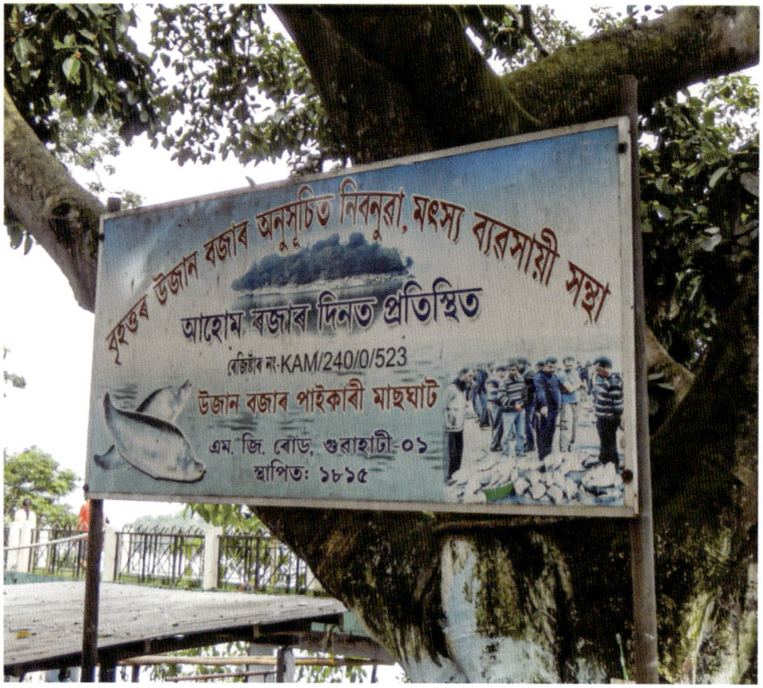

One of the oldest *maas ghat* or fish markets in Guwahati is located on the banks of the river Brahmaputra, in Uzanbazar, a residential-cum-commercial area. It's said that this *maas ghat* (fish port) dates back to the early nineteenth century, during the period of the Ahom dynasty. Today, fishermen from villages in North Guwahati come in boats to deliver the fish at this *maas ghat*. Each wholesaler invites bids from fish sellers, and every net of fish is auctioned. All the other sellers from Barpeta and other districts use carrier vans to deliver their quota to the market. They come to Guwahati twice or thrice a week, and if needed at other times of the week, such as festivals, to deliver fish at other fish markets. Many local fish vendors or hawkers buy fish from bigger sellers in Barpeta, and deliver fish to various localities on bicycles. The *maas ghat* sells local fish, while the markets in Garchuk and Fancy Bazar sell *salani* fish – or the fish that comes from outside the state which requires a *challan* or a receipt.

The *maas ghat* is a very busy place, employing a large number of migrant labour to unload the catch from boats, clean and prepare fish and the numerous processes of sale. Many cycles, *rikshas* and pick up vans are parked on the edges of *maas ghat*, waiting to be loaded with fish to distribute to different parts of the city. Wholesalers and sellers are constantly weighing and cleaning fish. A few men sit on a bench or a dedicated cubical structure and loudly shout numbers, inviting bids indicating quantity, quality and price. Sellers and contractors sitting in the core area note the nosily shouted numbers. At the peripheries, smaller vendors sit, selling small pieces of fish, usually the less preferred or cheaper portions.

A migrant vendor who came into the city from a village in North Guwahati, sits on the outer edges of the market. She sells coconuts and a few other vegetables, like edible ferns and lime. She said that most of the vendors who come from these villages buy a quantity of vegetables from a wholesaler in the north bank of the River Brahmaputra, and then take the boat to come to Uzan Bazar. They leave at dawn every morning and the commute takes them close to an hour. They return home by 2 pm, once their products have been sold for the day.

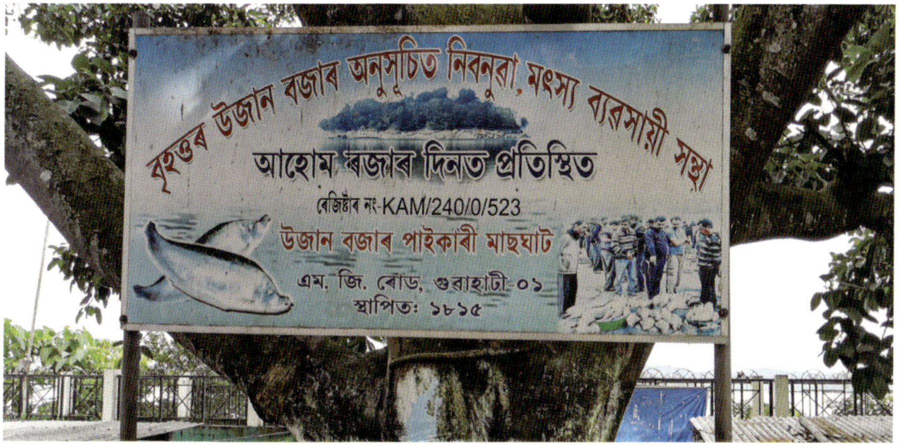

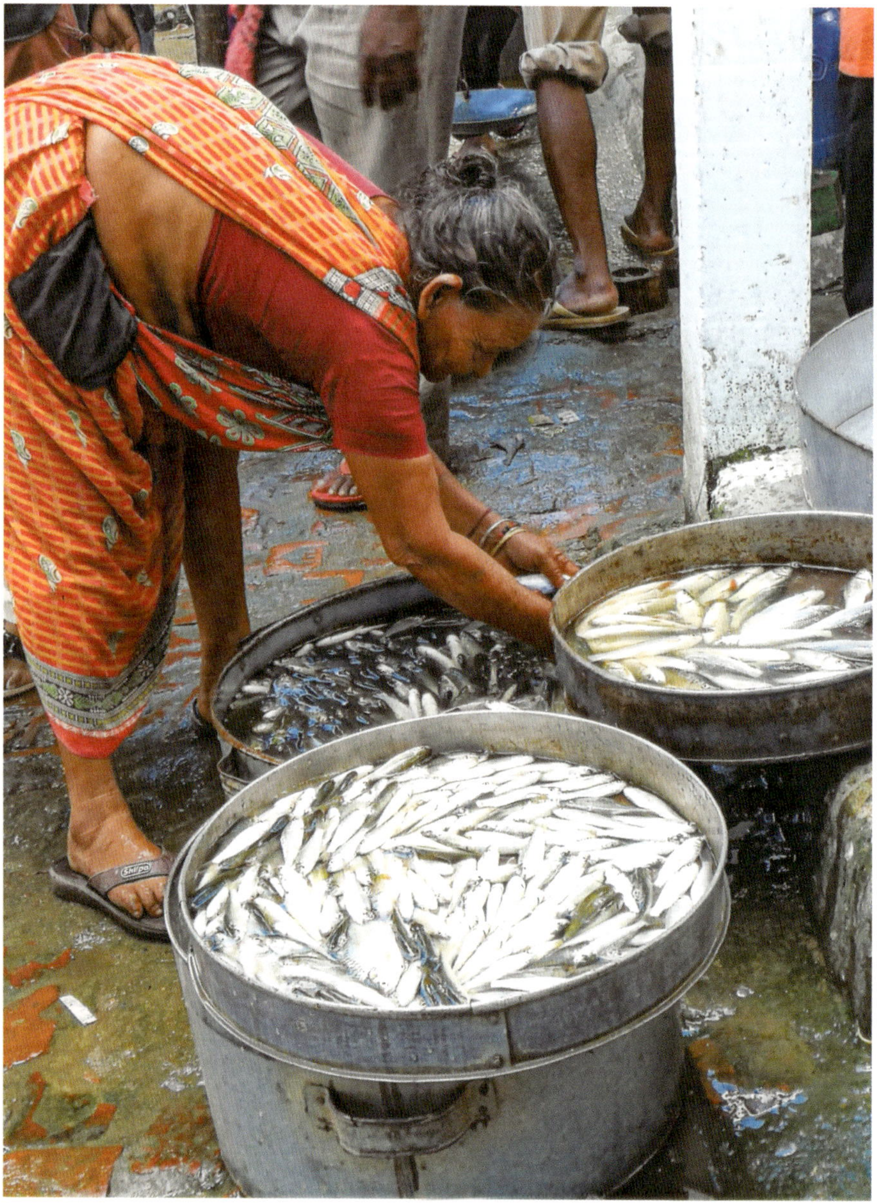

Fresh fish brought every day to Uzan Bazar *maas ghat*, fish market, Guwahati.

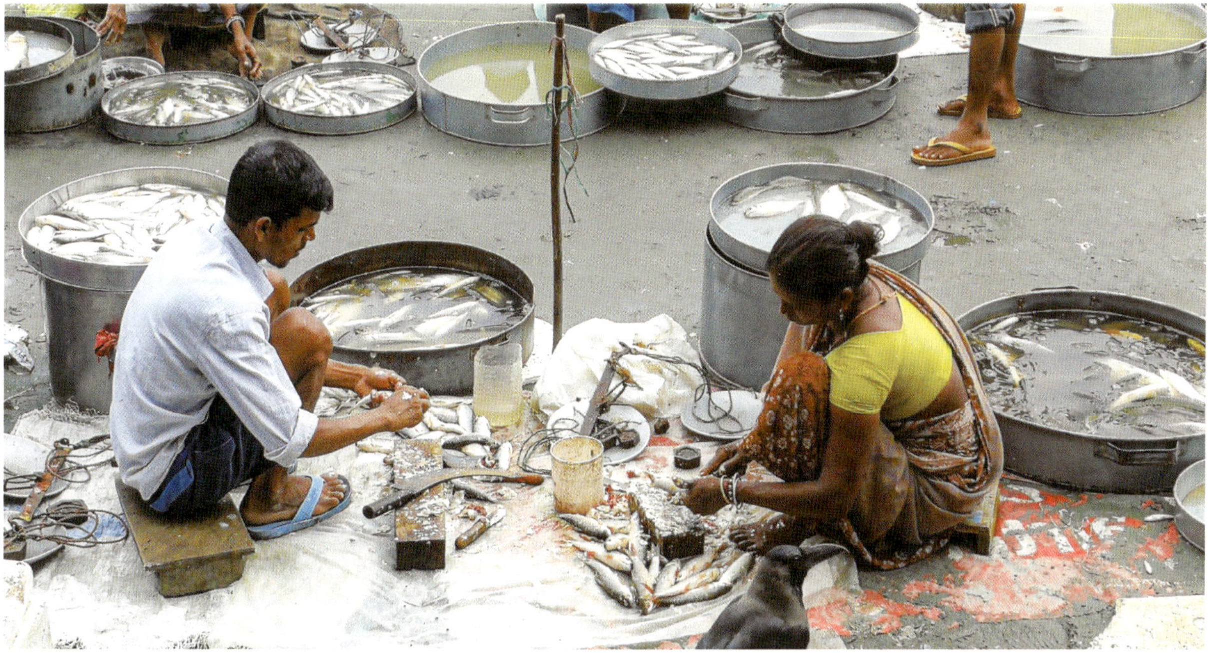

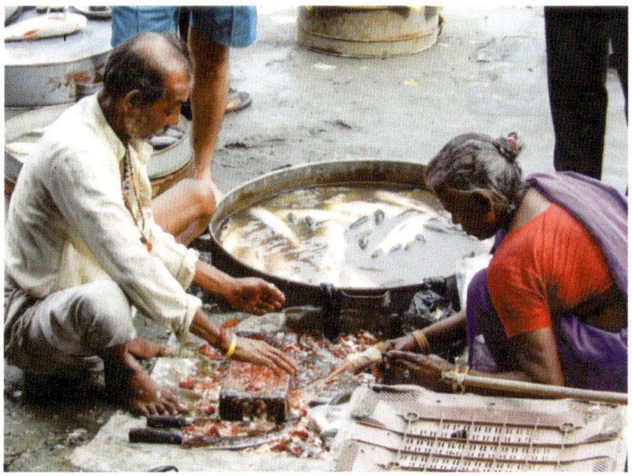

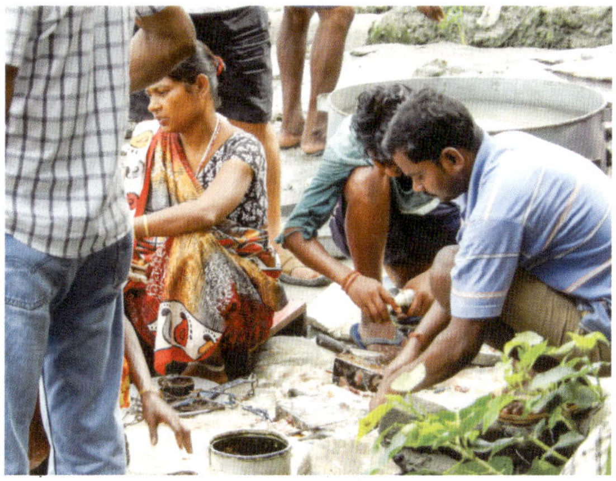

Fresh fish is cleaned by labour employed by small and large wholesalers, and prepared for distribution and sale.

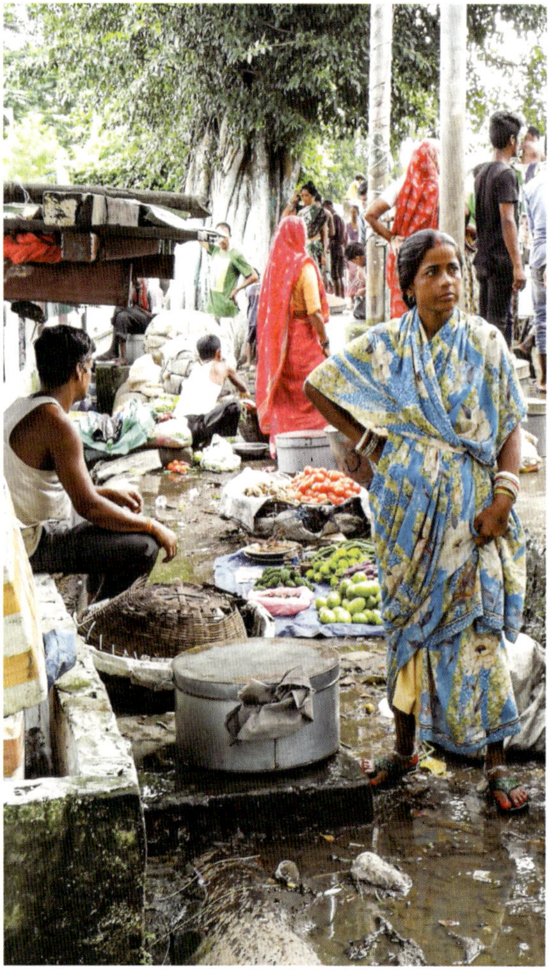

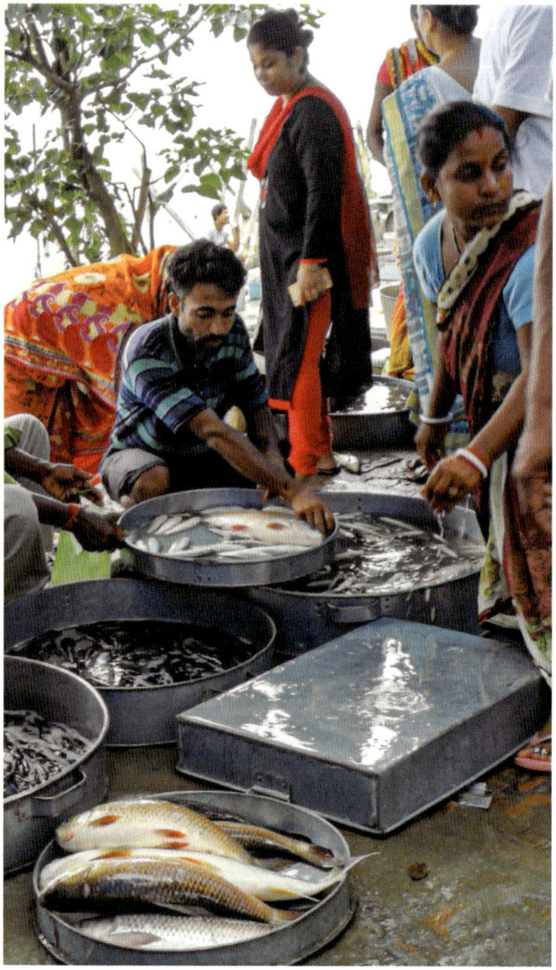

Women play a critical role
in the sale of fresh fish in Uzan Bazar.

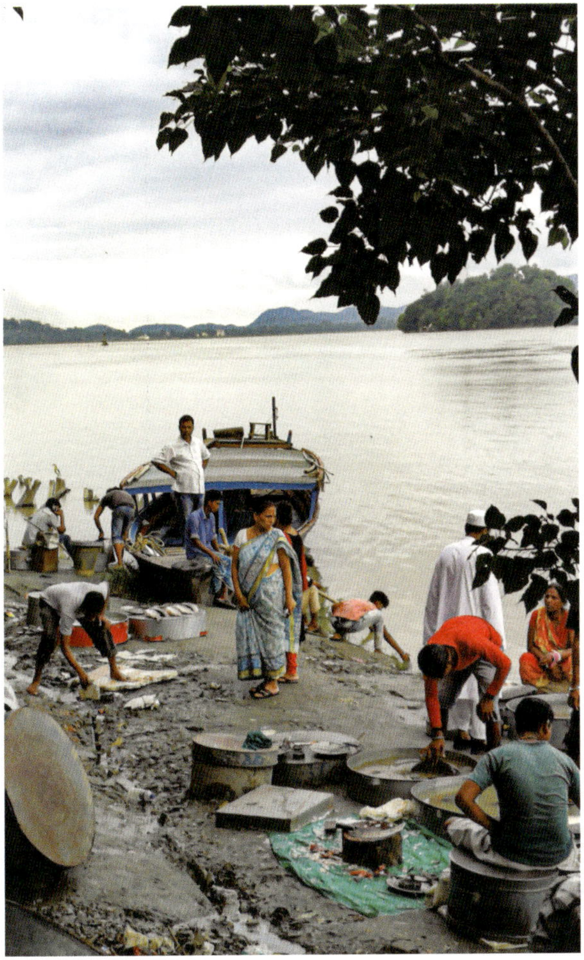

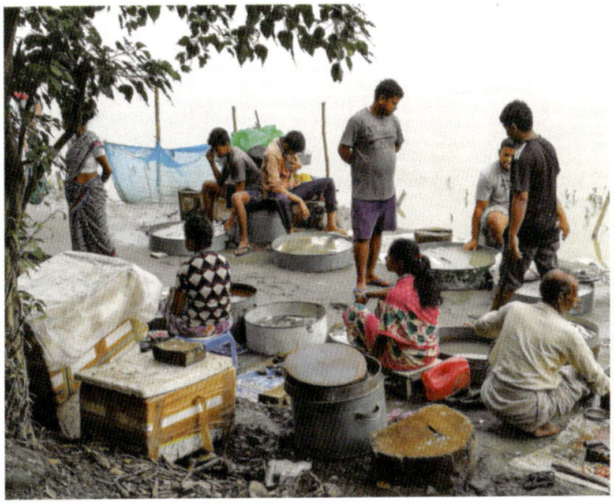

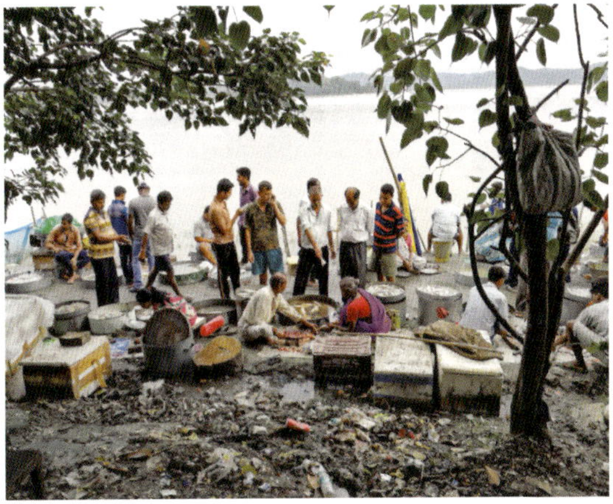

Fresh catch brought in by river boats to *maas ghat* is rapidly auctioned.

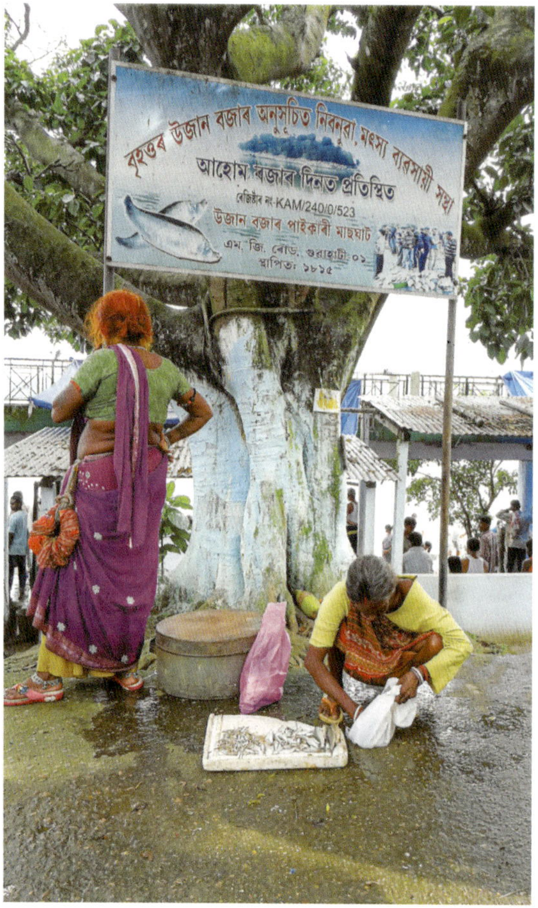

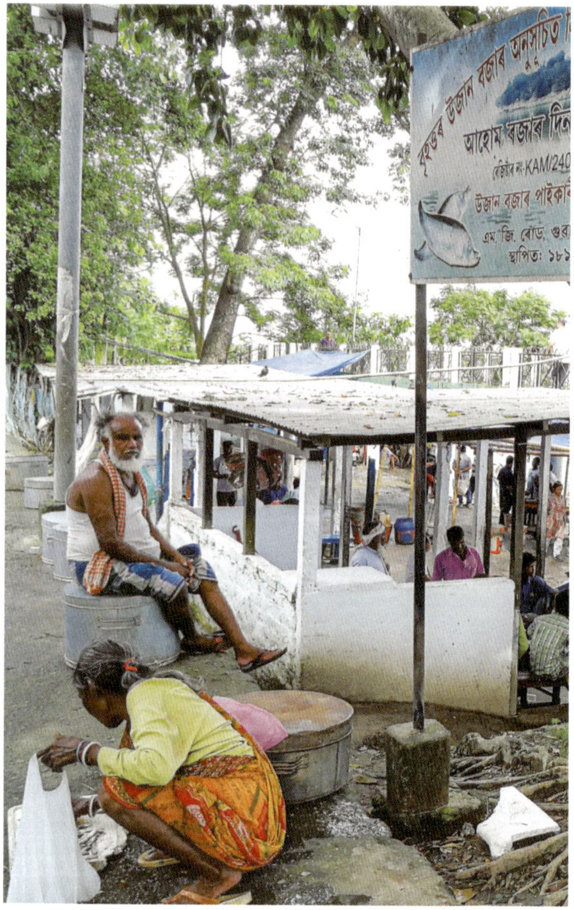

On the edges of the market, small sellers, usually women, sell cheaper fish.

Worlds of Work

Leather in Bootan Mandi

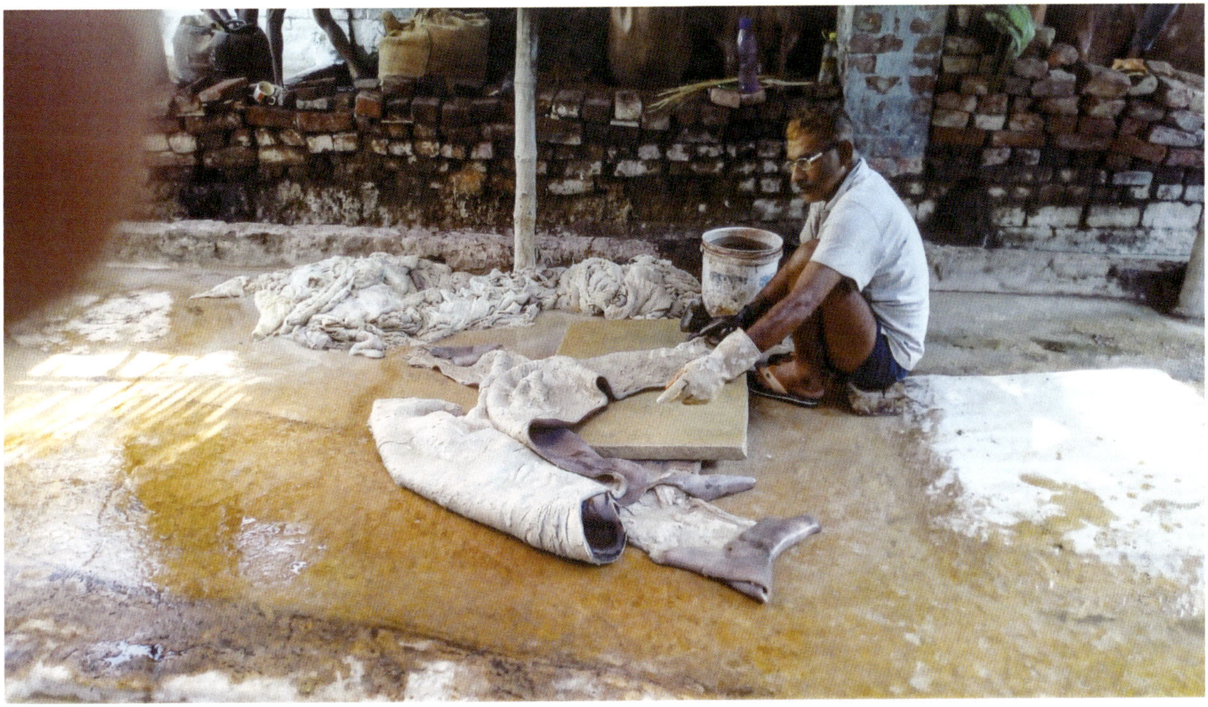

Converting skin to leather isn't easy. As material, leather needs to imitate the suppleness of skin. Unlike skin, it mustn't wrinkle or decay. Colonial military uniforms with their leather belts, boots and straps, gave a boost to leather tanneries established near cantonments. The cantonment in Jalandhar, one of the oldest in North India, benefited from the demand for boots and saddles. Labour intensive methods of tanning and curing create a demand for labour, pulling in migrants from different parts of India, who settle in cities like Jalandhar with flourishing leather businesses, particularly its 'leather neighbourhood', Bootan Mandi, and the newly established Leather Complex on the outskirts of the city.

Leather is big business in India. At the turn of the century, the Council for Leather Exports under the Ministry of Commerce concentrated on 'finished' leather goods to add value to leather. Medium and large scale leather enterprises benefited greatly from state policy. Nevertheless, small scale and cottage industries employ a huge number of people in the labour intensive processes required to convert skin to leather. These small scale workshops at the lower end of the social hierarchy have increasingly become an important focus of government policy.

The labour of migrants is critical to large scale and to artisanal enterprises. Migrant artisans, especially those skilled in flaying, curing and leather tanning become valuable members of the local community. In Jalandhar, many migrant leather artisans and leather workers settled in Punjab and in 2018, the year of the survey, had lived in the state for 30 years or more. The more recent migrants to Jalandhar are employed in larger leather factories, part of the Leather Complex on the outskirts of the city.

How is leather made? When a dead animal is skinned, its skin is flexible, elastic and quite resilient. When it dries – and it does that quite quickly – the skin shrinks, becomes hard and begins to crack. Getting the skin ready for tanning involves intense and laborious acts of washing, pulling, stretching, soaking, pounding and hanging of hides, acts that require intense physical labour.

When an unprocessed hide arrives at a tannery in all its rawness, the first thing is to wash it thoroughly to remove the blood, the membrane, the grease, or the dirt sticking to the hide and hair. Soaking and washing the skin and hide is hard, manual labour. The skin is placed in a salt solution and stirred frequently to ensure the gradual decrease of bacteria that can transform the skin. Though the soaked skin softens after a while, it still needs to be cleansed of the matter that associates it with life – fat, flesh, keratin (that makes up the weight of hair) and blood. Soaking, pounding and scouring the skin to remove these 'life' substances are the first steps in converting skin to leather.

Removing hair – an important by-product – needs careful handling. Hair is used for paint, shoe, horse and cleaning brushes. By and large, bristle is removed in abattoirs; some dressing of bristle is done in tanneries by leather workers.

Bootan Mandi in Jalandhar has a long history of leather tanning and shoe making. Migrants moved into Bootan Mandi, working as loaders or in the numerous processes of curing and tanning. Over time, the more skilled migrants became valuable members in Bootan's leather economy, greatly sought after and offered regular employment. Some were already familiar with flaying, curing and tanning, especially migrants who came from the areas around Kanpur and Rai Bareilly.

In Bootan Mandi, no carcasses of recently dead animals are flayed; the skins or hide arrive either from an abattoir or from rural suppliers and skinners in villages. Trucks or carts carrying hides arrive regularly in Bootan and are stored in small warehouses called *godams*. Warehouses employ migrants labour to load and offload hides from trucks and carts.

Liming to remove hair leaves the skin quite hard. It is also a process that is most closely associated with odours (Ayuz, 2009). Liming has to be carefully judged, for some products require lime to be left in while others do not. If the hide is required for harder leather commodities like shoe-soles, a small amount of lime is allowed to remain in the skin; otherwise lime is thoroughly washed out. Thinning the hide and making it softer and more supple needs additional soaking in deep pits. Hung back on the beam, the hide is washed and cleansed once again. The frequent washings prepare the skin for tanning.

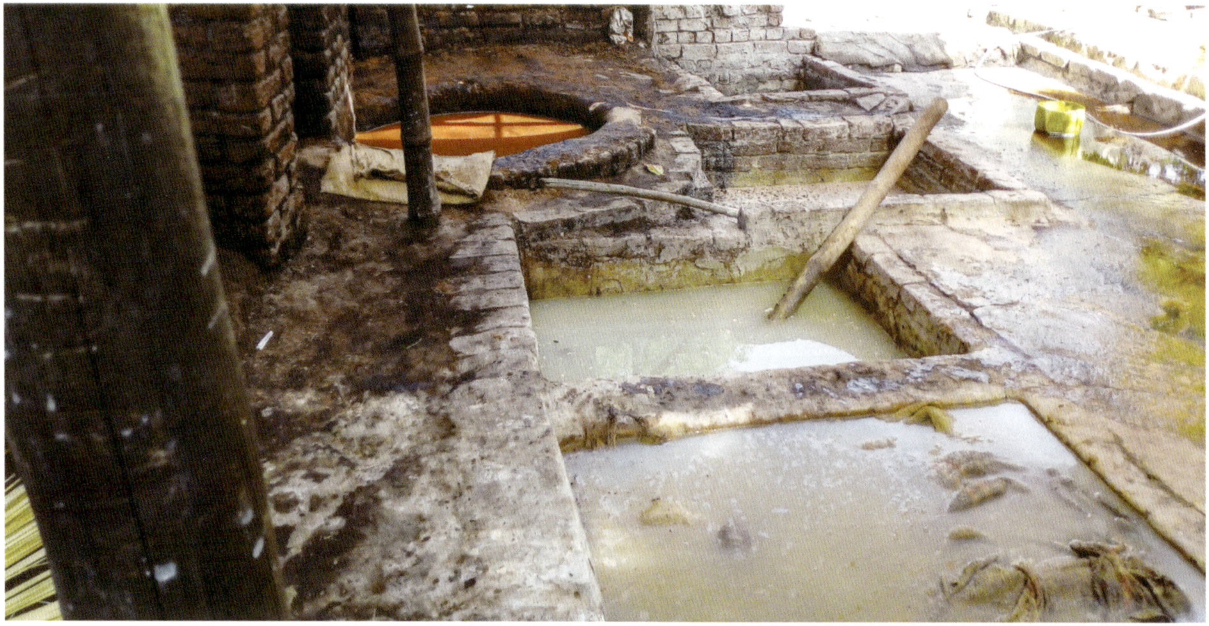

Soaking and Liming pits. Raw hide is soaked to remove hair, dirt and blood, and soften the hide.

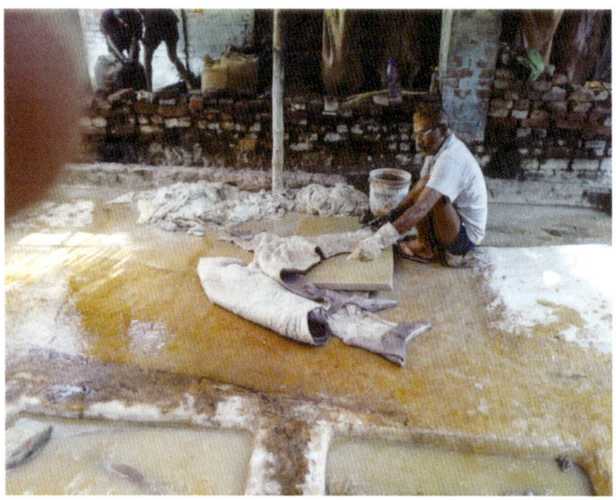

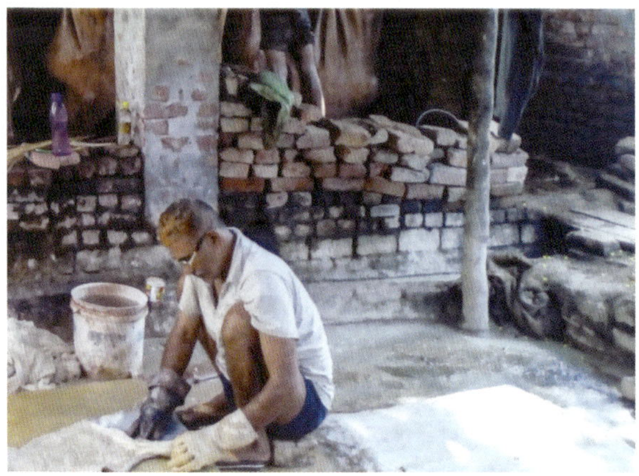

Splitting the hide into layers before tanning and drying.

Tanning involves stretching and pulling the skin. Stretching is important to 'open' the pores of the stiffening hide so that various substances used to keep the skin supple can be absorbed, or steep into the skin. Skin may be stretched on frames and soaked in tannin. The skin is stirred quite vigorously, so that the tannin can penetrate the pores. The skins are soaked in the astringent infusion of the bark of *babul* (*acacia arabica*) to make them less water soluble and able to resist bacterial decomposition. Post tanning, the hides are dried, readying them for their future use as leather. Vegetable tanning thickens the skin and makes it malleable, though in comparison to the more modern – and now more common – process of blue chrome tanning, vegetable tanning makes the skin less soft. Leather that has been tanned in *babul* bark is most suited for saddles, luggage, belts, furniture and products that require harder quality leather. If very soft leather is required, post tanning and drying the leather is dressed in oil in a process called currying. Again, soaking, cleaning and rubbing are necessary, all of which need hard labour and considerable skill.

Chrome tanning, developed in America in the late 19th century was adopted in India by colonial run and managed tanneries. Chromium(III) compounds are used in place of vegetable tanning, replacing tree bark in favour of a chemical process. With chrome tanning the skin fibres become grey-blue, which is the reason why this process is often referred to as 'wet blue'. Quite apart from the fact that chrome tanning is a much quicker process, it also produces leather which is very soft. Wet blue or chrome tanned leather is used for handbags and shoe uppers. Dyeing leather in various colours – red, yellow, brown – entails men standing in large vats of dye and stamping on the softening leather to evenly distribute the colour within the fibre. These are more common to Middle Eastern leather processing though small businesses based in Bootan advertise leather dyed in numerous colours. Migrant labour is critical to this process.

Ayuz, Fazli, Odor: An important problem in leather industry https://www.researchgate.net/publication/270892028 [Accessed 8 December 2020]

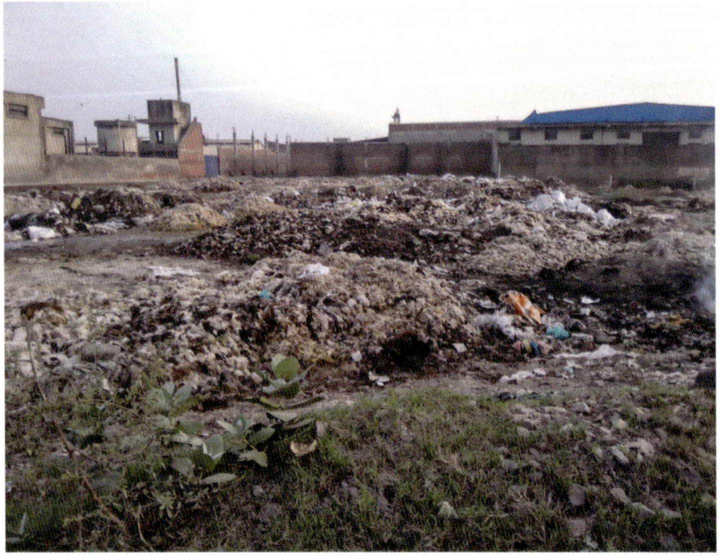

Waste animal hair.

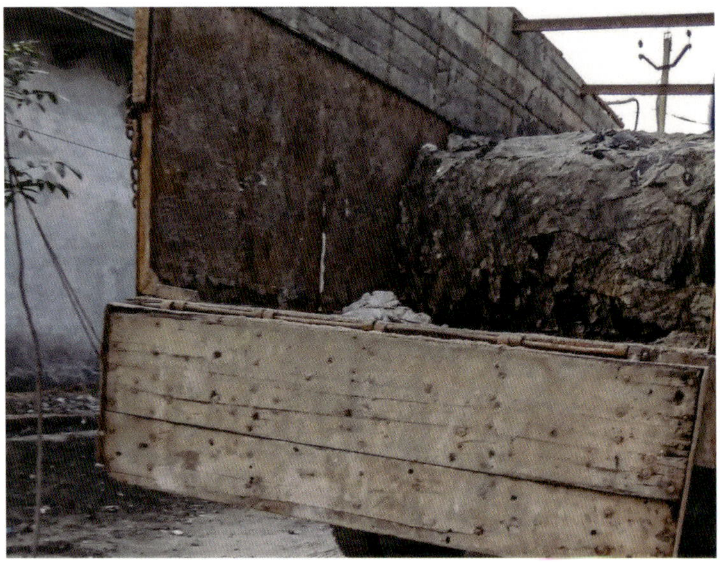

Hides arrive at the Chamra Mandi, the hide market in Bootan Mandi, Jalandhar.

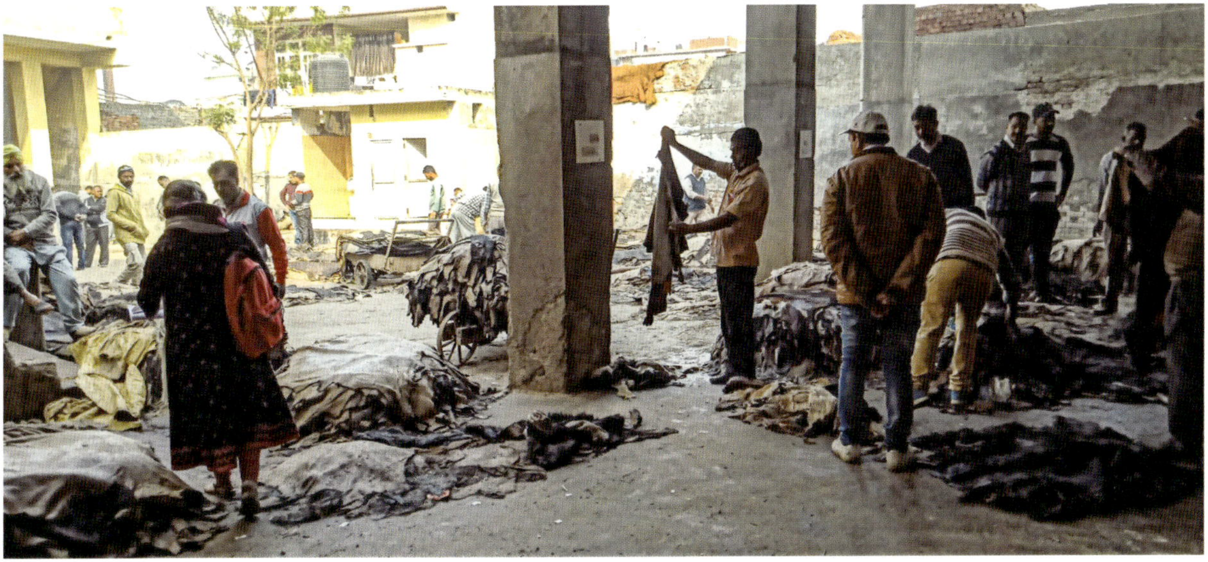

Auction of hides at
Chamra Mandi, Jalandhar.

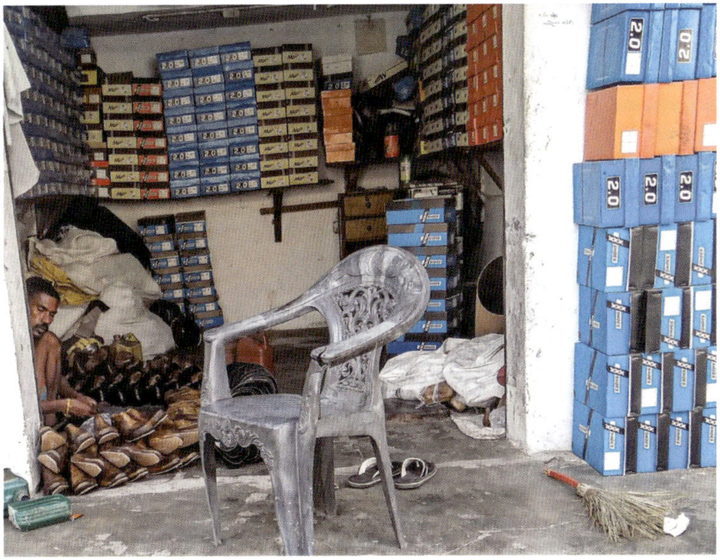

Workshop, Bootan Mandi, Jalandhar.

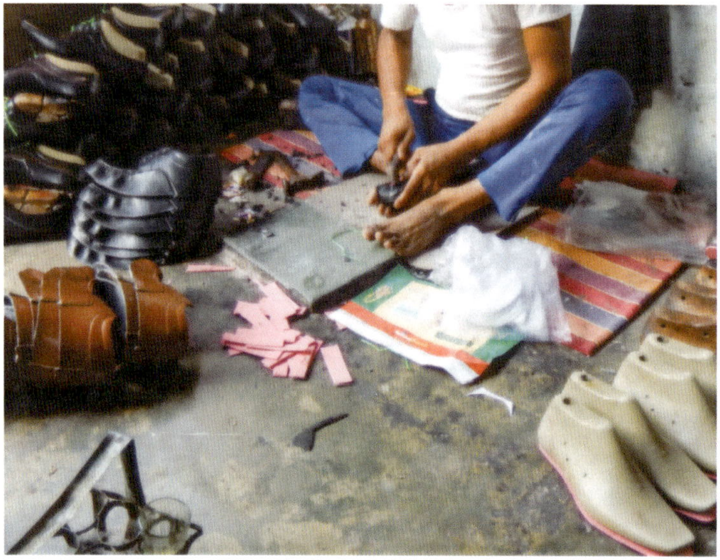

Shoe uppers being cut in a small, artisanal workshop in Bootan Mandi.

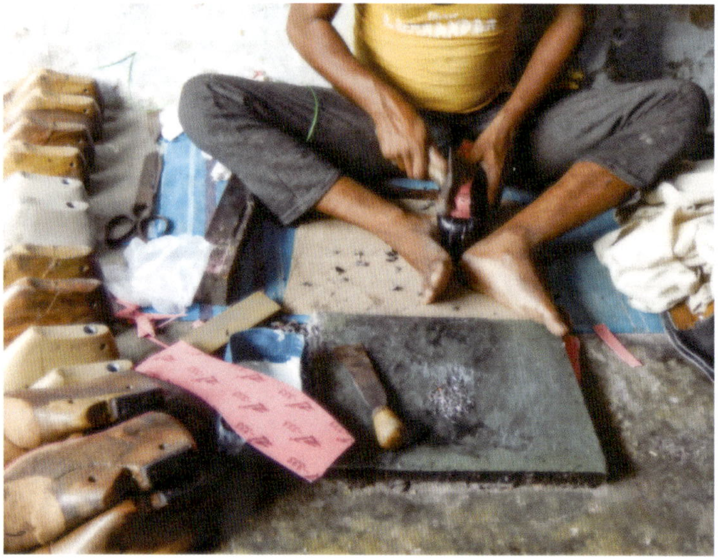

Shoe lasts and uppers, an artisanal workshop in Bootan Mandi.

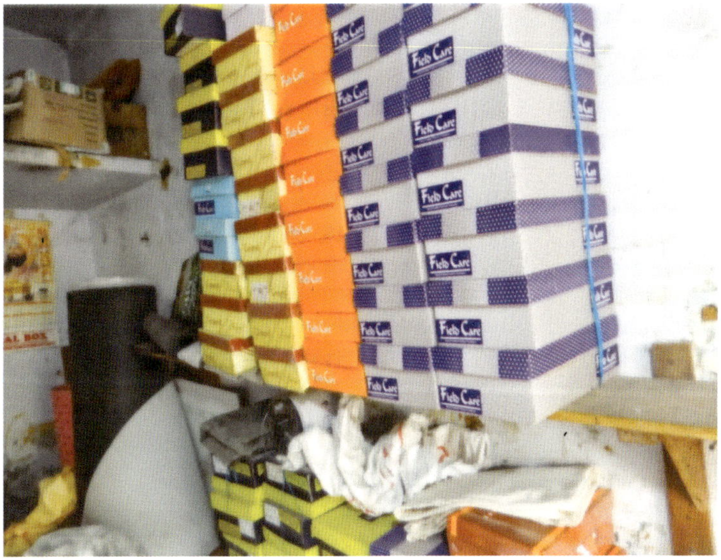

Locally made shoes sold at a small outlet, Bootan Mandi.

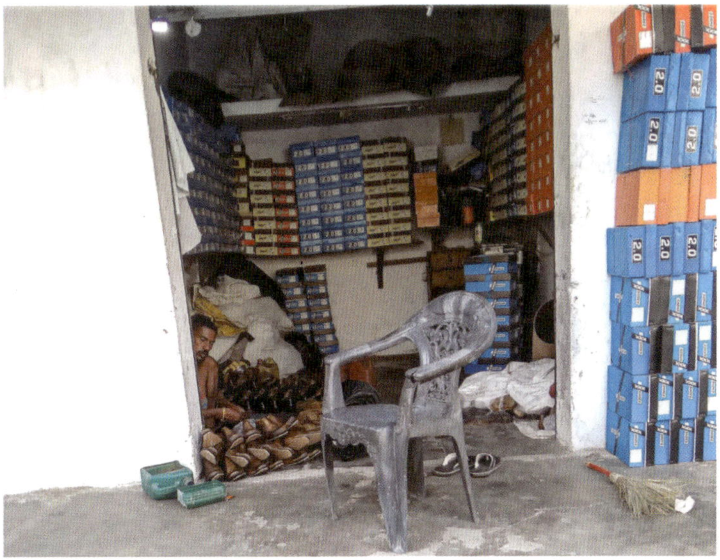

Juta dukan, shoe shop of locally made shoes, Bootan Mandi.

Worlds of Work

Synthetic Shoes and Slippers

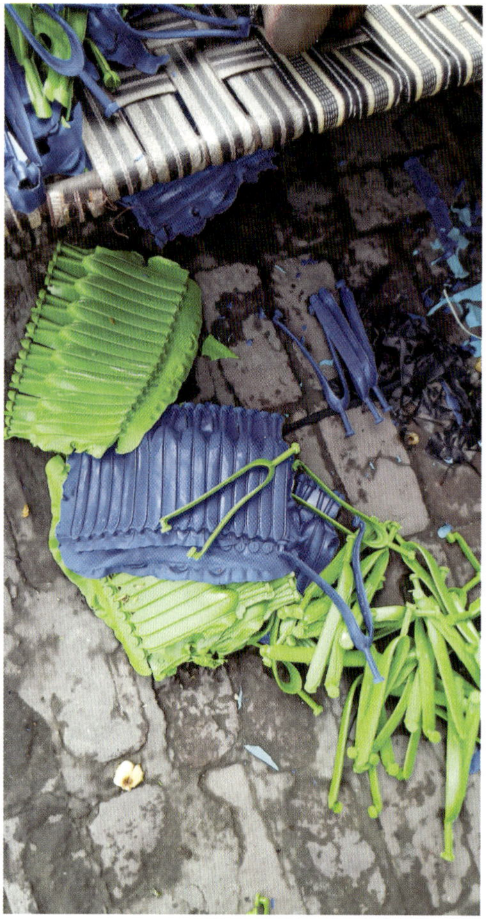

Moulded 'blocks' of fibre straps need to be manually cut to make pairs for slippers.

Quite apart from leather tanning and processes for which Bootan Mandi is justly famous, twenty first century Bootan Mandi is becoming known for the number of small enterprises engaged in making synthetic fibre sports and walking shoes. An entire lane of Bootan Mandi is dedicated to stitching synthetic shoes. The business in synthetic shoes and goods has increased more rapidly in comparison to the number of workshops that continue to make leather boots and shoes. The demand for synthetic sports and leisure footwear is perhaps the clearest indication of the commercial challenges that confront leather.

Migrant labour is central to the small and medium enterprises engaged in making synthetic footwear. Some processes – cutting straps of *chappals* (slippers) or fixing tips of shoelaces – involve manual labour. These processes are farmed out on a piece rate system to women of migrant households, who work as home-based workers to complete the product.

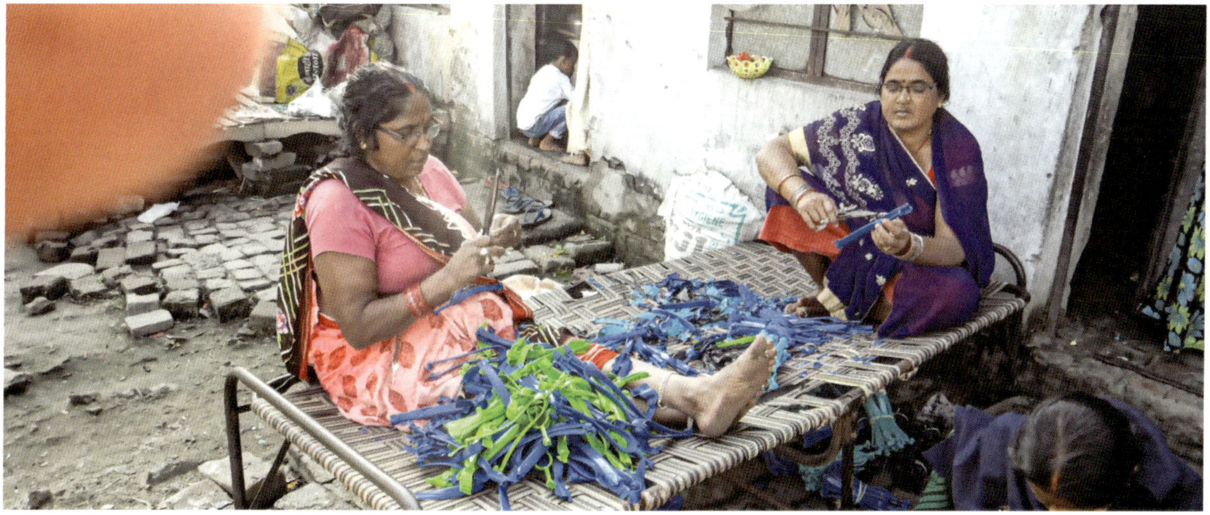

Migrant women cut the straps for slip-on footwear.

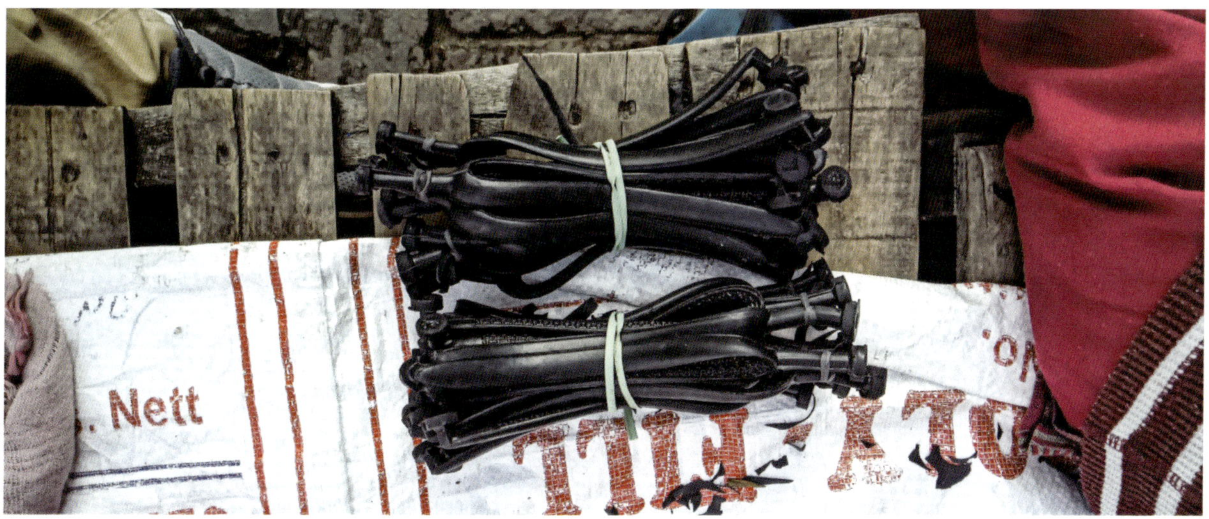

Cut and completed, slipper straps are tied in bundles;
the home-based woman worker is paid by the number of pieces in a bundle.

Worlds of Work

Grain Mandi

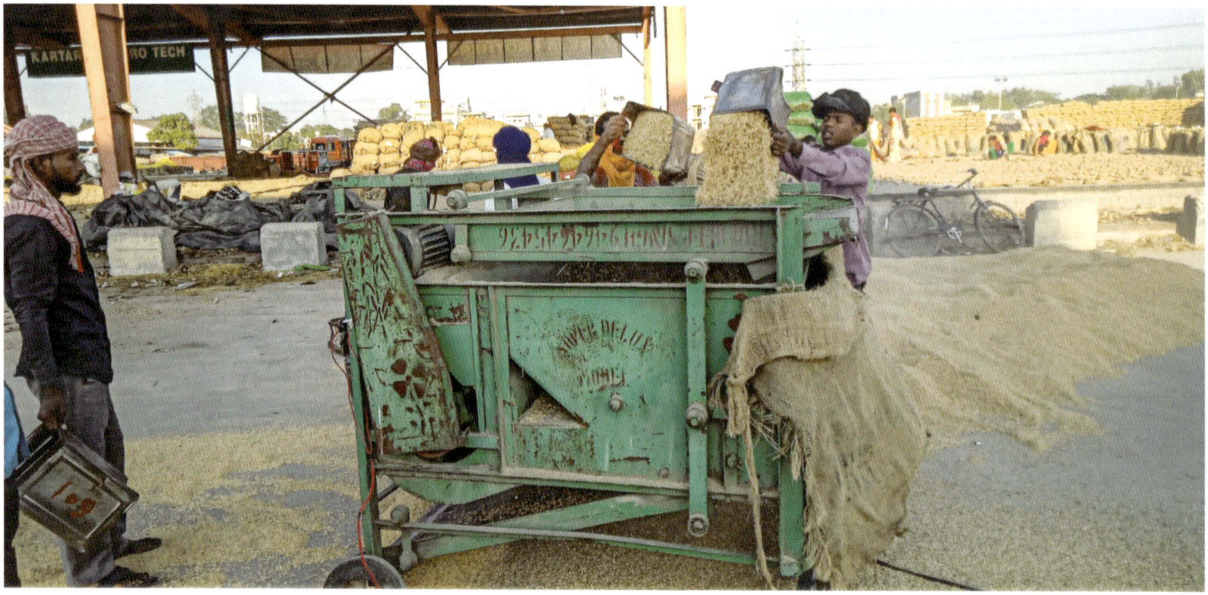

Extract from field notes – Jalandhar, November 2019

Today, Bharti and I went to *Sabzi Mandi* in Jalandhar to talk to migrant workers machine-drying paddy and stitching jute-bags for the grain. We went to an establishment in Maqsudan from Bawa Nahar. Bharti went in first and I joined her after parking the two-wheeler. When I reached, Bharti was talking to Ashok, a worker who was busy drying rice grain. Another worker was working on jute-bags. Workers were engaged in swiftly filling machines that dry the rice grain, before filling gunny sacks. They had to work fast, keeping up with the machines.

I observed another worker cutting jute-bags. Most of the jute-bags were torn. His task was to cut them up into portions to make them reusable. The torn pieces were collected from shops in the *mandi*, cut and then delivered as whole bags back to the shop. Each worker gets paid ₹ 1 per jute-bag. Shop owners employ different people for stitching these portions together in the desired sized. Some portions which were rejected would later be used to make cardboard.

One of the workers told us that they come here in the morning, very early around 4 or 5 am, and they keep working all day. They commute by auto-*rikshas*. They do not have any holidays, not even on Sundays, though the Mandi is closed. Income is very low, and they cannot afford to take an off-day. Despite working continuously, they are barely able to manage their expenses. They say they won't be able to stay afloat if they don't work (*chhutti nahi karte; chhuti karenge to khane ke liye kaun dega; kar-karke nahi hota, to kaam nahi karenge to kaise hoga*).

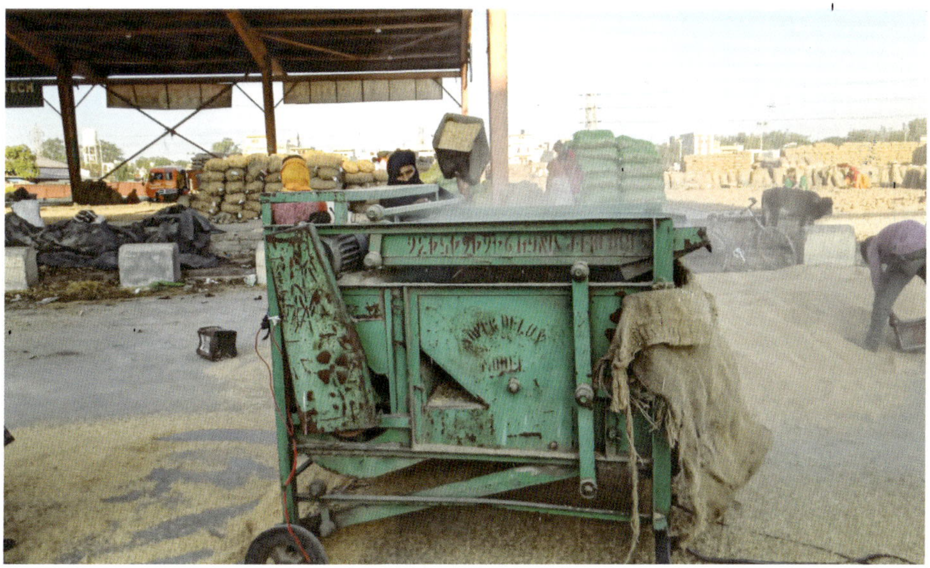

Drying paddy before it is bagged in gunny sacks.

Worlds of Work

Bora – The Omnipresent Gunny Sack

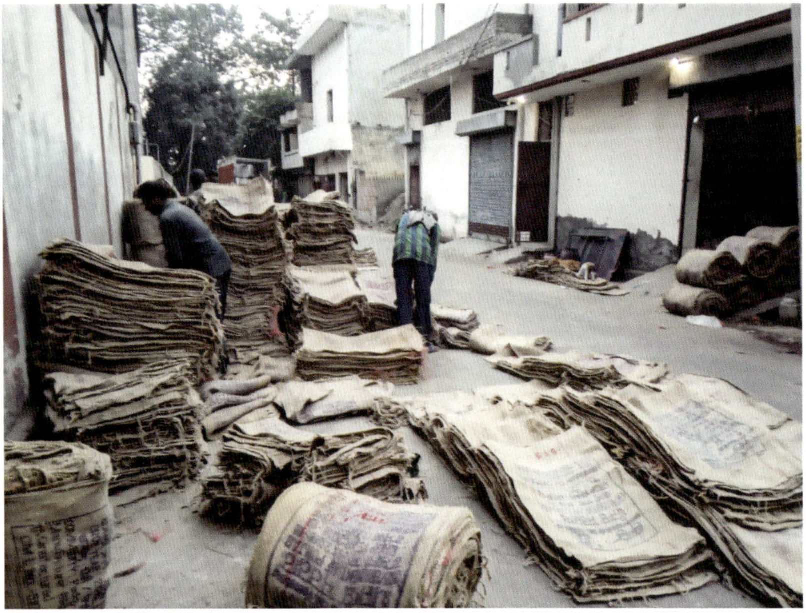

No grain or vegetable *mandi* is complete without the indispensable *bora*, the coarse gunny sack, woven of jute or hemp. Grain and perishable commodities – wheat, rice, potatoes, onions, fresh vegetables are transported across urban landscapes, encased in gunny. Quite apart from the convenience of storing and transporting grain and produce, the durable gunny sack is used as a measure – the half quintal *bora*; the *pachees kilo boriyan*, the twenty-five kilo sacks. Perishable goods stored in gunny rarely spoil because gunny is a porous, breathable fabric.

Warehouses – *godams* – of gunny are essential for grain merchants and sellers. Every gunny *godam* employs migrant workers to cut and separate pre-stitched sacks that are rolled into huge and heavy bales of gunny.

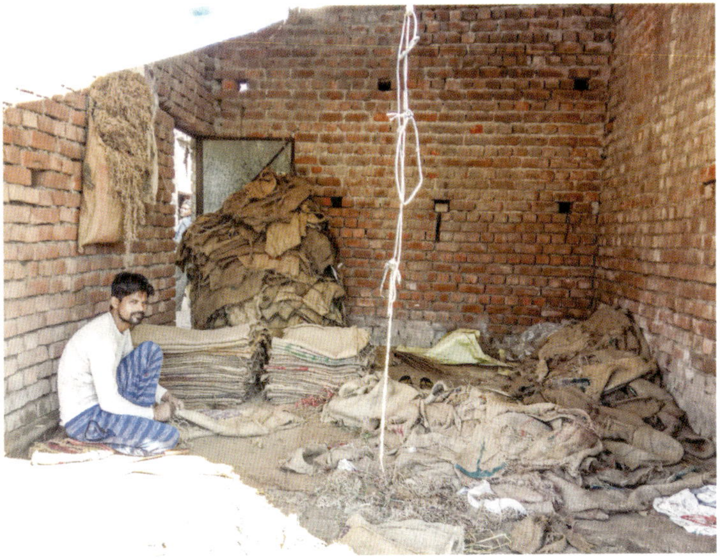

Stitching gunny bags to be filled with grain.

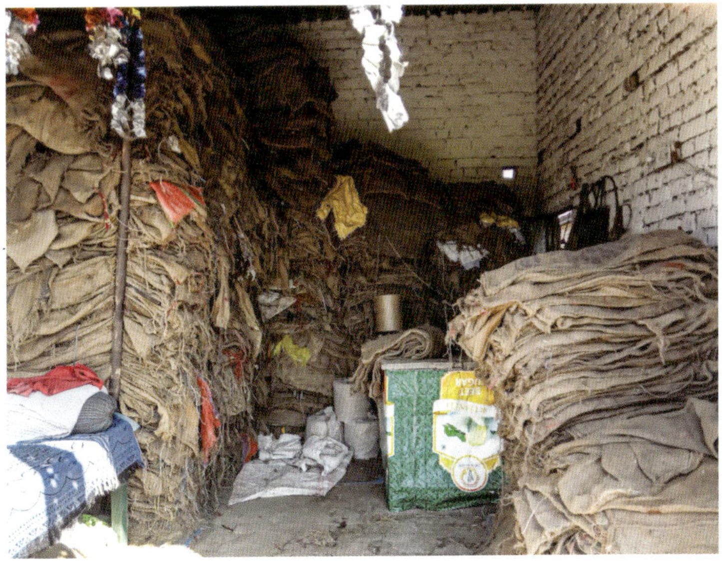

A store room for gunny bags, doubles as the sleeping quarters for migrant labour who work in grain mandis.

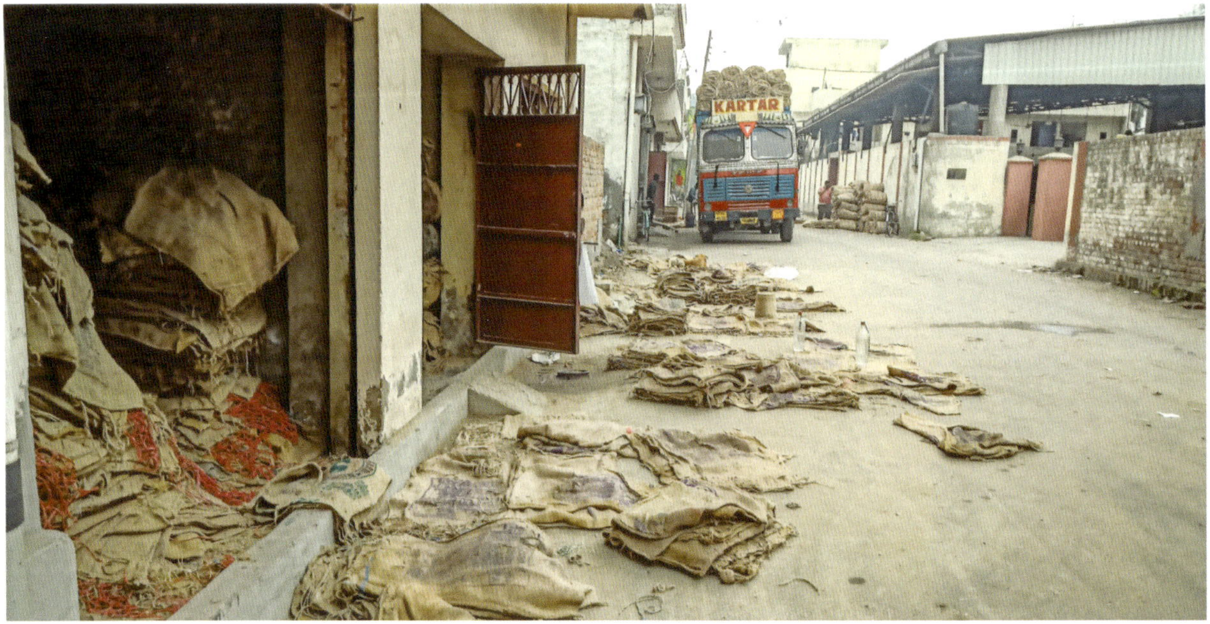

Gunny *godam*.

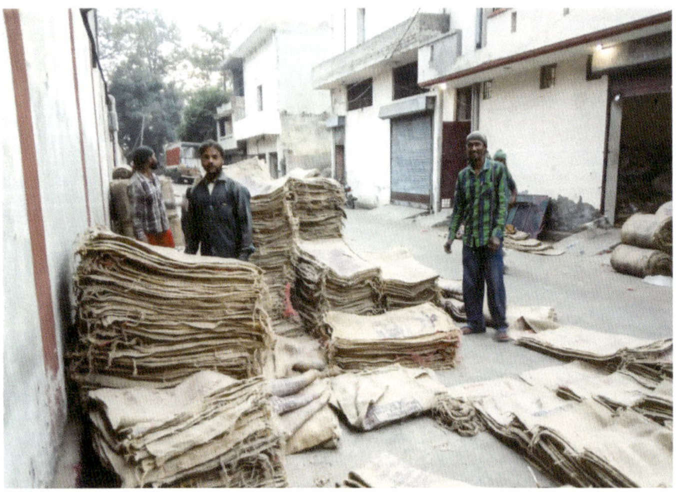

Segregating differently-sized *boriyan*.

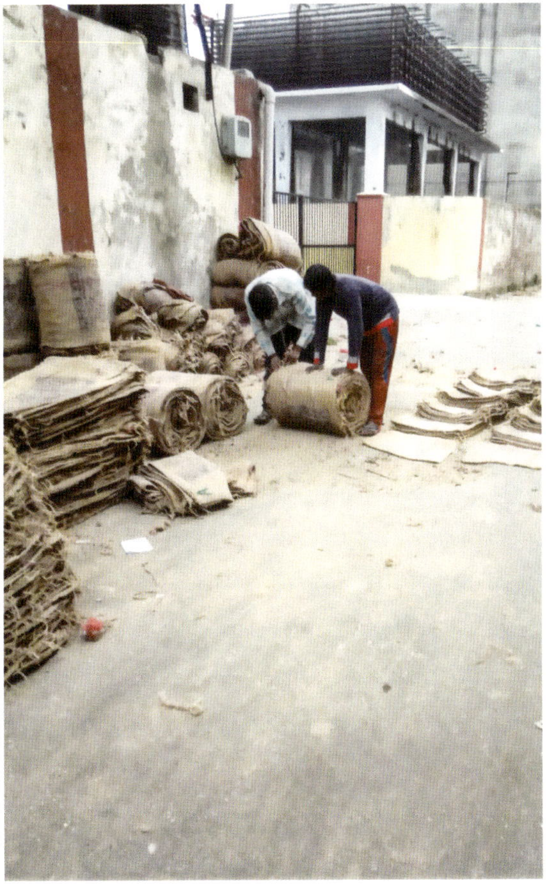
Unrolling bales of pre-stitched gunny sacks.

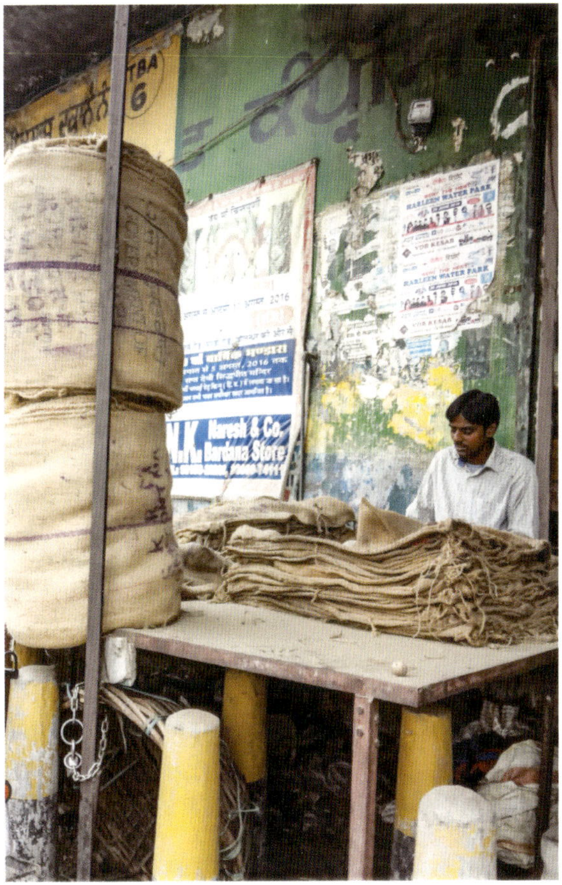

Hisab-kitab – counting sacks.

Living in the City
Pavements and Homes

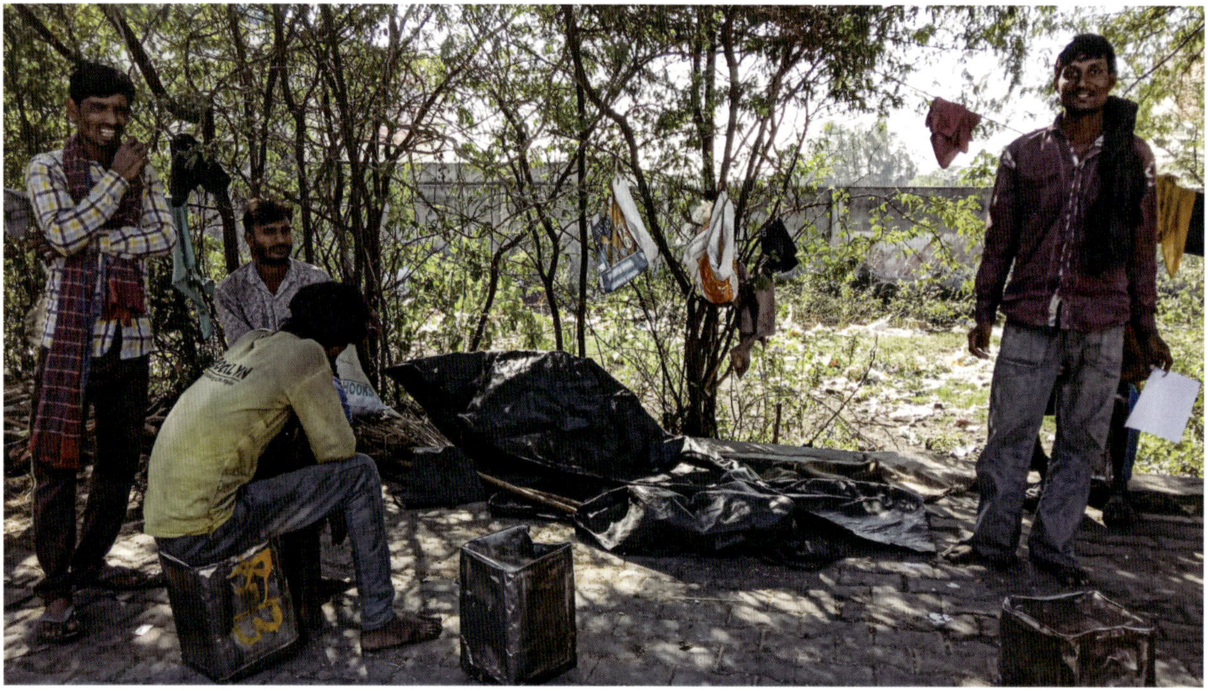

The common idea of 'a roof over one's head' underlines our ideas of shelter and 'home'. For mobile populations of migrants, a key element is the floor. The fact of a slightly raised, *pucca* paved stone or brick floor, is invaluable when a home is impermeant. Paved *pucca* floors doesn't necessarily mean they are safe. What's valuable is a floor slightly raised above street level, demarcated and distinct from surrounding spaces like the street or any *kaccha*, mud packed space. Pavements of stone and brick remain comparatively dry. That's what is important.

Though pavements are ubiquitous throughout the city, not all of them are available for migrant housing. Elite localities may have the most durable and well-maintained *pucca* pavements, but the rights to use them are restricted, if not wholly unattainable. Around city centres and official complexes, living on pavements is prohibited. Pavements abutting shrines are more accessible, potentially able to be squatted on. Around construction sites, broken pavements provide floor space for fragile rooves and small cooking hearths. But these are temporary. And very soon, without being asked, migrant workers with their families will move. The city isn't always available to everyone. For migrants their marginality is indexed on the constantly shifting homes that are part of their working lives.

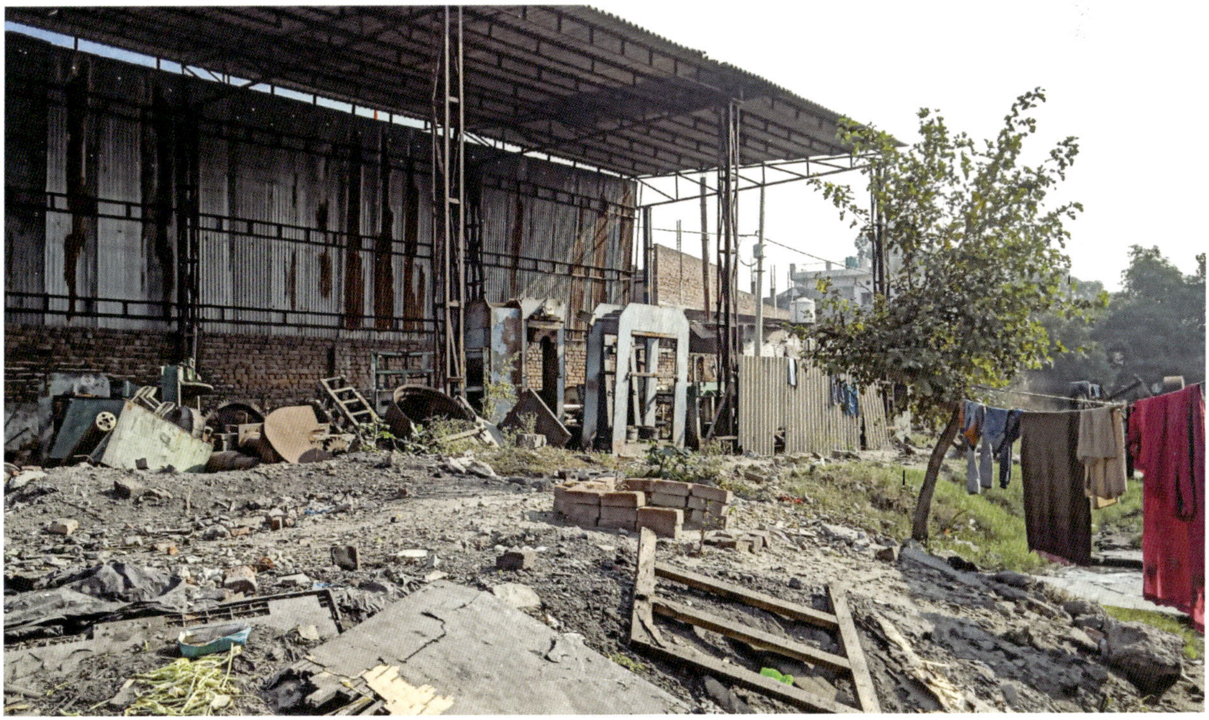

Migrant housing at a tyre factory dumpsite.

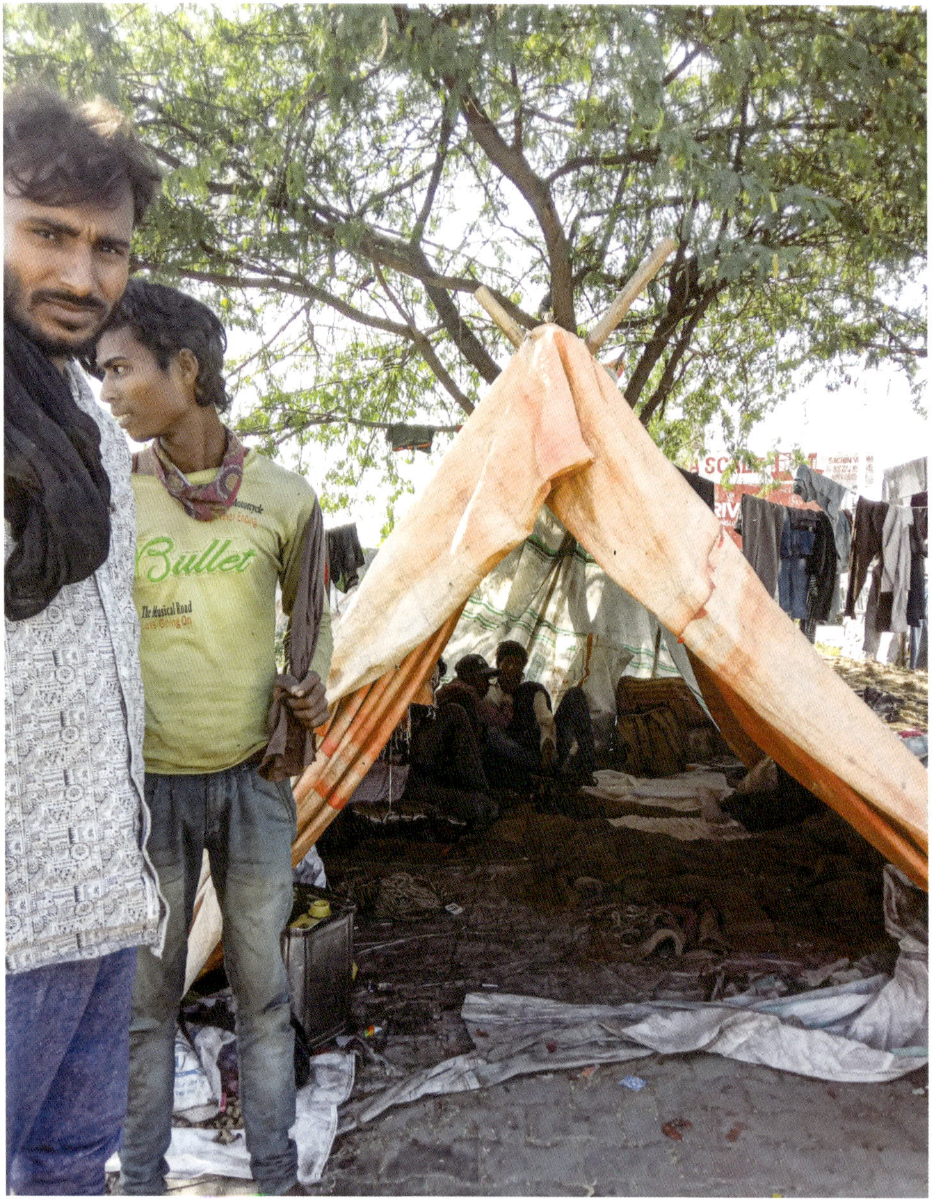

Migrant paddy workers set up temporary shelters, Jalandhar, July 2019.

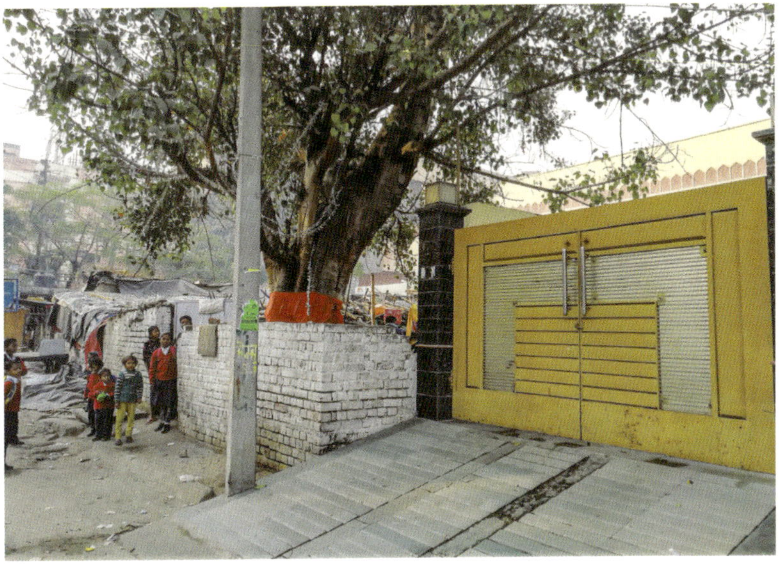

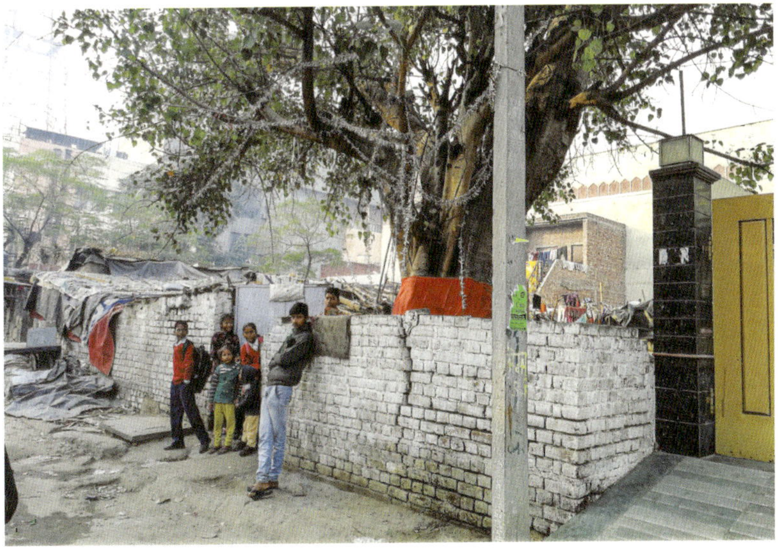

Low walled temporary shelters on a pavement, at the back gate of a boutique hotel.

Living in the City

Under the Flyover

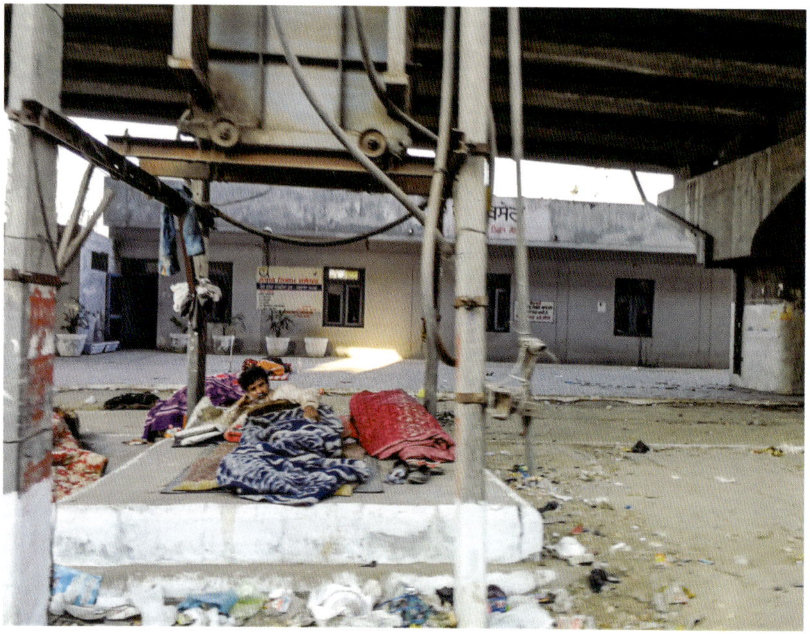

Flyovers are passages through the city – they are 'routes' between nodes and literally bypass everything that is urban and urbane. For poor migrants, the flyover is a sheltering, though thunderous, roof. Spaces under flyovers seem transient and temporary but are spaces that are at once a place of stay, of work, and precarious livelihoods.

Flyover living is bare life. Just living, not life. Merely biological life rather than how life should be lived. The most likely inhabitants of spaces under flyovers are low skilled, recently arrived, migrants. Living lives of precarity and continual displacement, small groups of migrants spread their meagre belongings under flyovers. Flyover living is a testament to the growing power of resource extractive industries, structural transformations and neo-liberal agrarian economies that have forced people to leave homes and families in search of employment. The barest shelter under the flyover is probably the best many low-income migrants can hope for.

Pandemic life

On 29 April 2020, soon after the pan Indian lockdown, 27 containment zones were identified in the city of Jalandhar notified by the District Magistrate. The zones were identified based on cumulative cases reported and the doubling rate.

A month later, on 28 May 2020, a report in the daily newspaper *Indian Express* noted that a flyover in Jalandhar on NH No.1, on the Pathankot bypass, had become home to hundreds of migrants since mid-April 2020. Migrants started living under the flyover in the hope of getting permission to enter a Covid screening centre, the last stop for the Shramik train journey to their homes of origin. The screening centre was just across the road from the flyover. Shramik train tickets were issued after a medical check at the screening centre. The report stated, "there are no public toilets and no facility for washing hands. But over the last 10 days, makeshift huts have come up."

[https://indianexpress.com/article/india/punjab-hundreds-of-migrants-make-flyover-opposite-covid-screening-centre-their-temporary-home-6422998/]

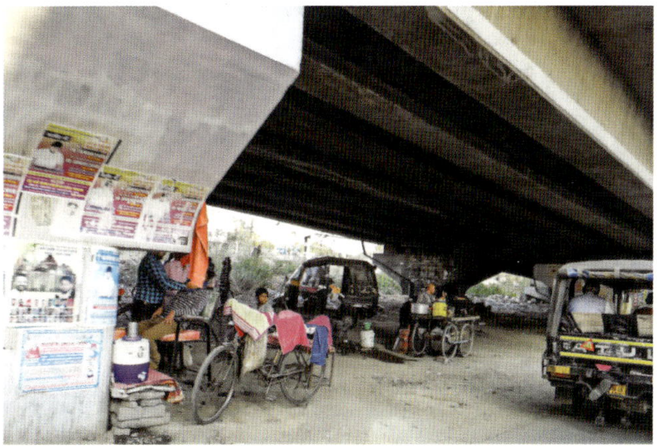

Living insecurely under a flyover.

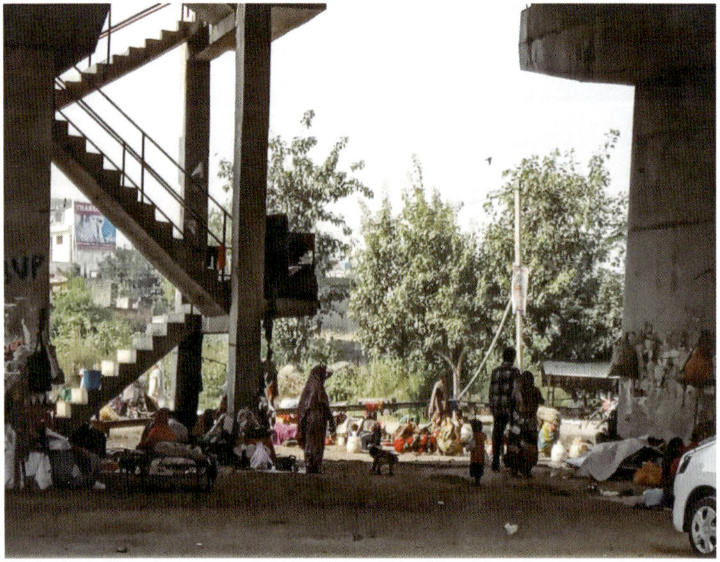

Under the DAV bridge, Jalandhar, October 2018.

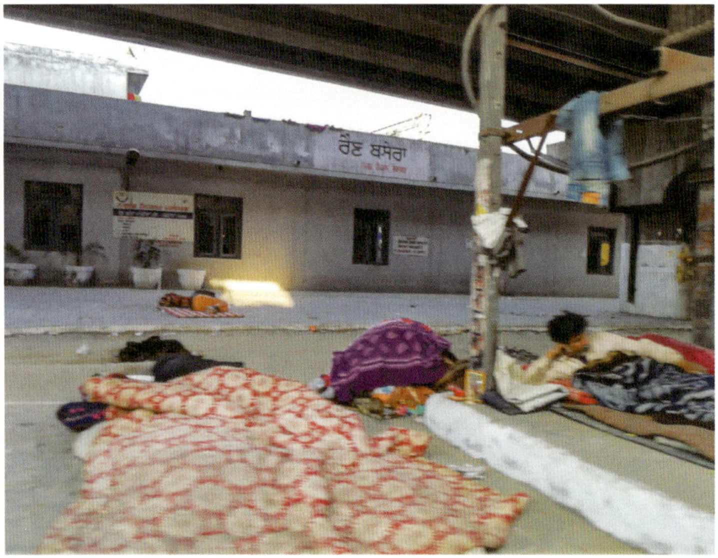

Bare shelter provided by the city government in a *rain besera* (night shelter).

Living in the City

Migrant Homes

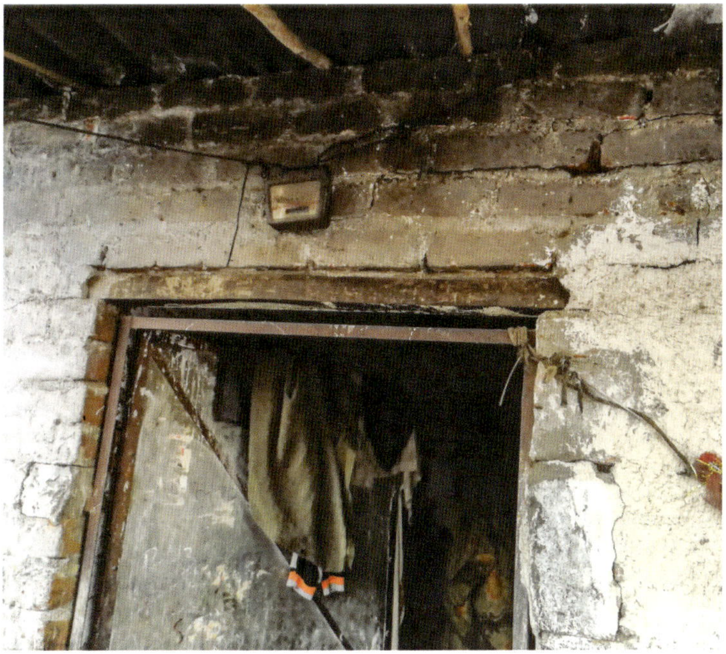

Where is home?

Migrant dwellings in cities raise a fundamental question: 'where is home'? The question hinges on the realities of constant movement that underlines migrant lives. Census data in India tries to tie the question 'where is home' to the 'place of last residence'. For migrants, place of residence is only a partial answer to 'where is home'.

'Where is home' is entangled with 'where do I belong'. Narratives of migration describe migrant lives as biographies bifurcated by frequent movement, temporary locations, and split families. In the literature on migration, the use of terms 'origin', 'destination', 'place of residence', 'place of earning' indicate hybrid homes and a fragmented sense of belonging. Words and language indisputably show us the patchwork that makes up the sense of 'home' and the disjointed, uneven, uncertain response to 'where is home'.

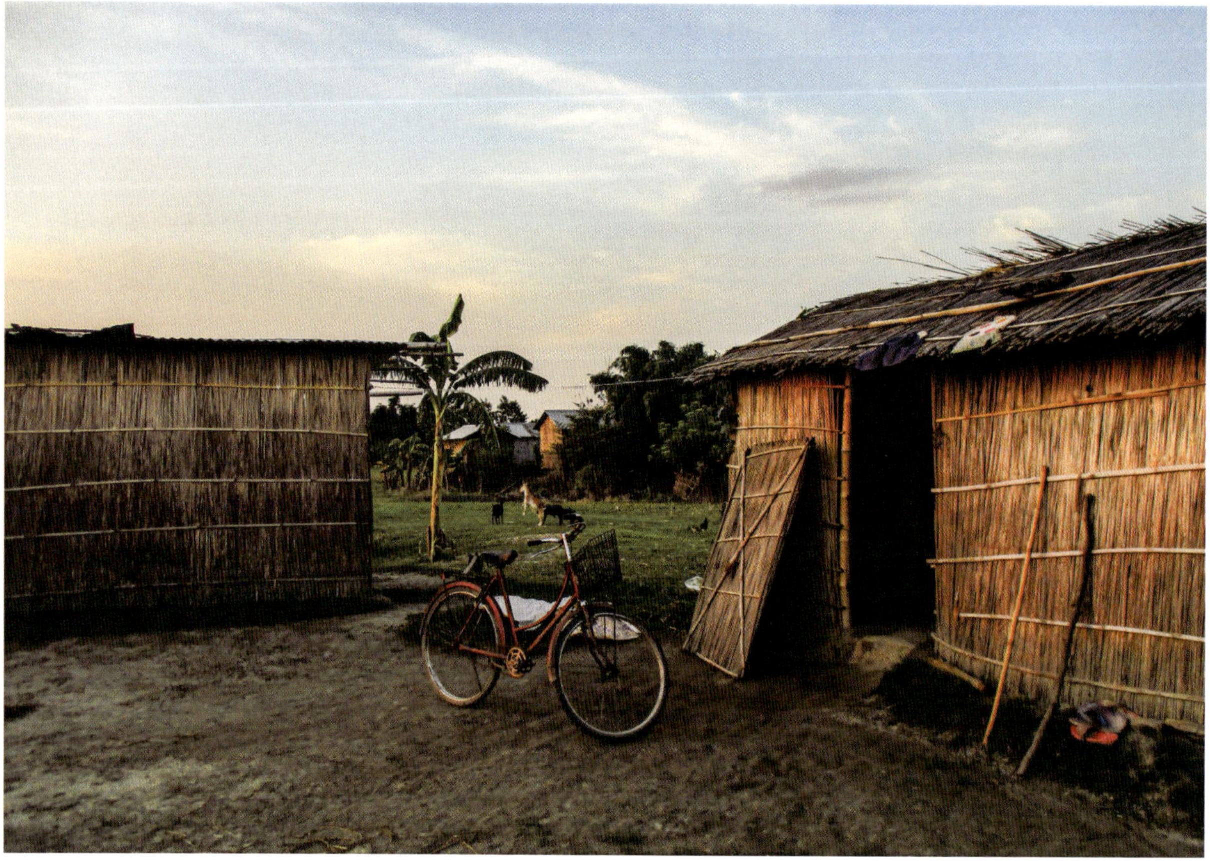

Gaon ka ghar – place of origin.

For low-income migrants in India, 'where is home' is not just a question about a house. It is also about connections and networks that have important survival dimensions. Networks in places of origin support the search for jobs, finance loans, provide family care, food, and information and access to welfare or justice. The networks in places of origin exist along with networks created in places of destination. Both sets of networks are the substrata for migrant survival.

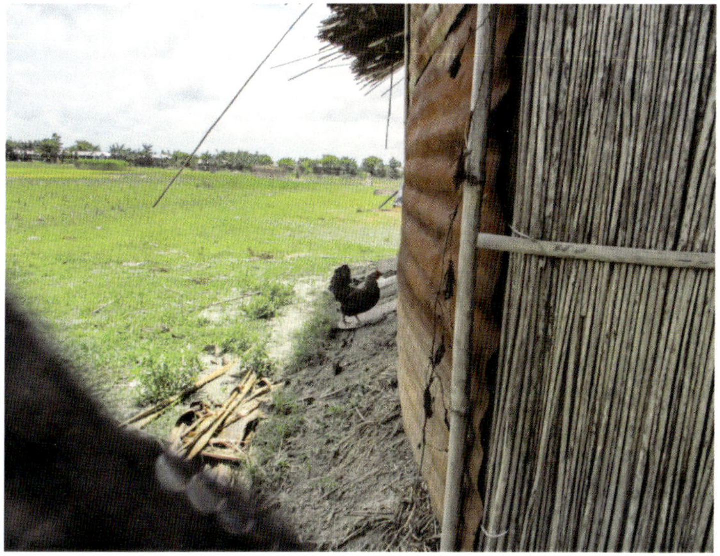

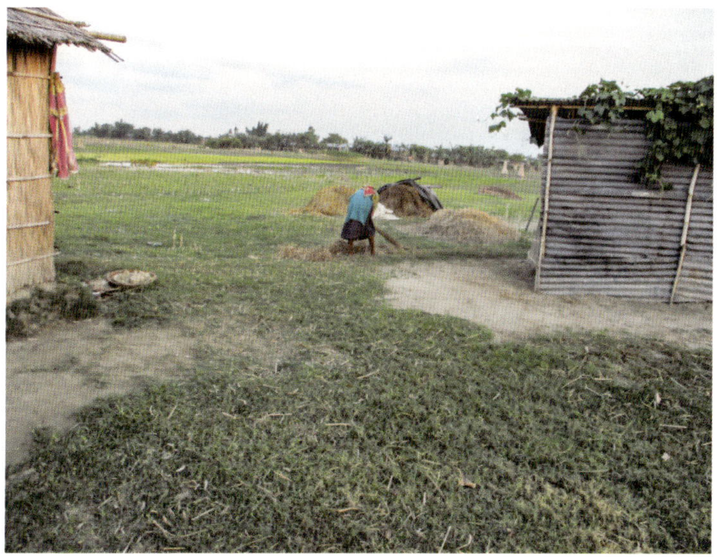

Gaon ka ghar is a real and an imagined place. It is spoken of as a place of clean air and unadulterated food. Urban migrants speak of a sense of loss of the *gaon ka ghar.*

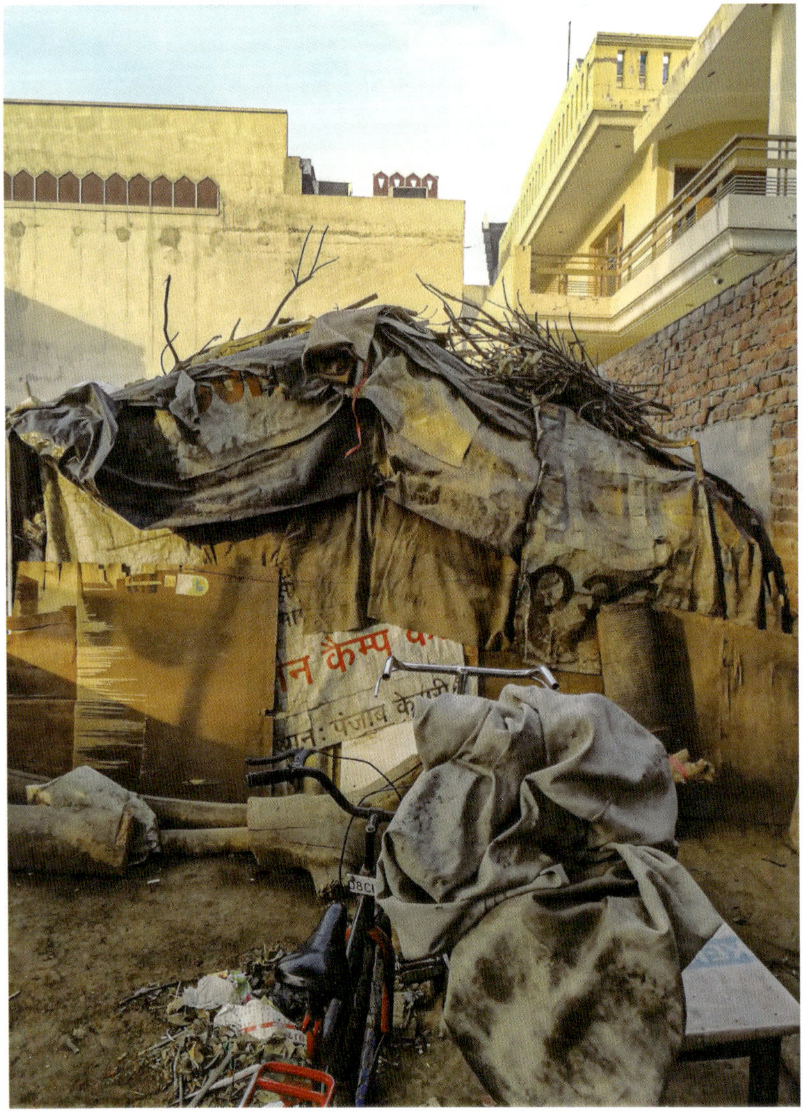

Precarious homes

Living in the city isn't secure. For migrants, modes of living in the city run the entire gamut from squatting in a place, to paying rent for a room. There is an intermediary form of living which is anchored in the legitimate use of space for a specific period of time; but the closure of that space results in a loss of a place to live or rest. Migrant workers employed in small eateries (*dhaba*) or restaurants might be allowed to sleep on the floor or tables of the *dhaba*-restaurant at night. But during the day, they have no claim on that space. Others employed in workshops or small manufacturing units are permitted to construct temporary shacks on the peripheries of their place of work. The moment employment is terminated, home disappears. 'Home' is time bound as is the 'house'. Both depend on the immediate context of employment.

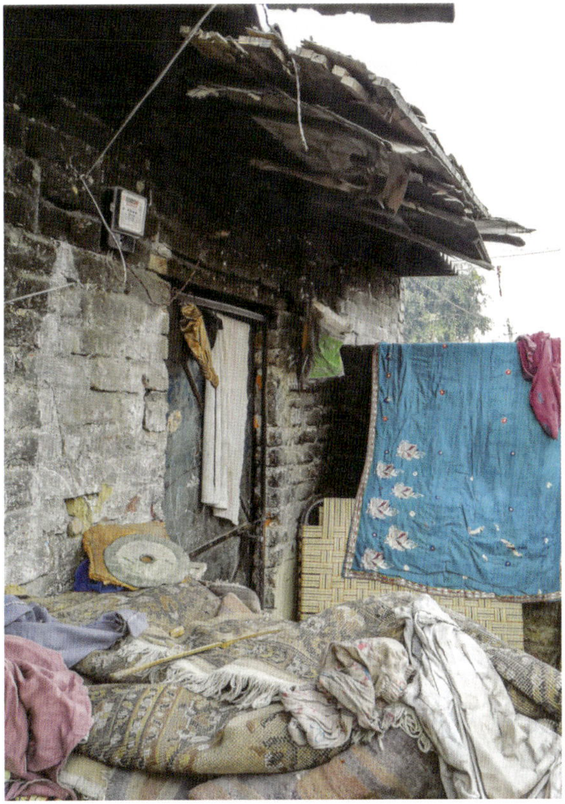

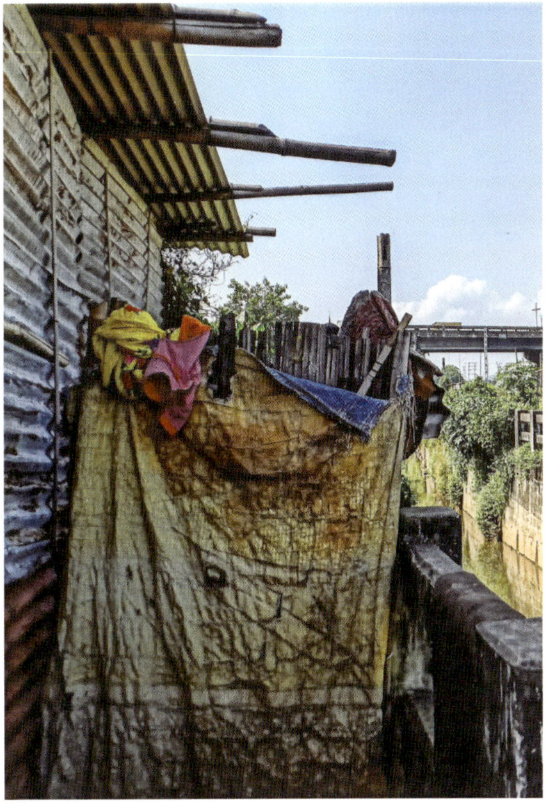

Temporary shelters at the periphery of working spaces.

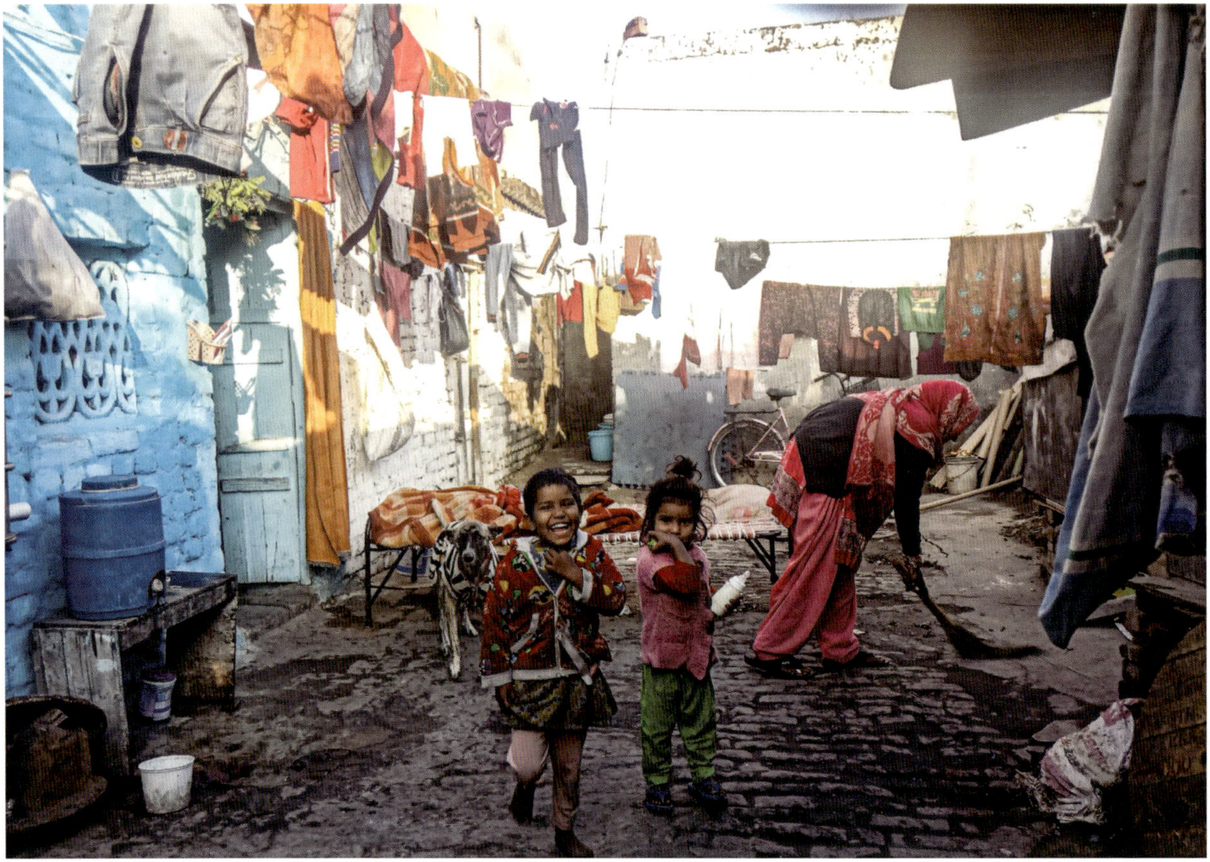

Migrant households

What then is a migrant household? Everyone who has arrived at one go? Where the children are? Everyone related by blood or marriage? Everyone who pays a share in running a household? Everyone who shares a source of water or a single electricity meter? Anyone who shares an earthen *chula*? Is a household member someone who is connected to many different households through money networks, enables money to move and is also a mobile bank? A kind of social ATM? Do they evoke 'home'?

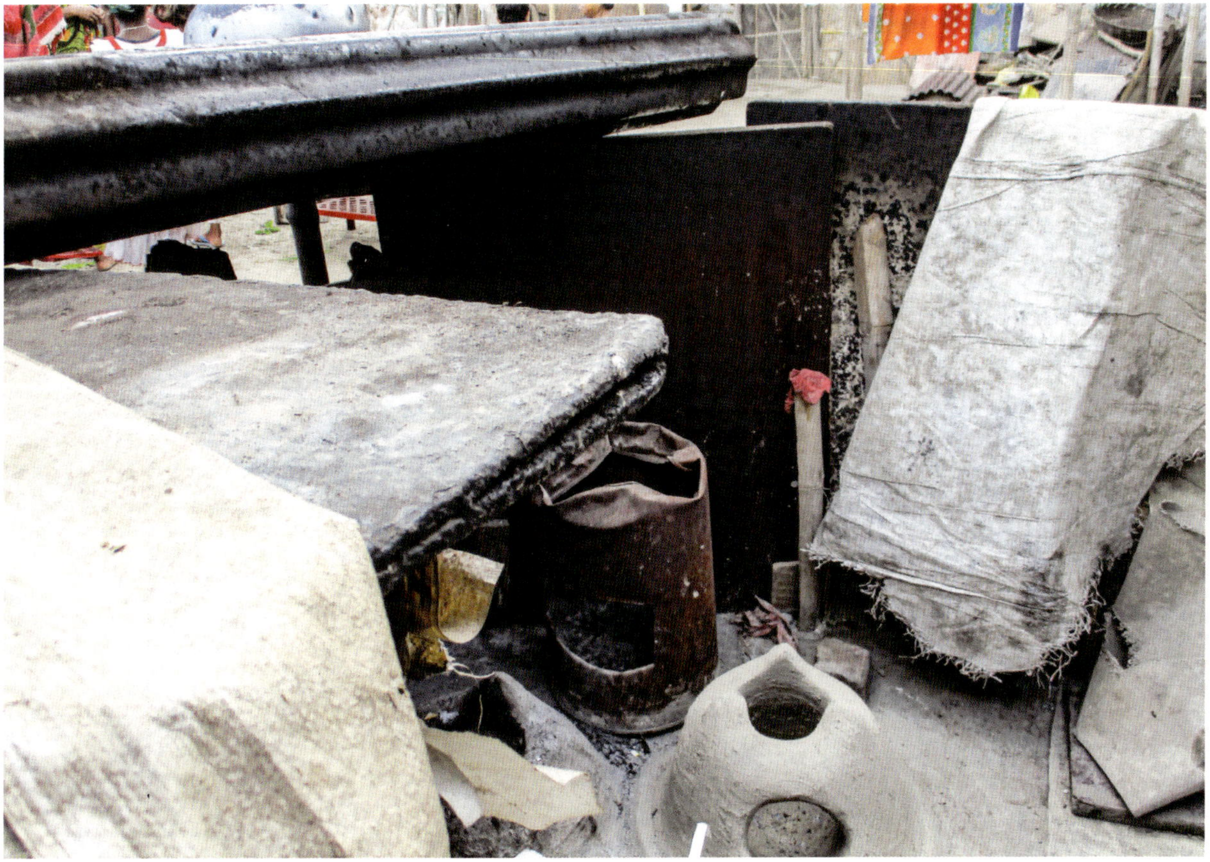

Paucity of space and shared *chulas* or cooking stoves create migrant networks.

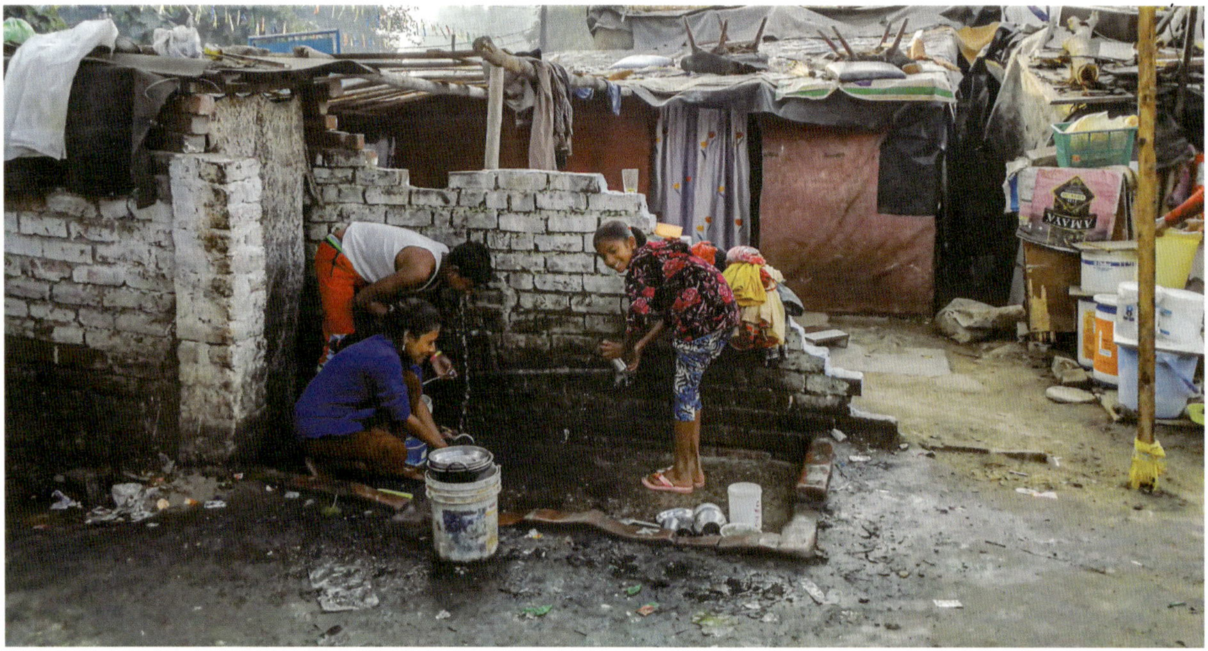

A common water pump is a place of meeting, and shared lives.

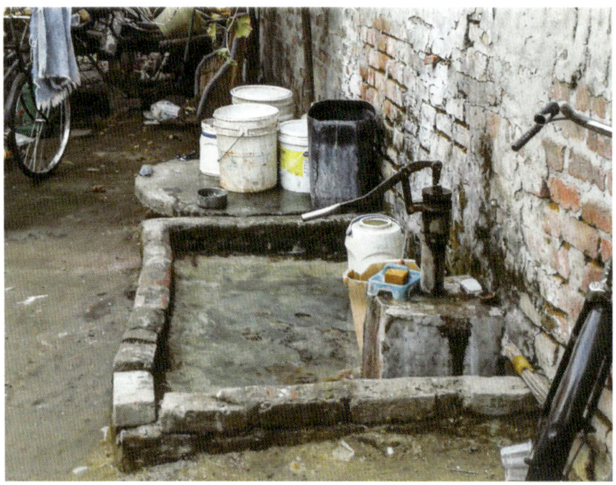

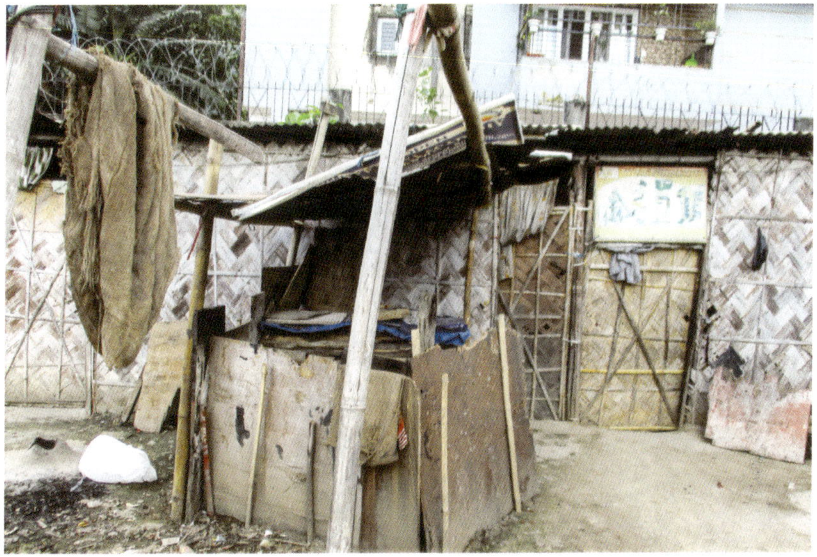

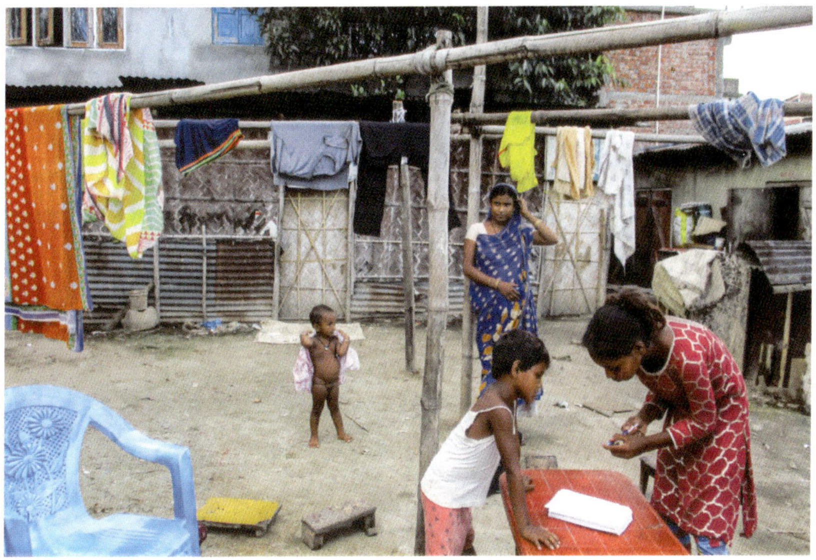

Bamboo shacks around a shared courtyard, Dhirenpada, Guwahati.

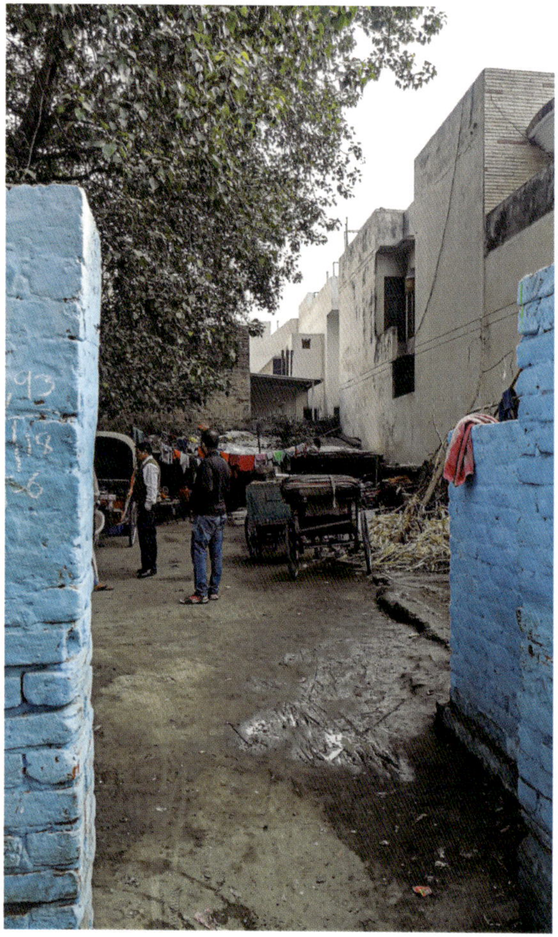

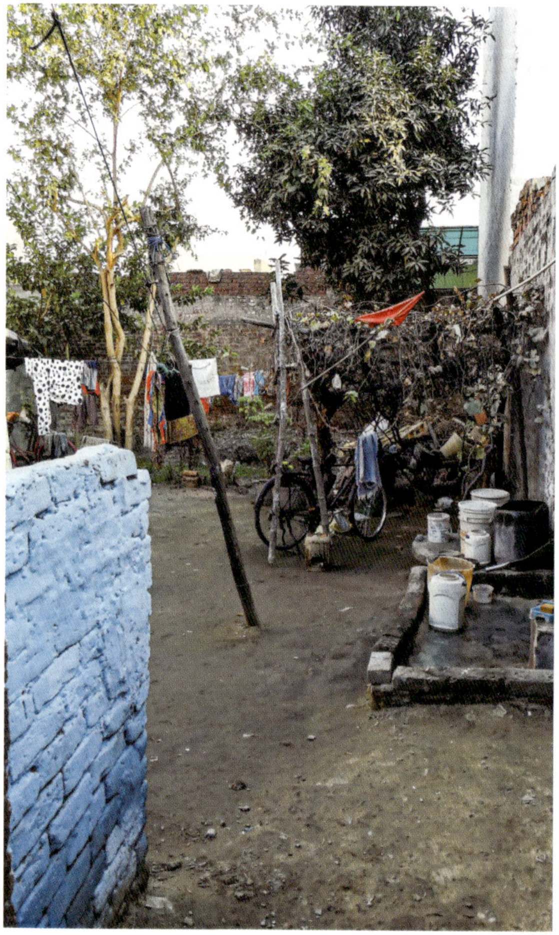

Evoking home: Painted brick.

Paint is a symbol of minimalist claims that migrants make on an urban landscape. The claims are neither antagonistic, nor exaggerated. Painted brick half walls suggest that people who live behind [or next] to them are 'clean', modest, untroublesome, and have an aesthetic imagination that doesn't threaten the genteel view for middle class neighbours.

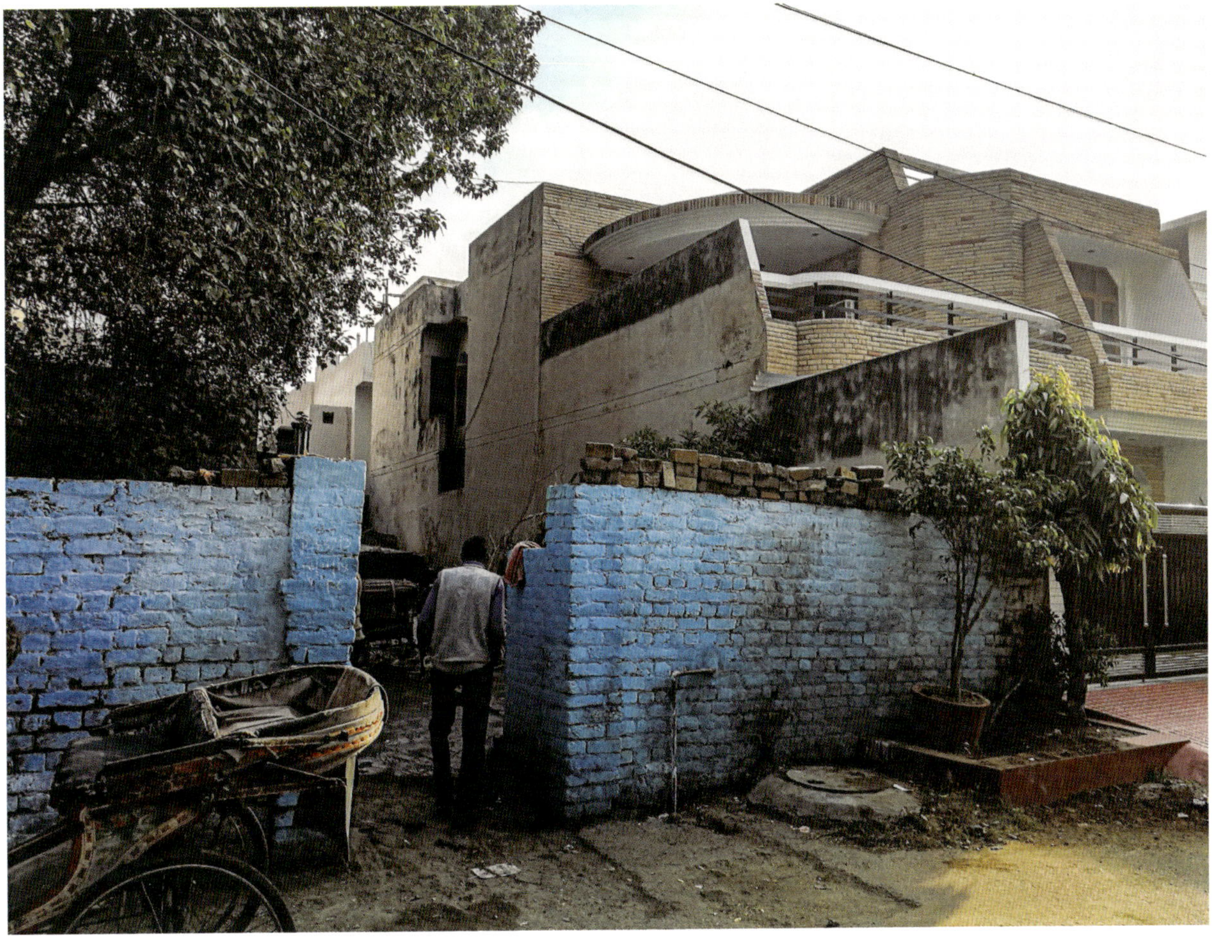

Painted half walls distinguish migrant settlements from upper class neighbourhoods.

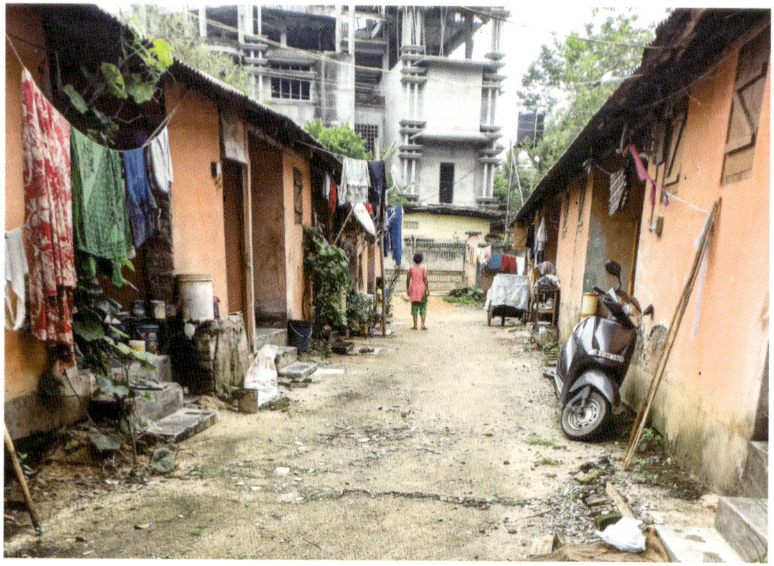

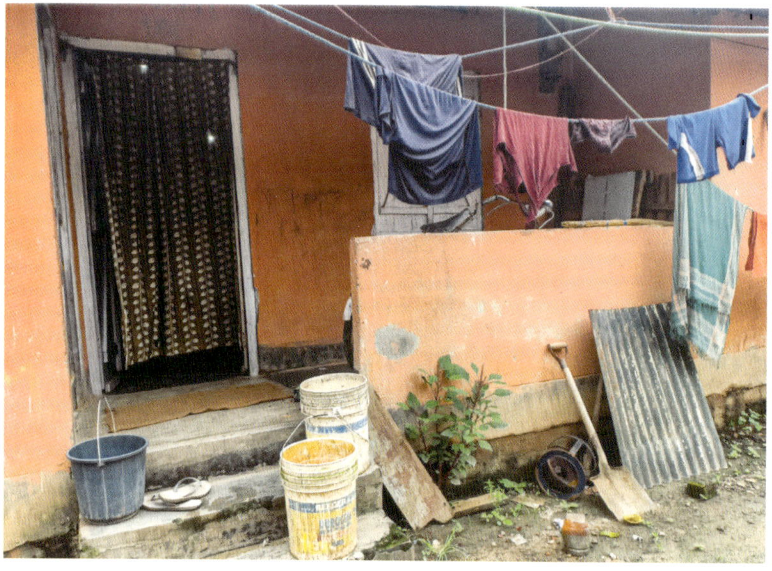

Longer term migrants invest more to make their homes aesthetic. The pale coloured walls present the migrant household as inoffensive and orderly.

Living in the City

Rooming Houses

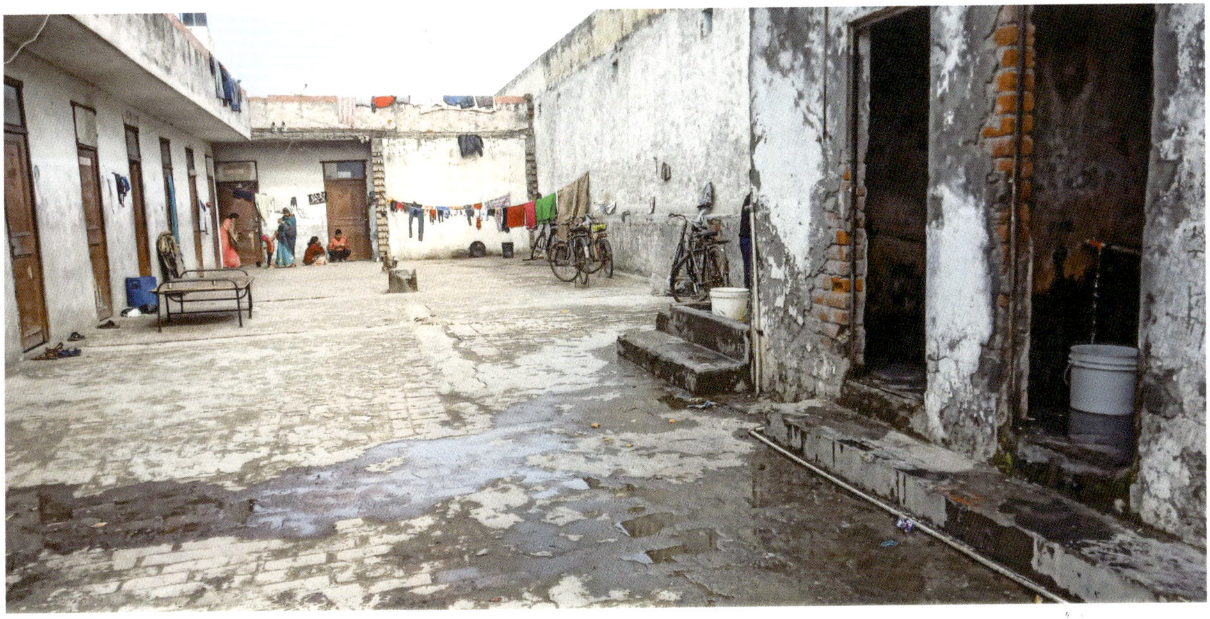

The economies of cities depend on the labour of migrants. Estimates suggest that in Jalandhar, migrants form 25 per cent of the population. The 2011 national census suggests that migrants form about 15 per cent of Assam's urban population. Cities like Guwahati and Jalandhar have large pools of migrant labour. As the city of Jalandhar expanded, it ate into surrounding farm land. Municipal rezoning laws resulted in a re-classification or recategorization of agrarian land as special industrial zones. Such re-classified areas are a distinct and identifiable site for migrant housing. Former agriculturalists have become urban rentiers, and converted their fields to housing structures 'custom built' to rent out to migrant families.

The basic plan is a set of rooms built around a common courtyard. Rudimentary – often meagre – water and toilet facilities are shared by all the tenants living around the courtyard. Though small, rooms are shared by entire families, but represent 'independent' family homes.

Renting a room is an expression of a tentative foothold in the city. A rented room ties the migrant to the city. Longer term migrants are most likely to seek and rent rooms in such purpose-built accommodation. If they can afford it, migrants pay rent in advance for these rooms and shared facilities. Some migrants forgo or postpone going back home to villages if they have paid rent in advance.

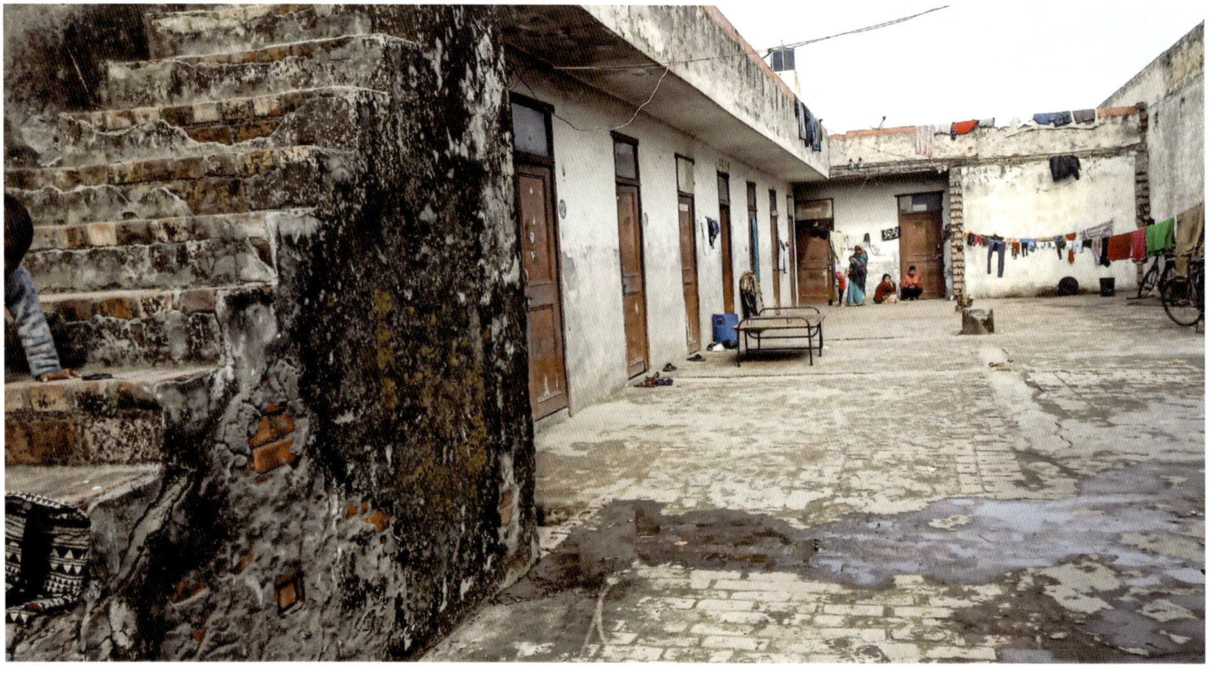

Rooming houses, around a courtyard, with shared toilet and water facility,
Peer Daas Mohalla, Jalandhar, January 2019.

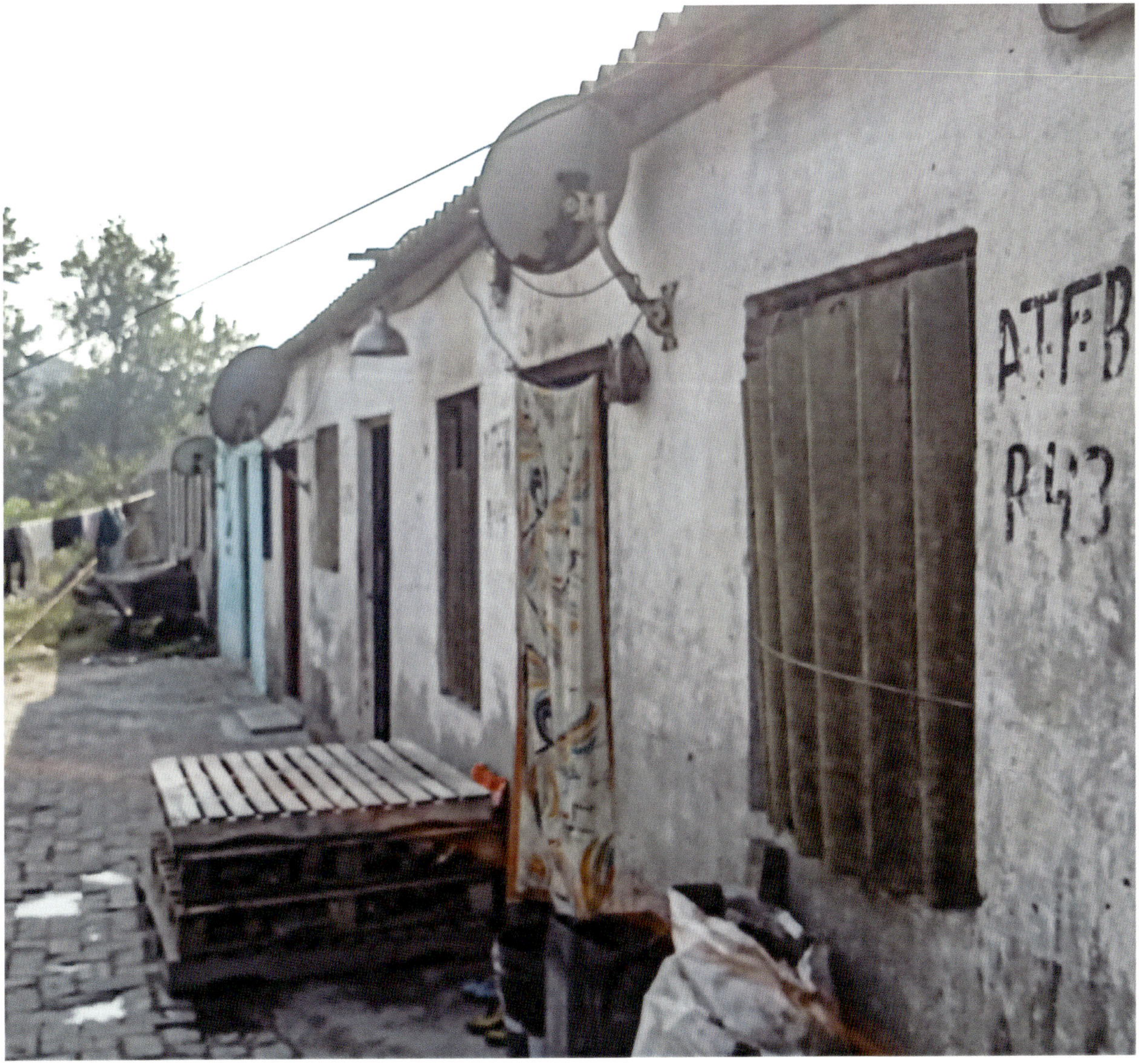

Rooming house, Focal Point, Jalandhar, November 2019.

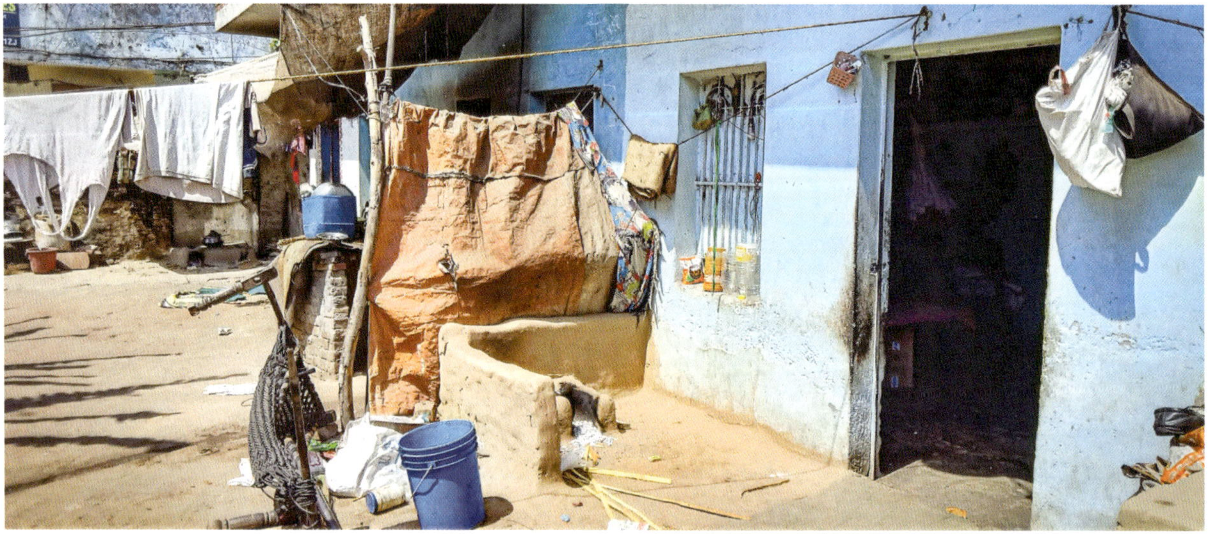

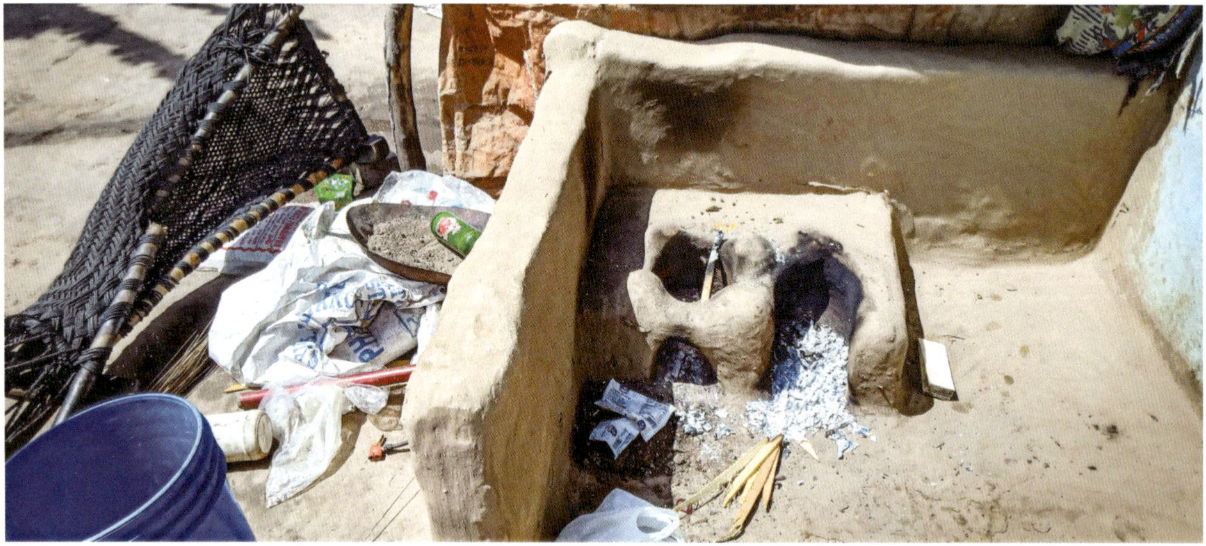

Sanju's room and *chula*, the family cooking hearth, Saini Colony, Jalandhar, March 2019.

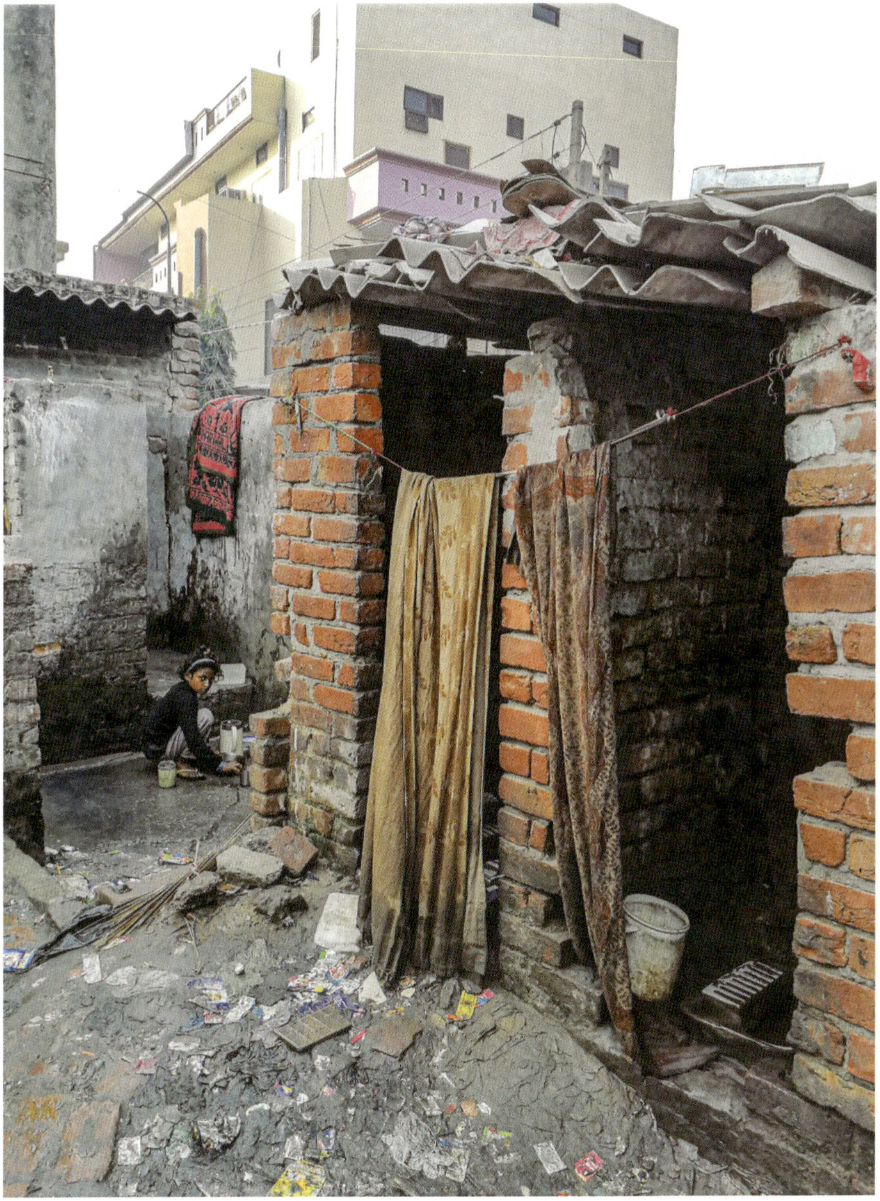

Basic toilet facilities,
Guwahati, October 2019.

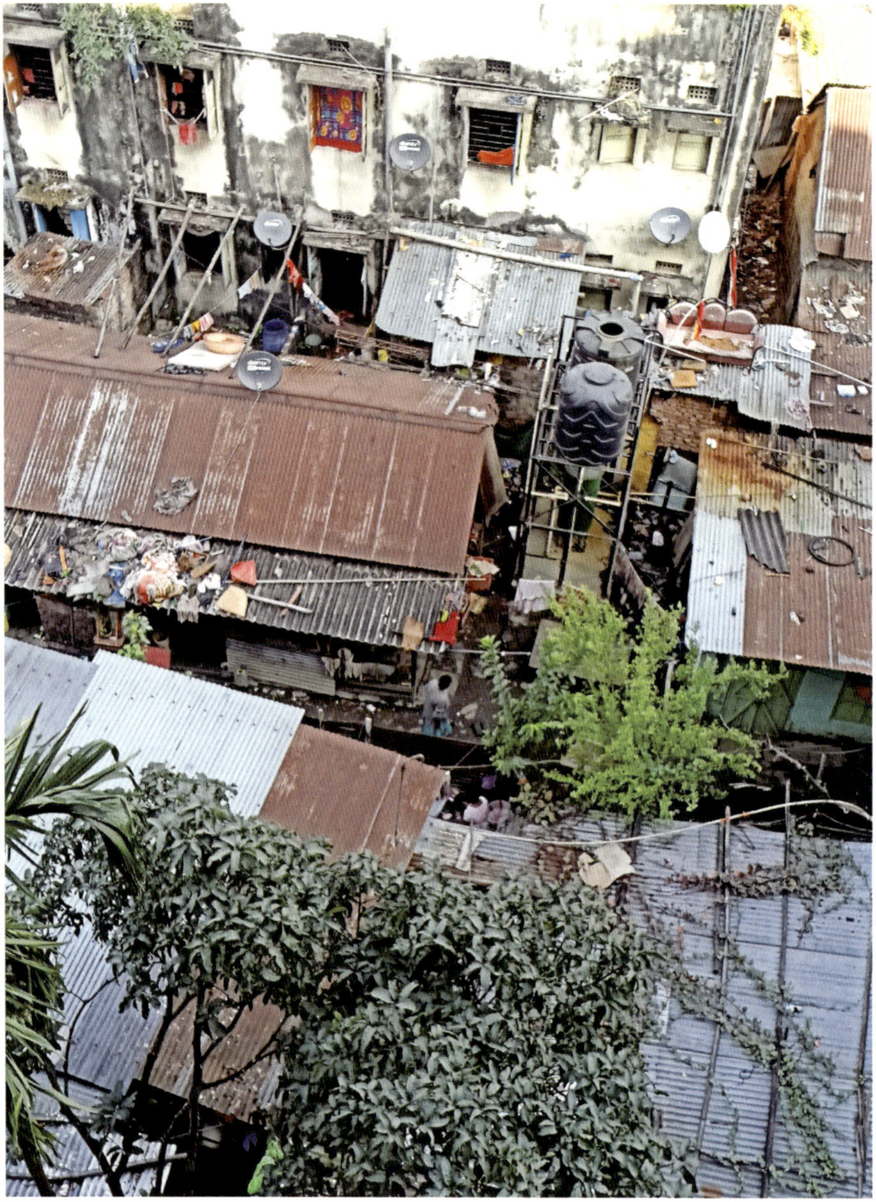

Aerial view of migrant rooming houses, Guwahati.

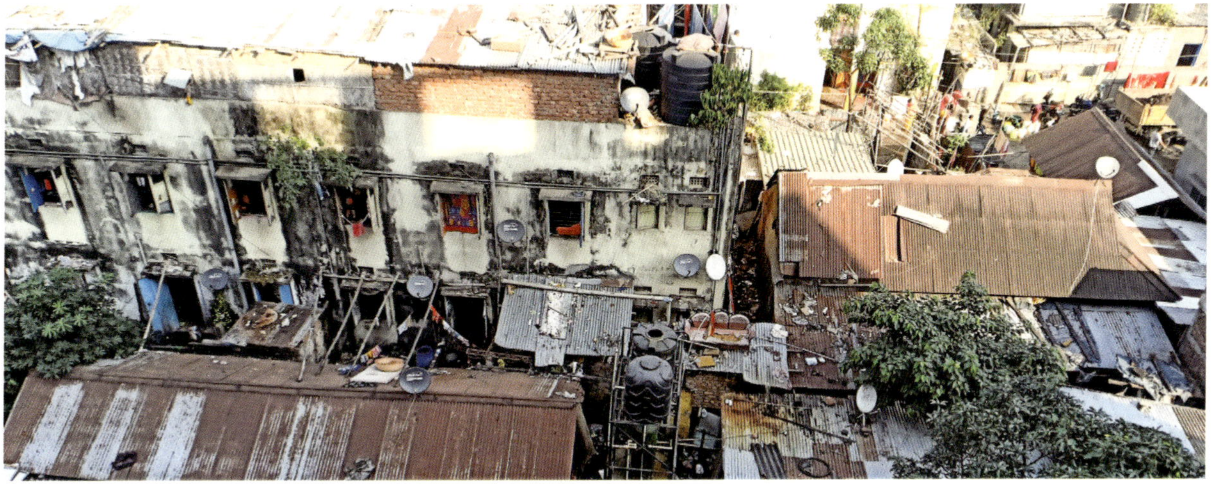

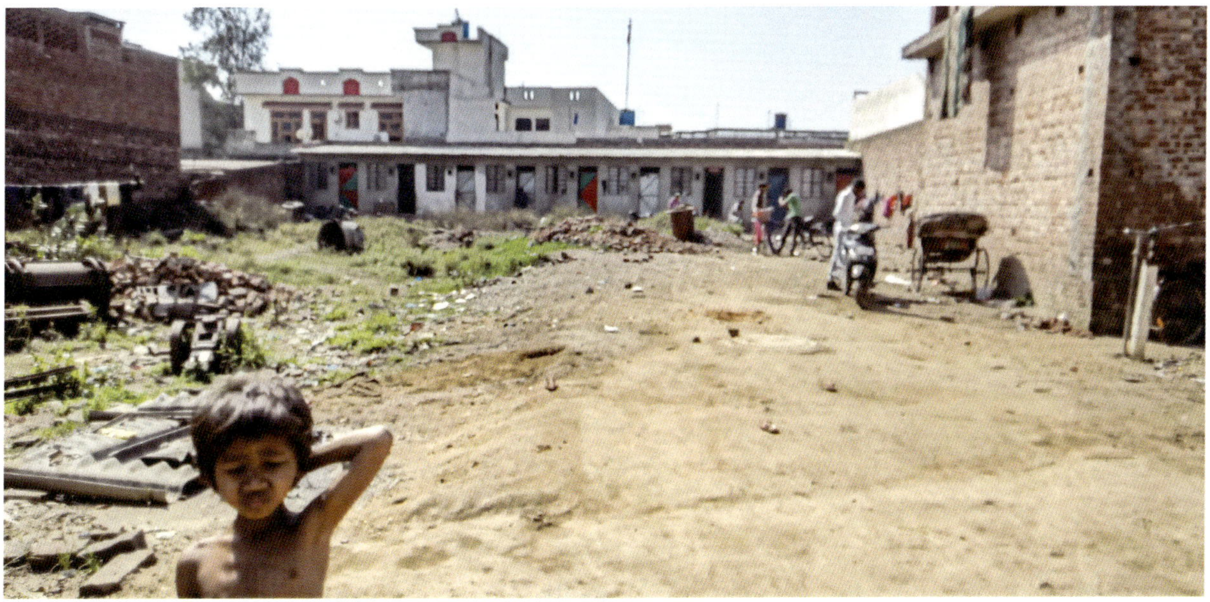

In the shadow of a middle class housing block, migrant labour lines.

Settling in
Migrant Bazaars

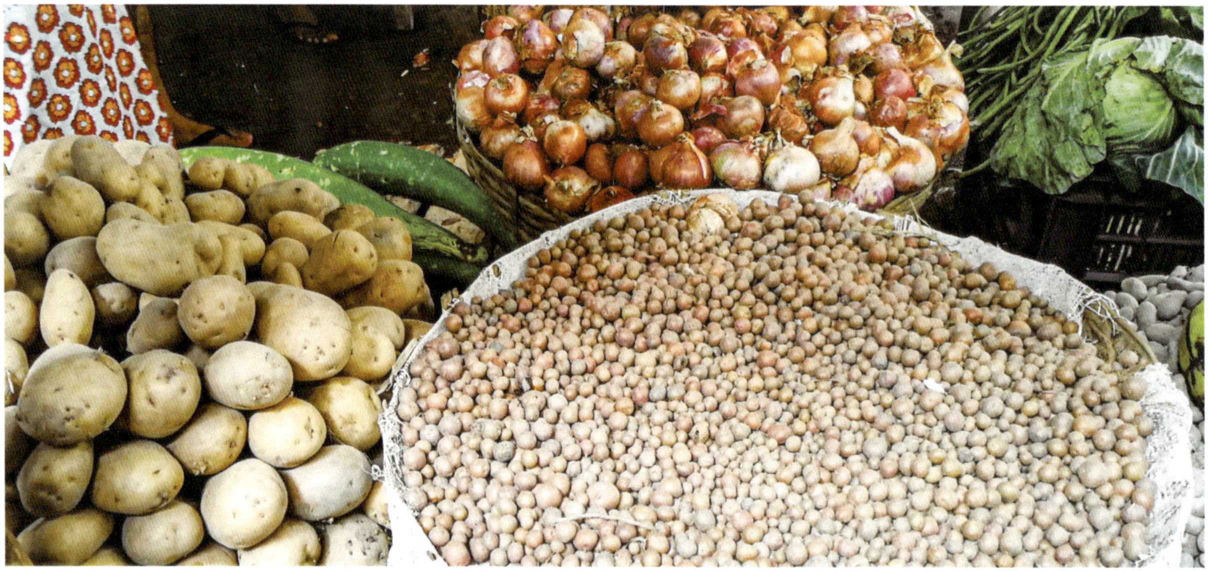

For most city dwellers, pavements are passages. For urban migrants, pavements are usually the only places available to set up shop. To call a portable basket of goods, or a few goods laid out on a torn plastic sheet a *dukan*, a shop, is somewhat of a misnomer. Nevertheless, in the language of goods and food, the little pavement *dukans* are important documents of migrant lives and the spaces of migrant settlement.

Migrants source goods from 'home' through a series of networks. Buses that bring migrants to cities also bring goods. Some local shopkeepers stock goods that are popular among segments of migrants from specific parts of India. These are disbursed to individual migrants or to smaller, mobile sellers who traverse the areas where migrants live and work.

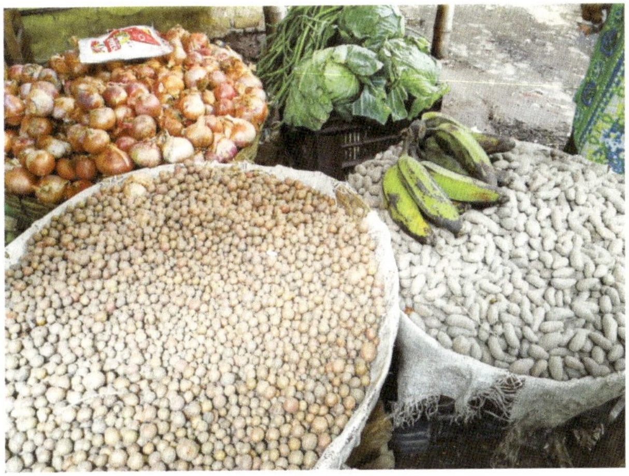

Raw bananas are rarely used in Punjabi cuisine but are popular in eastern India cuisines.

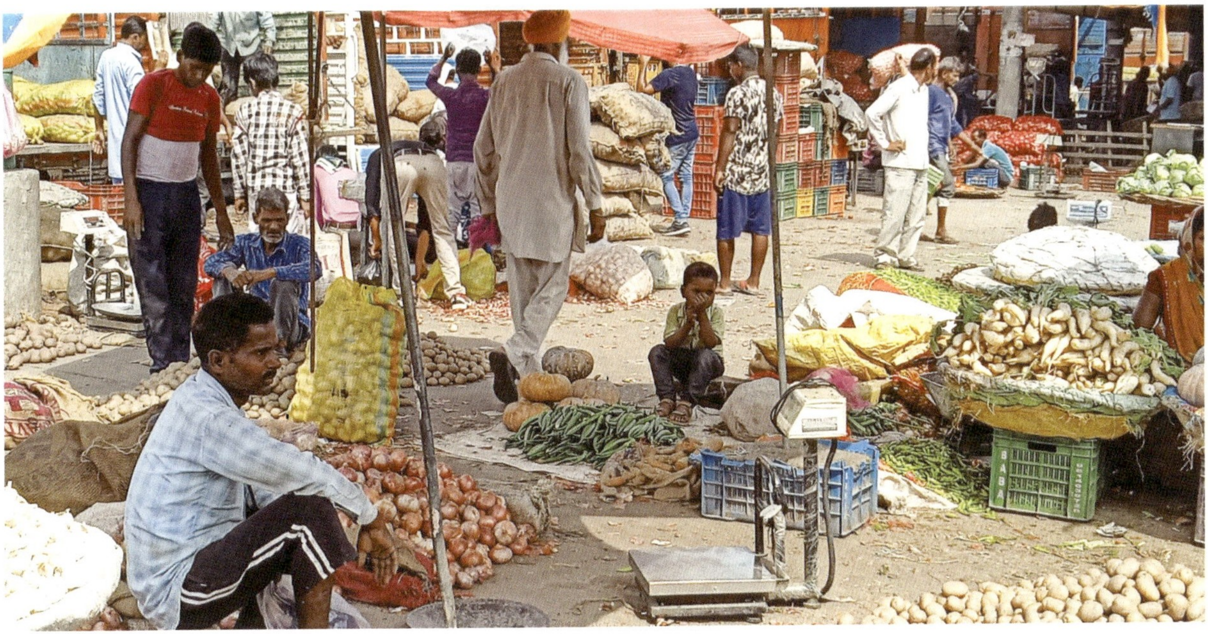

A young migrant boy selling a few pumpkins and ridge gourd, Maqsudan *Sabzi Mandi*, Jalandhar, July 2019.

Settling in

Migrants and their Festivals – Chhath Puja in Jalandhar

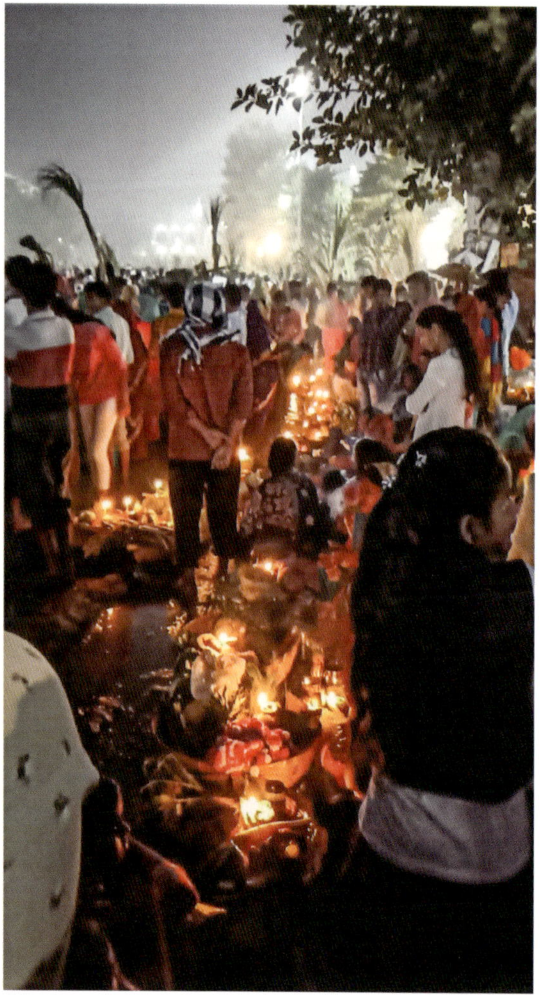

From fieldnotes Jalandhar, 11 November 2018

On 11 November 2018 while having breakfast near Maqsudan *Sabzi Mandi*, Bharti and I saw a market had come up on the main road, near the bus stop. The entire area was full of items required for Chhath celebration. Since Chhath, a puja to the Sun and to Chhathi Mata, is a largely eastern Indian festival, and certainly a major festival among Biharis, we thought that migrants from Bihar would be return home for the period of Chhath. But in fact, a significant number of migrants from Bihar celebrate Chhath in Jalandhar. We noticed that the market had many items like bamboo baskets, small scoopers – *soop* – foods such as *dalia* and other foods and fruit including sugarcane, coconut, *Dabha Nimbu*, *singhada* (water chestnut) particular to Chhath rituals. Cosmetics and other eatables were also laid out in baskets and plastic sheets.

This market was bustling and full of goods not usually seen in the everyday pavement *dukans* with their meagre goods set up by migrants for migrants. The spectacle of this market drew our attention, heralding the forthcoming Chhath festival.

Chhath is not celebrated by Punjabis. A woman vendor told us that many of the items like *Dabha Nimbu*, a variety of citrus that are larger than the normal lemon, were especially brought all the way from Bihar. Migrants were also discussing whether fresh water would be available in a nearby canal, as many ceremonies require flowing fresh water. They told us they had approached the canal operator to ask about the release of water into the canal.

We learnt that a bigger market had been established along the Baba Canal on the Kapurthala Road. We went there and saw another market had come up on other side of the road from the usual market. Both markets were more than usually crowded. Many auto-*rikshas* were waiting to take migrants to other markets or back to their accommodation with their puja supplies.

We also wanted to see the market in Focal Point, opposite Sarb Multiplex. We had heard about it from Lakhbir Singh, one of the people we interviewed. Though smaller than the Baba Canal market, we decided to go there and also see the Chhath puja. On the way to Focal Point, we saw another big market for Chhath items near Doaba Chowk (close to the Devi Talab Temple).

From fieldnotes, Jalandhar, 14 November 2018

Bharti and I left for Devi Talab Mandir early in the morning, by 5.45 am. Sunrise was to be at 6.50 am in Jalandhar of the 14th of November. We wanted to secure a good spot from where to observe all the Chhath puja ceremonies. Even though it was very cold in the morning and we had reached well in advance, there were large number of people already there. Some had stayed the night; some had come hours in advance to await the sunrise. Devi Talab Mandir is near an industrial area. The temple is devoted to Goddess Durga. It stands in the middle of a pond, the *talab*, which is divided roughly into four parts for the immersion. To accommodate more people, water was also poured into an open area near the temple, though the depth was only a few inches. We walked around in the crowd for a while to get a sense of the festivities. About 15 policemen were stationed there, coordinating the movement of around 50,000 (conservative estimate) people. By and large, most policemen were either sitting or patrolling the peripheries.

When people started offering prayers (*Aragya*, offering water), it started getting very crowded. We moved to a gallery at the entrance of temple, which was at a higher level and we were able to observe everything quite clearly. Some groups had put up food stalls offering various items such as tea, toast, *kheer* and *halwa*. for devotees. The makeshift food stalls were evidence of migrants catering to migrants on this religious occasion.

There was a traffic jam on the road in front of the temple as people began to leave. Since this was a main highway, heavy trucks had been permitted entry by this time. Unfortunately, the traffic police had not blocked the entry of the trucks, to prevent the jams. In our view, either the traffic police have very little idea about how many migrants are in the city or they really don't care about the numbers affected by the inconvenience of traffic jams on Chhath puja mornings. At the same time, the police presence indicated some minimal dialogue between migrants and authorities. It is highly likely that some arrangements were made as migrants are now also a major vote-bank in the city.

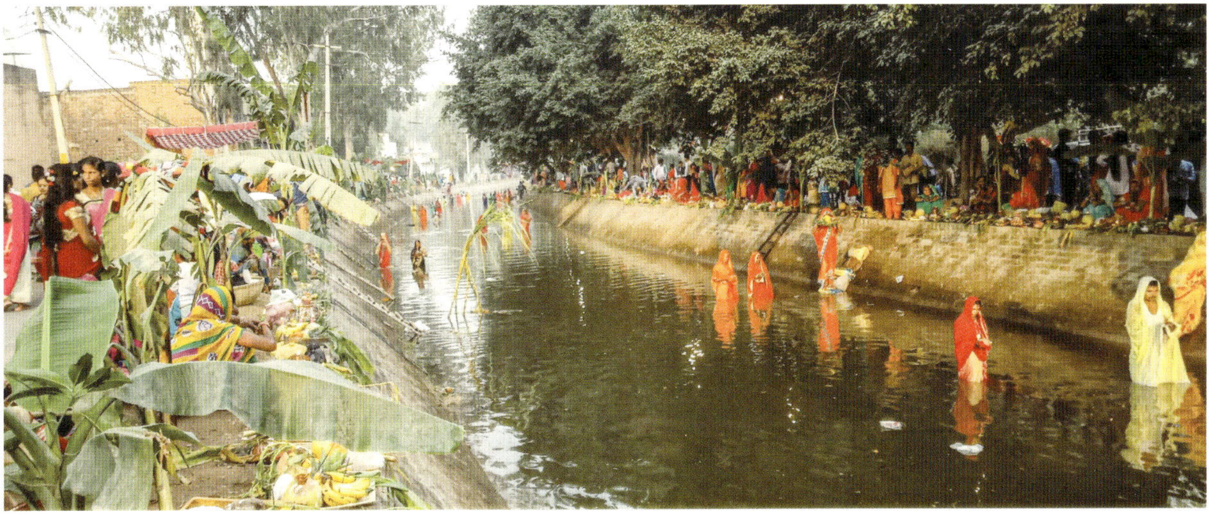

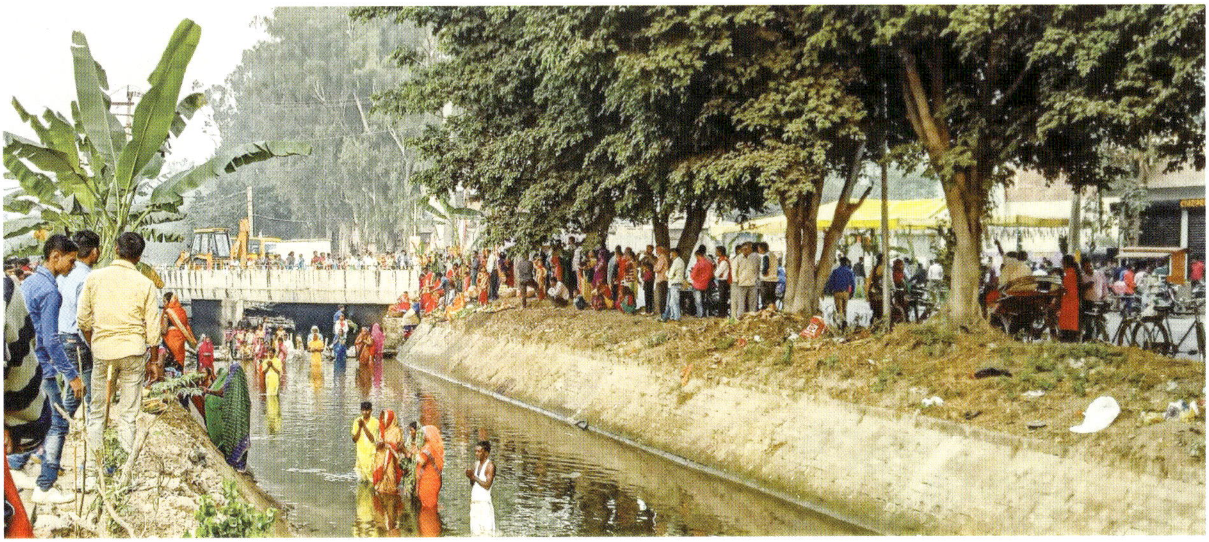

Standing in the flowing water of the canal, Baba Nahar, Jalandhar, migrant women from Bihar, dressed in orange, yellow and red *saris*, regarded as auspicious colours, present oblations to the Goddess, Chhati Mata.

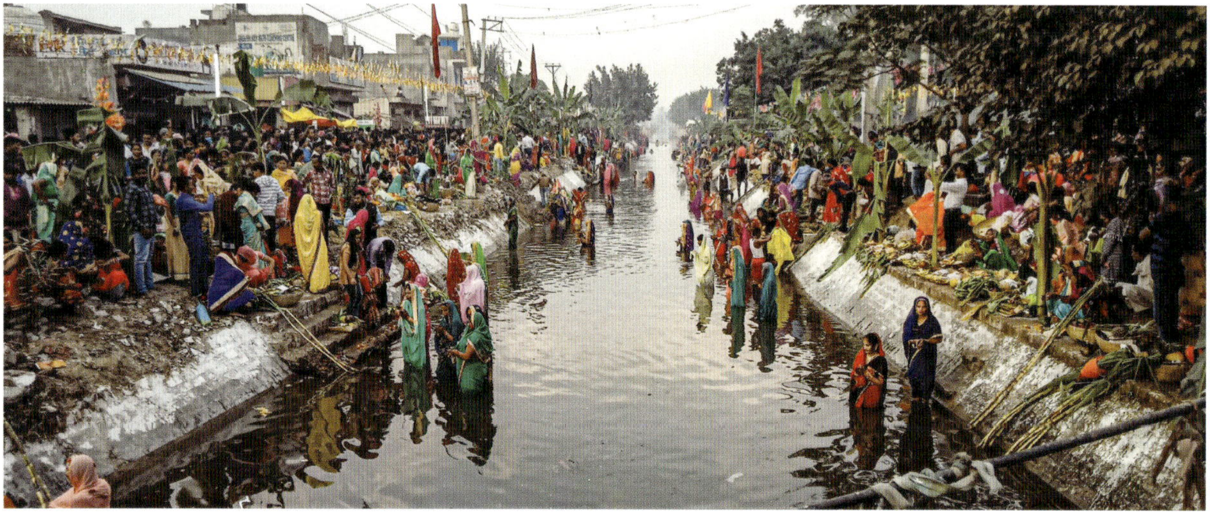

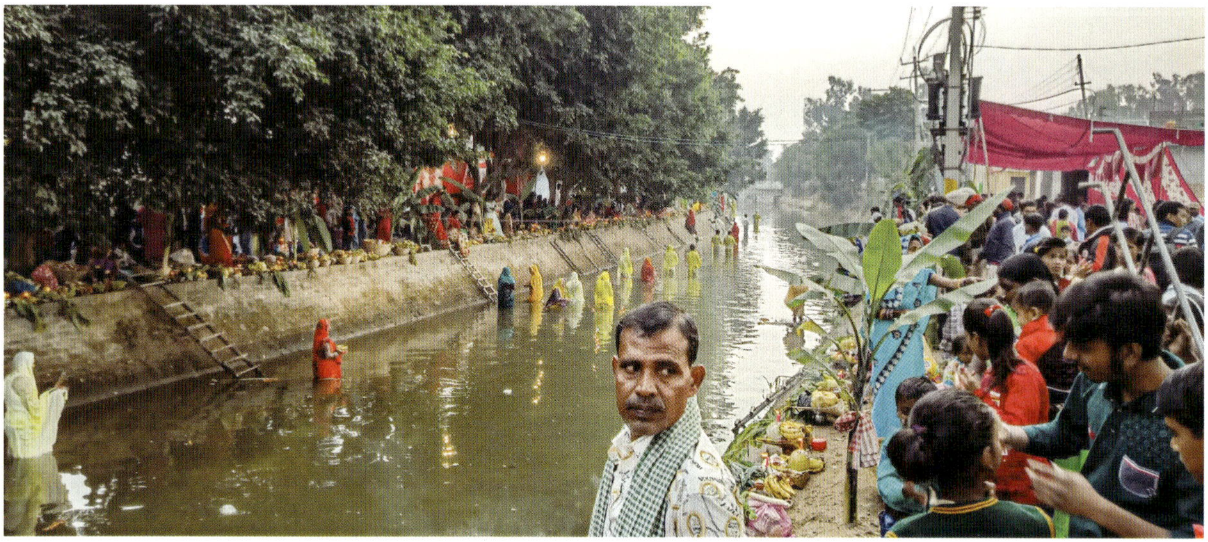

As the dawn breaks and the day advances, many more migrants gather around Baba Nahar, while the women make offering to the goddess.

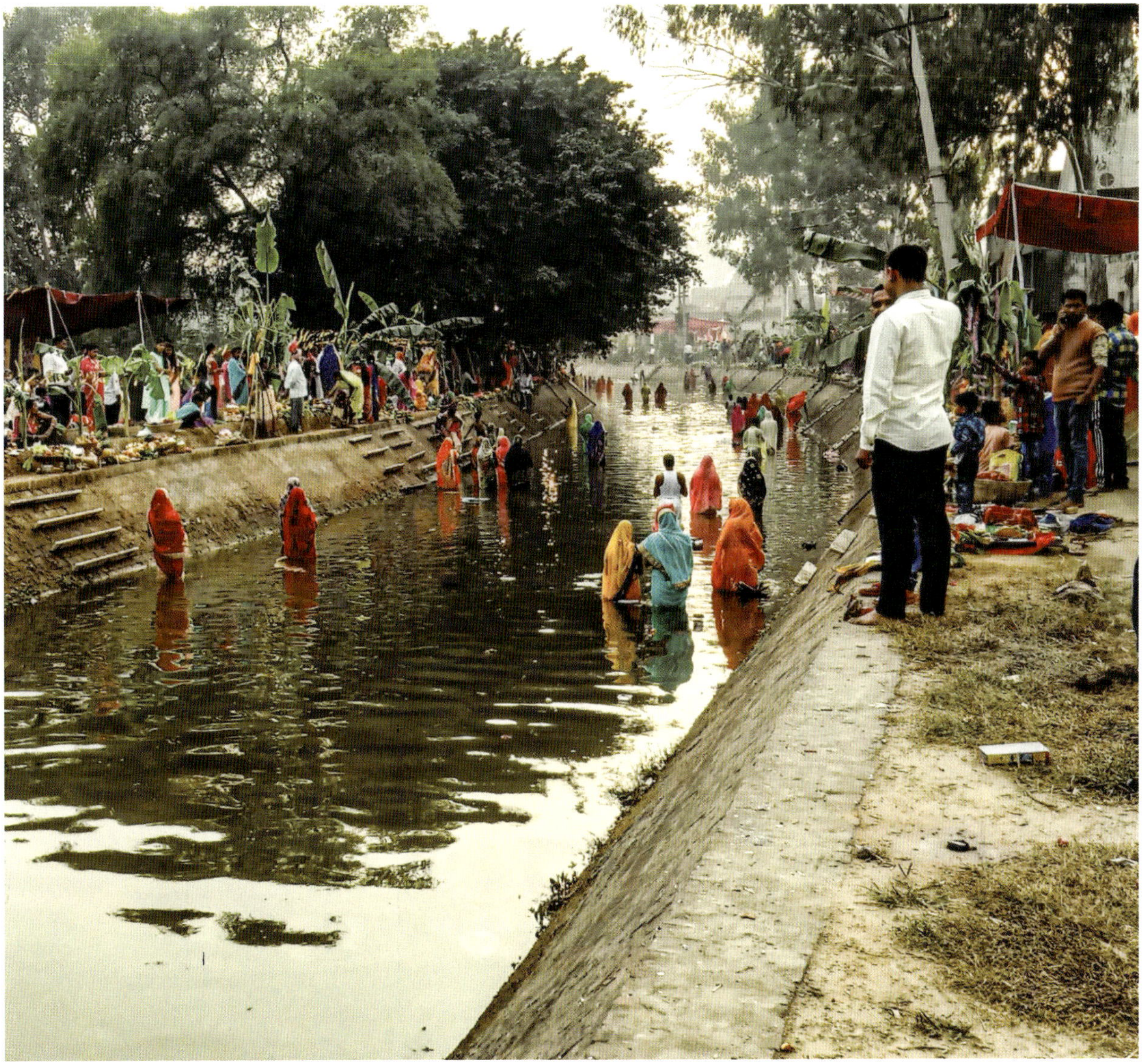

Mingling with devotees, migrant vendors selling ritual offerings, sit along the side of Baba Nahar.

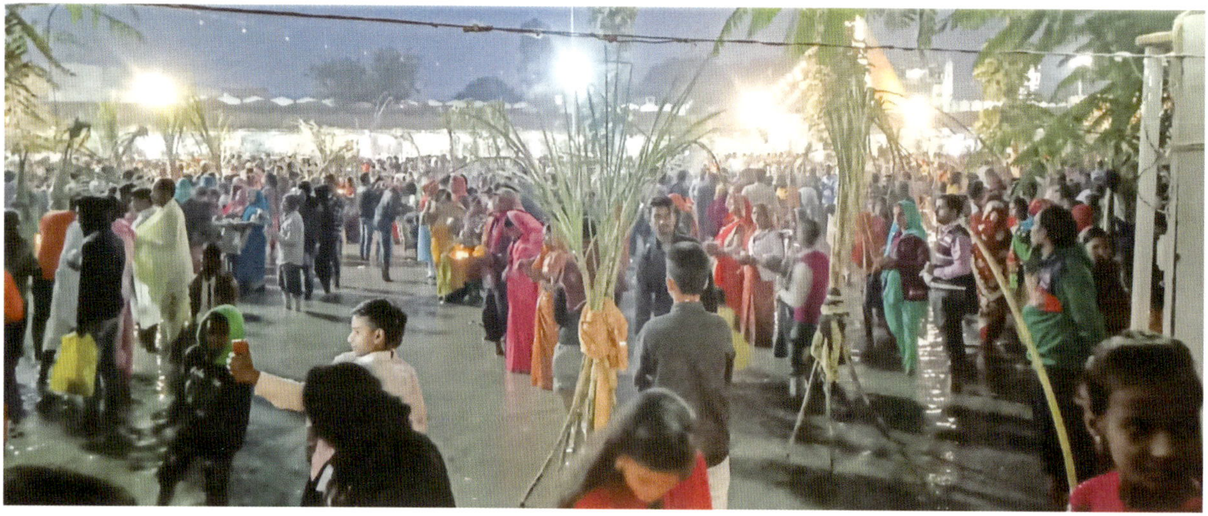

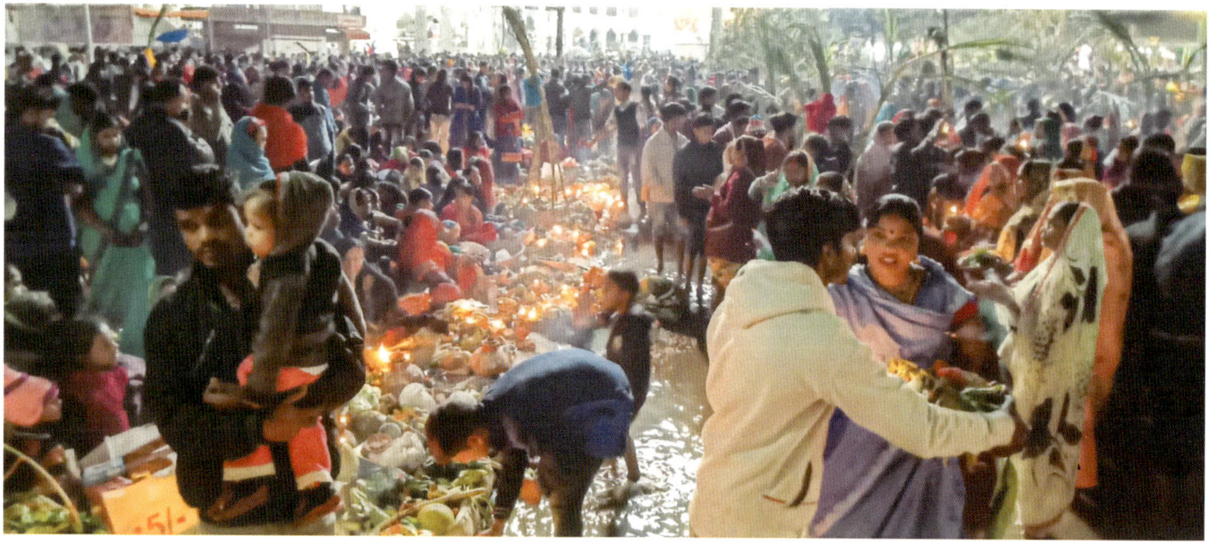

Late evening Chhath puja rites.

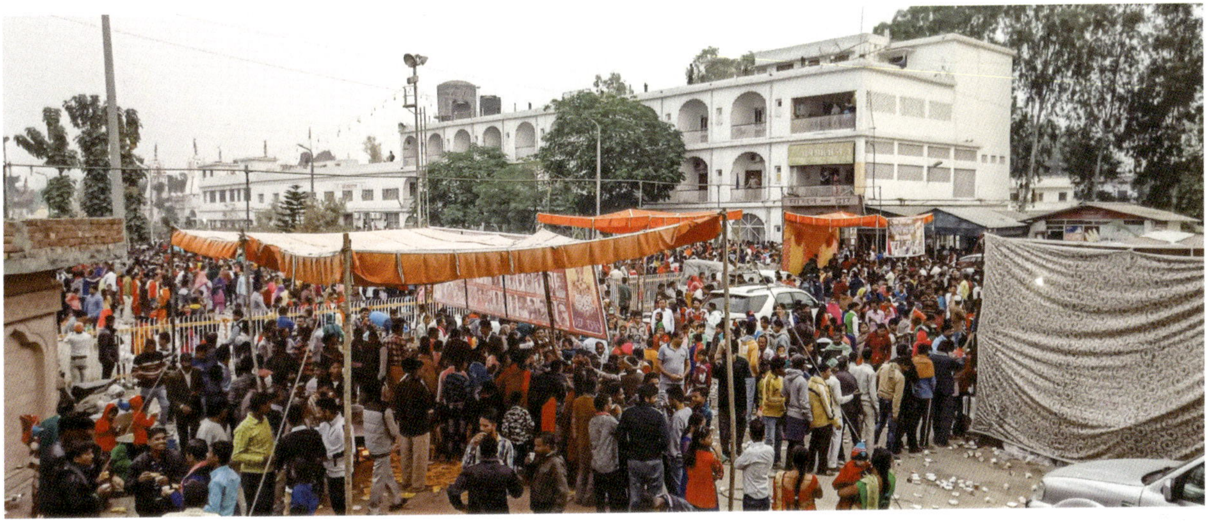

Crowds of migrants gather outside Devi Talab Mandir.

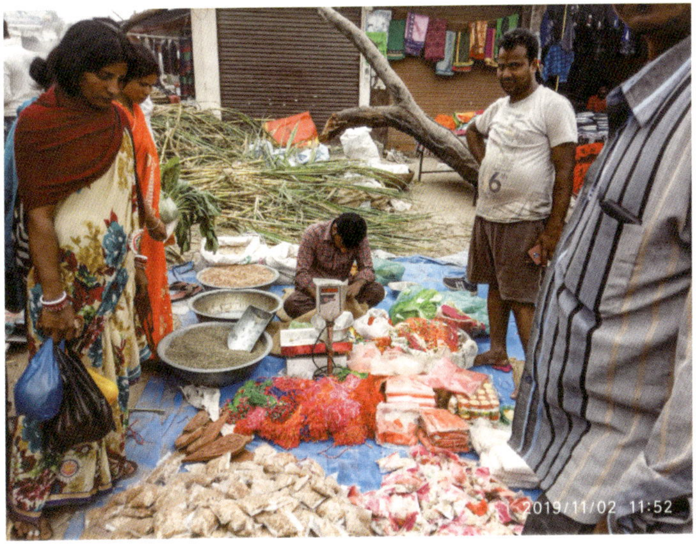

Women gather to buy *Mauli*, the threads that symbolise the powerful hair of the goddess, and packets of *sindhoor*, auspicious vermillion powder, worn by women to symbolise fertility. In the background, stems of leafy sugarcane.

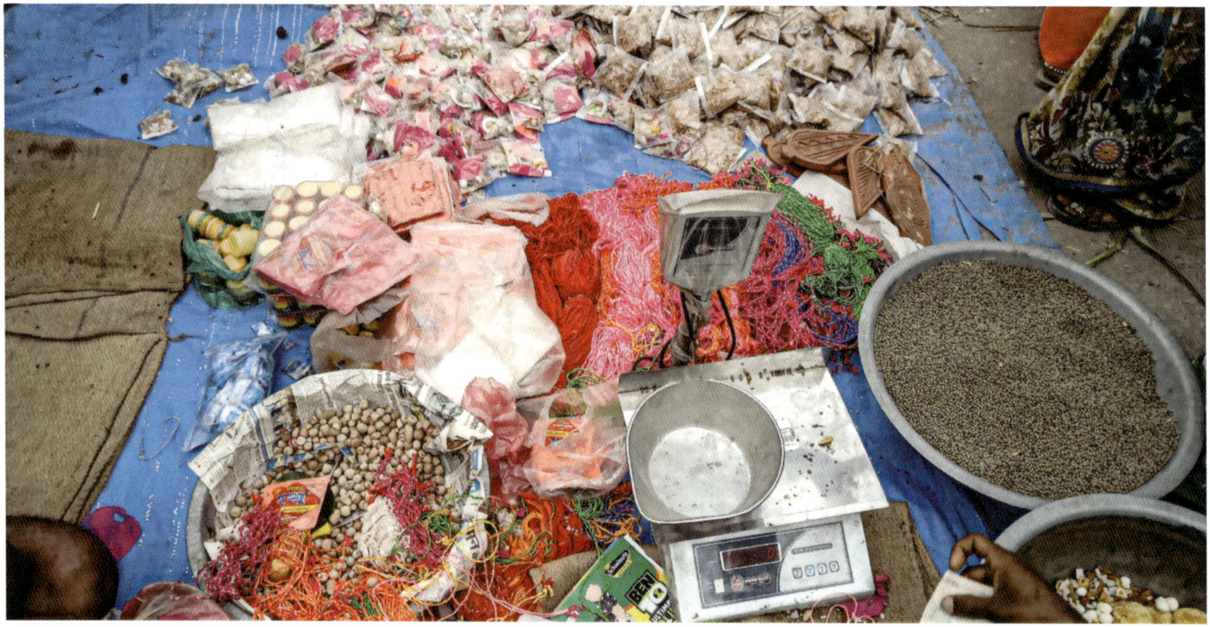

Heaps of *mauli*, *sindhoor*, *divas* (mud lamps), *supari* (betel nut) for the puja *thali*, the trays of offerings.

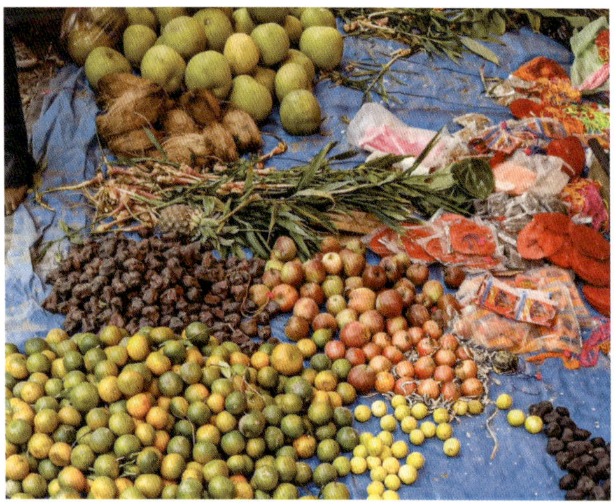

An array of *Dabha Nimbu*, a citrus fruit, larger than a lemon, and water chestnuts sold along the edges of the Baba Nahar.

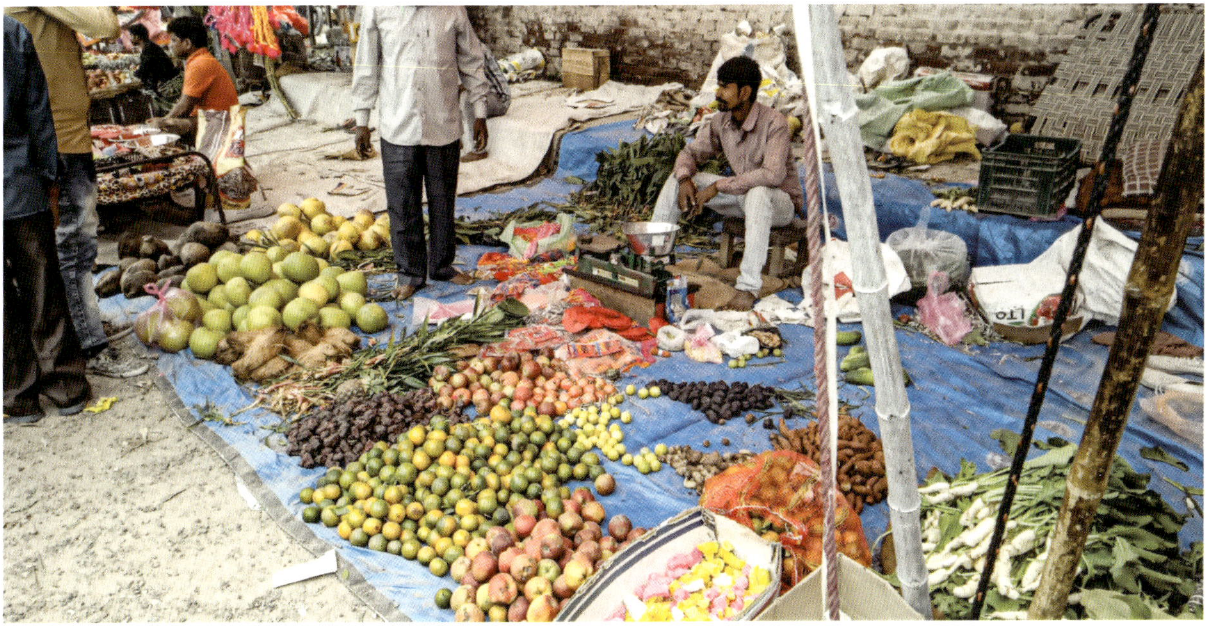

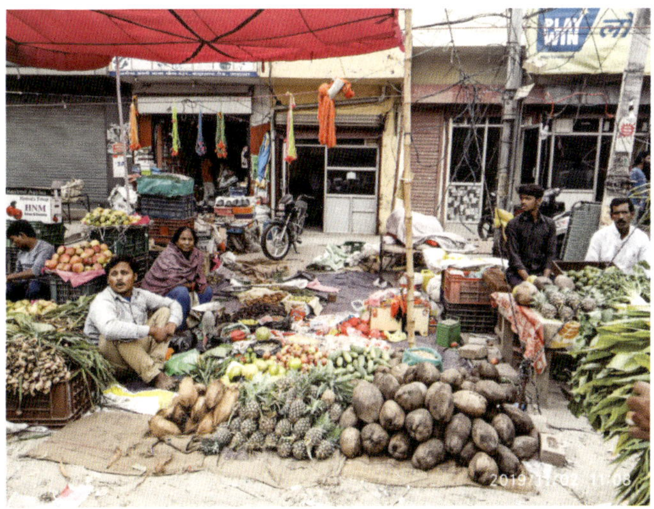

Bazaars, run by migrants from eastern India, spring up near locations where Chhath puja is performed.

Welfare in the City

Illness and Health

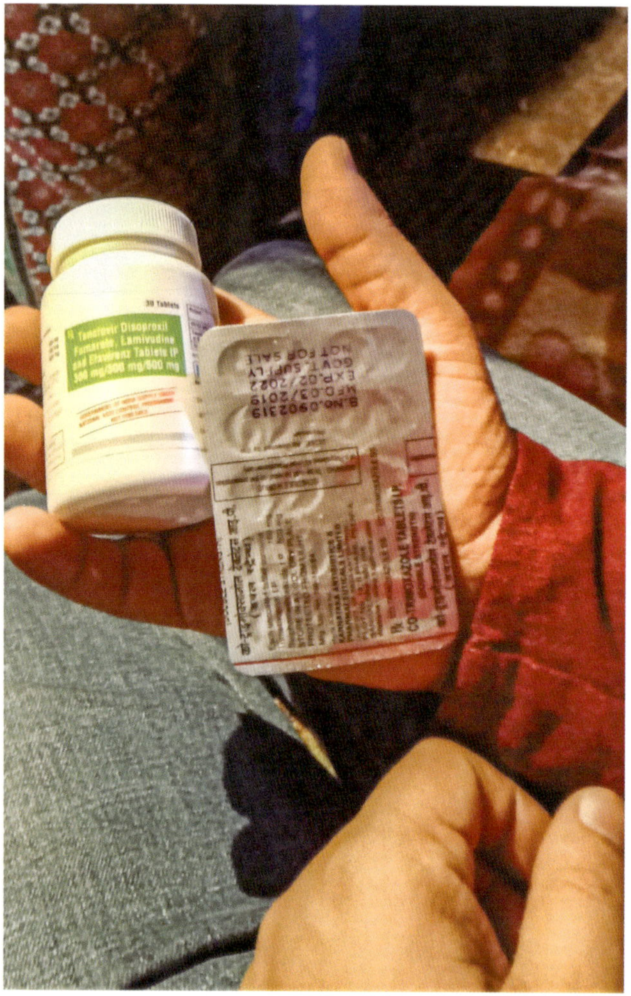

What effect does precarity have on migrant bodies? Right across India, the scarcity of health services available to migrants is appalling. Few employers take care of sick migrant labourers. If a migrant person suffers grievous injury or serious sickness, they are more likely to travel back in their injured state to villages or homes from where they migrated, to seek care and medical attention. Though private health care is available in the city, it is expensive. As an option, private health care is a poor one. Despite the high costs, a key reason to access private pharmacies is that they do not require identity documents. In Guwahati, anti-CAA agitations created tension and directly affected the ability of migrant workers to access formal, government health-care facilities and hospitals. Almost 57 per cent migrants interviewed in Guwahati used private pharmacies. Areas where migrants live are usually ringed around by a network of small clinics and private doctors who dispense *goli aur sui ilaj* (pills and injection treatment). The outcomes of such treatments are unclear.

What happens when a migrant person gets seriously sick? Mapping low income migrants and their health seeking practices during the course of research, it was evident that a breakdown of health and the impossibility of finding health care in cities compels migrants to return to their homes of origin. This is especially true for those who suffer accidents or longer term illnesses. In the absence of state issued documents that entitles citizens to access government hospitals, even pregnancy and birth are reasons to return home. Returning home is not a permanent move. It is part of a circular pattern of arriving-returning-coming back that is intrinsic to migrant movements. In the literature on circular migrations, economic reasons are offered as the key reason for migration. There is little attention to the absence or paucity of health care in cities, and *health* as the reason for circular migration. The 2020 migration visually recorded in media images, are underwritten by the very real problem of the almost complete absence of accessible public health care or medical facilities for migrants. For internal migrants this absence is a lived reality. Migrants walking down highways in 2020 are evidence of this lack.

Coming back to the city after an illness (or pregnancy) severely and adversely affects wage levels, which are often lower than before. Migrants who returned to cities after the pandemic lockdown in 2020 almost universally reported receiving lower wages than previously.

Personal or family crisis can throw a rural households, ability to sustain themselves out of gear. A single emergency can be a disaster, disrupting entire households. An injury to one member can force a rural household to migrate because earnings cannot absorb the costs entailed in coping with a health crisis.

Extract from fieldnotes – Jalandhar, September 2019

When their daughter was severely disabled after suffering a fall while gathering fodder for cattle from a high hilltop, D. and her husband were forced to leave their village, to earn enough to care for their child. In Jalandhar, both worked as labourers in a factory manufacturing valves, nuts and bolts. Because their documents were incomplete, state or government facilities were not easily accessible. Private clinics though readily available, were expensive. Despite the expense, D. and her husband have spent a large part of their wages on the care of their daughter.

In the course of fieldwork interviews, the couple showed a photograph of the daughter's injured feet to the researchers, Bharti Kumari and Anurag Sharma. In the photograph, the feet are at rest. It's an affective image because the feet, though at rest, are not inert. They ask us to consider the biography of this body and those who need to care for the person with injured feet. It's the marks of hurt, the signs of suffering that flesh out the biography of the person and of her household which was forced to migrate. Through the image, D. and her husband spoke of many things - their daughter's pain and disability, the arduous treatments undergone, the precarity of the household. The photograph of the feet is the 'back story', the 'why' of migration.

Extract from fieldnotes – Guwahati (7 August 2019, Fancy Bazar, Guwahati)

R., a man in his 40s, worked as a loader in a busy market area in Guwahati. He had left his family back home in Bihar and came to Guwahati to earn. It is a common practice for men in his village to travel long distances to earn money. During the interview, as we were talking about experiences of ill-health and health-seeking behaviour in Guwahati, an older man (another loader) approached us and listened to our conversation that took place by a cart used by loader for ferrying goods from shops, and commented that the man I was speaking to was not well two years ago and the government hospital asked for INR 20,000 for his treatment. He said that they don't treat us Biharis well. Only after this, R. narrated another recent experience to us. He had very high fever while working in the bazaar. Initially, he went to a private clinic in the bazaar and spent about INR 3000 on medication. As things didn't get better, his friends and relatives took him to the government hospital. The doctor told him that he had dengue. The hospital staff said that he needed to be admitted to the hospital for a few days and it would cost him around INR 20,000. He said, "I didn't have that much money saved; it is a very large amount for someone like me. If I had saved money, I would send that home. They were trying to extort money from me here." After consulting with his relatives and family, he went back to the village within 3-4 days of the interview.

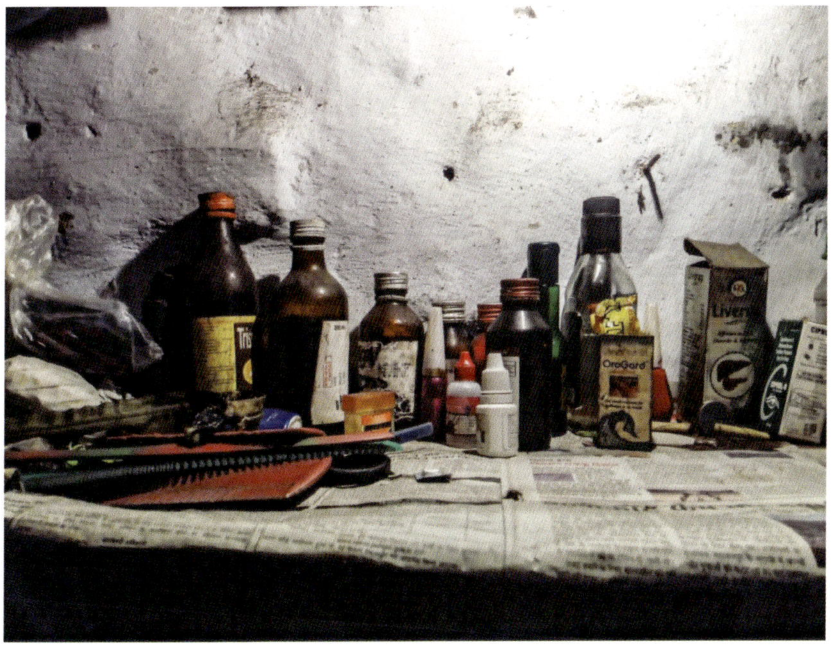

Variously dated, bottles of cough mixture, mouth paint and eyedrops are carefully kept in a small niche in a migrant workers home.

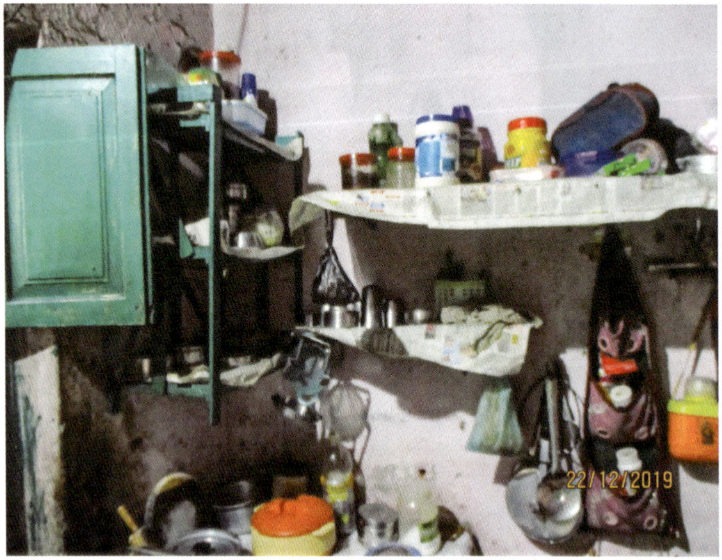

An assortment of medication in a migrant home.

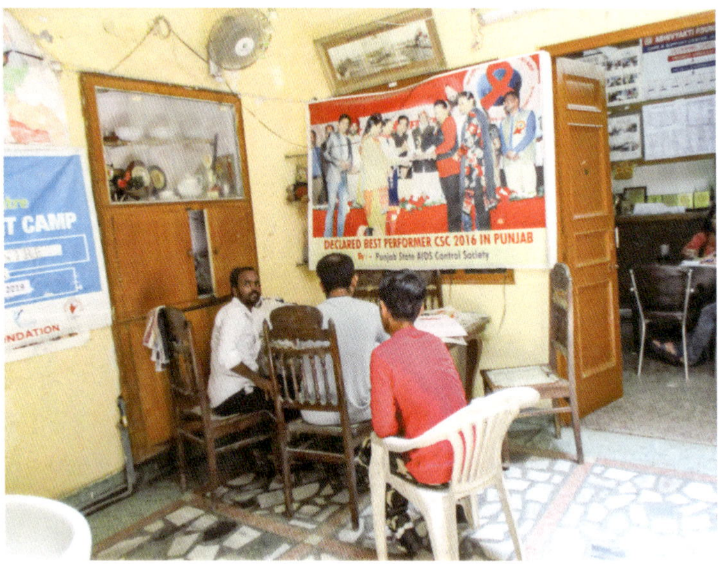

Interview with migrant workers in progress at an AIDS camp in Jalandhar.

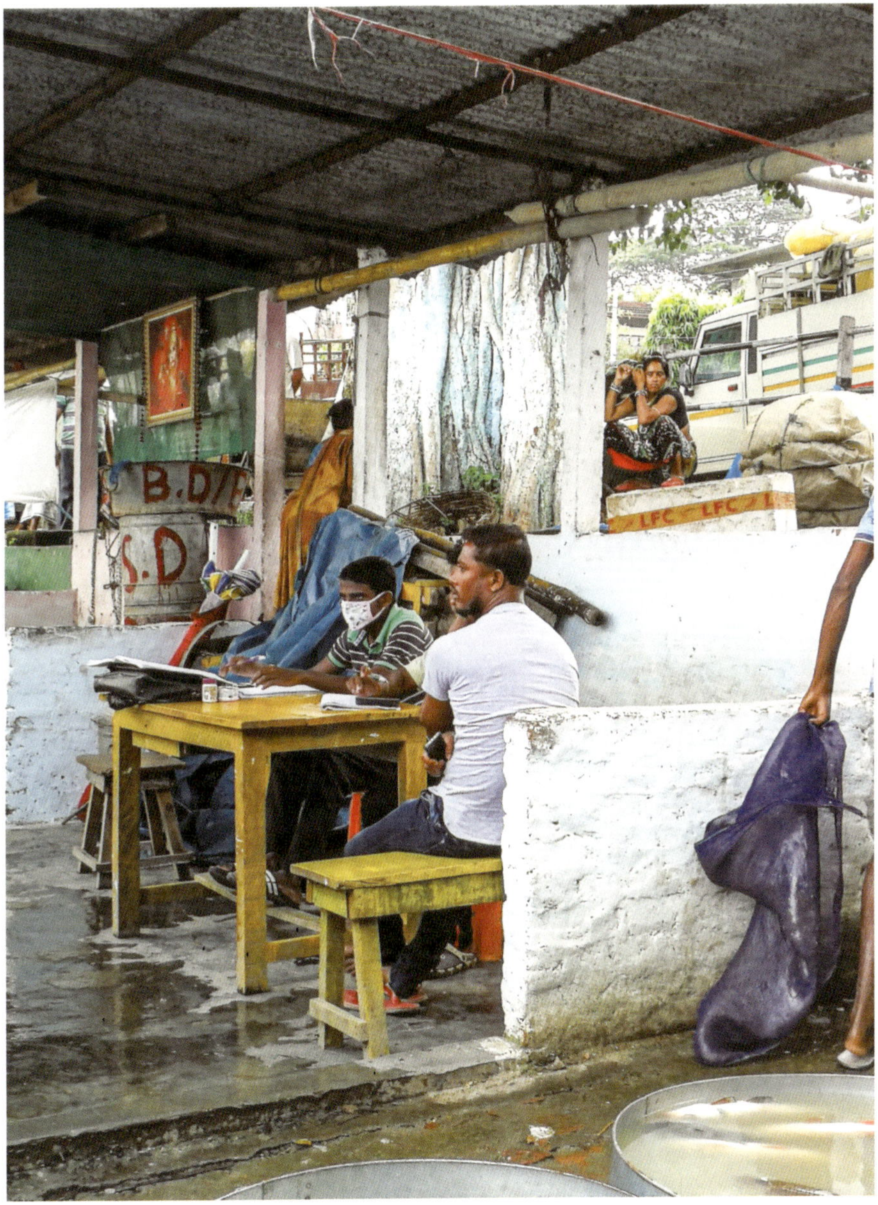

Covid protocols at the Guwahati fish bazaar.

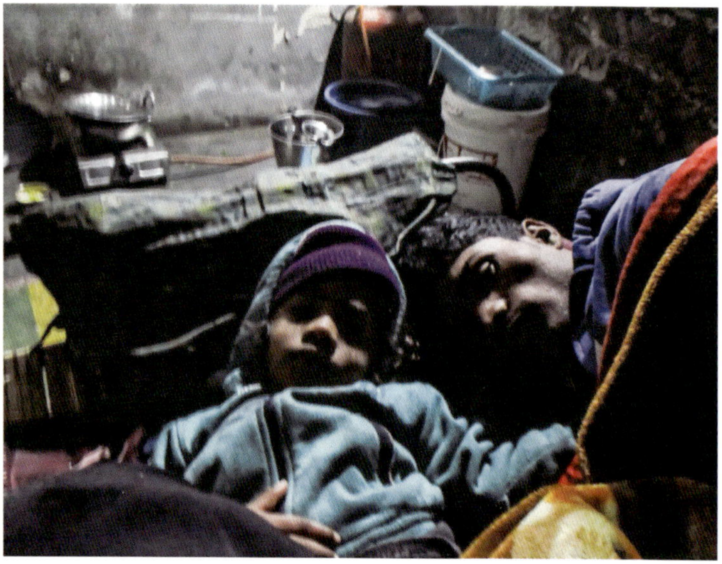

During an interview and a photovoice session, a migrant woman takes a photograph of her sick husband and child, to convey the condition of precarity in which the household now lives because of illness.

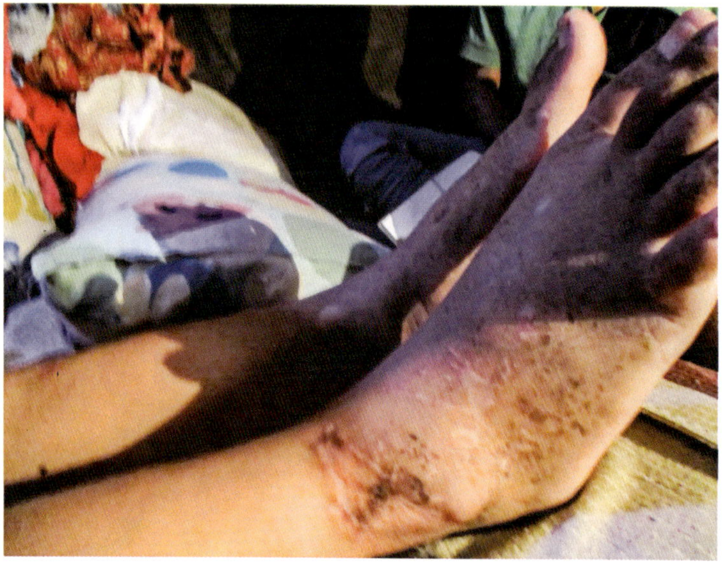

An image of her daughter's injured feet enabled D. to speak of her family's need to migrate.

Welfare in the City

Migrant Children

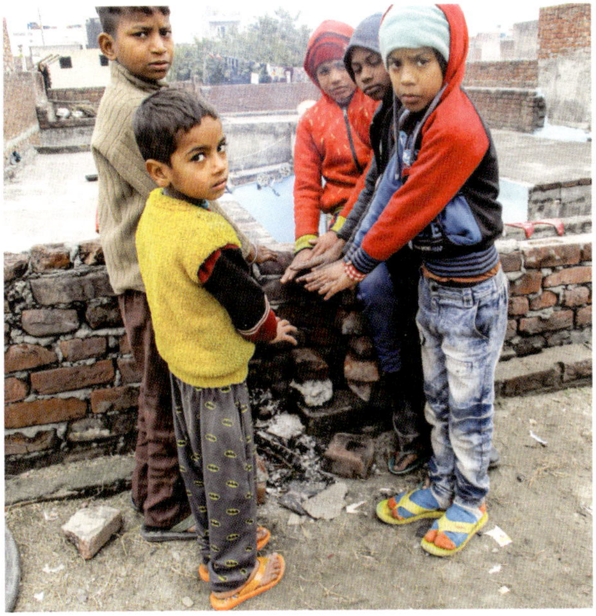

What does mobility and migration mean for children? In 2021, vaccinations, inoculations, gaps between shots, and calendars, are on everyone's minds. For migrant children, there is no consistency in the documents or calendars or other periodic follow ups. ANMs or ASHA workers do not have any chart or knowledge of a migrant child's health and inoculation biography. The likelihood of such children slipping through the cracks of public health systems is extremely high. It is perhaps one of the reasons why extreme levels of 'wasted' children have been recorded in global health statistics for India.

The efforts at schooling for migrant children is marginally better. Provisions in different states make some initial schooling a possibility. But employment opportunities for parents govern the length of stay in a city, which in turn have an immediate bearing on the continued schooling of migrant children. Migrant parents make extraordinary efforts to send children to urban schools. Tuition classes, or money paid for schooling and extra tuition, are a key part of household expenditure. In fact, education for children is a fundamental reason for initial migration. School calendars or education requirements are reasons to postpone visits to places of origin. Money spent on children's' education affects the ability to return home for periodic visits. Migrants who had worked and stayed in Guwahati and Jalandhar for ten years or more, offered children's education as a key reason for their length of stay in cities.

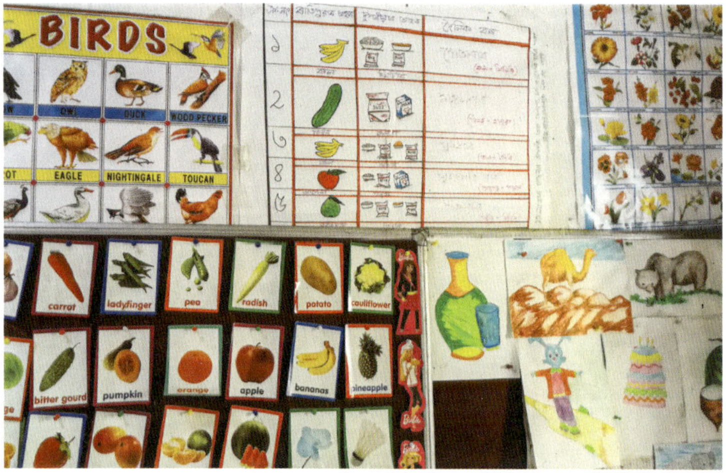

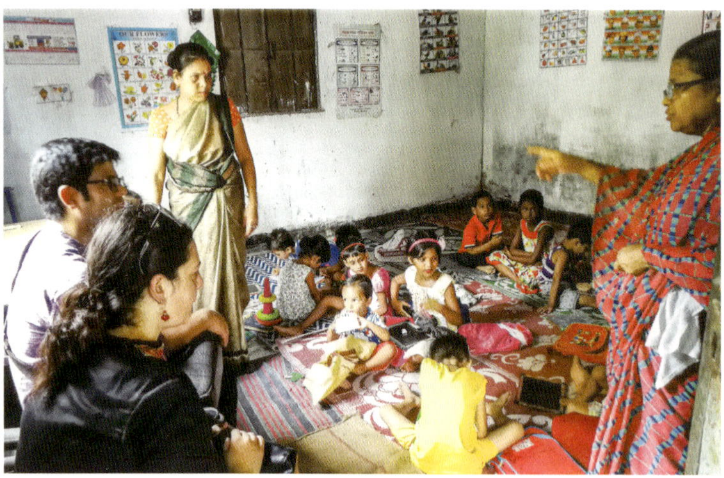

Children's education is a key reason to migrate to cities.

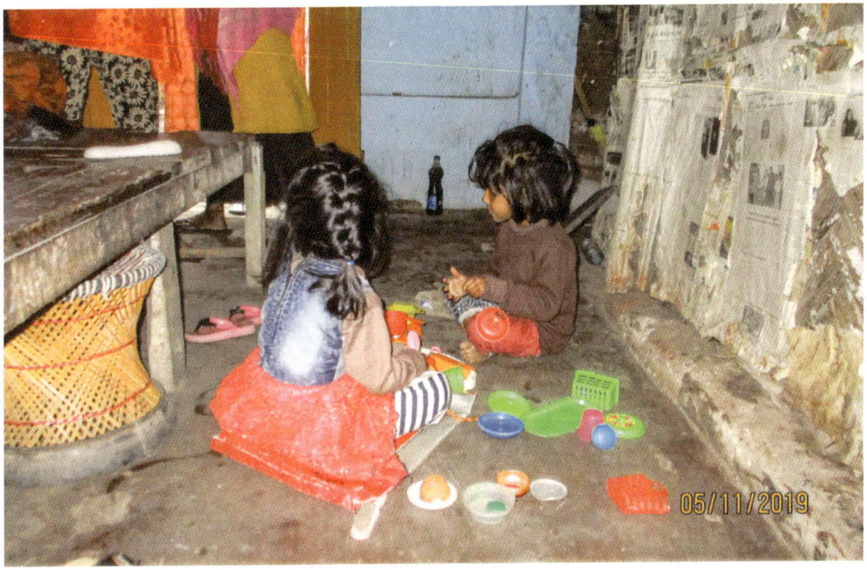

A great deal of effort and money is spent by migrant parents on their children's welfare.

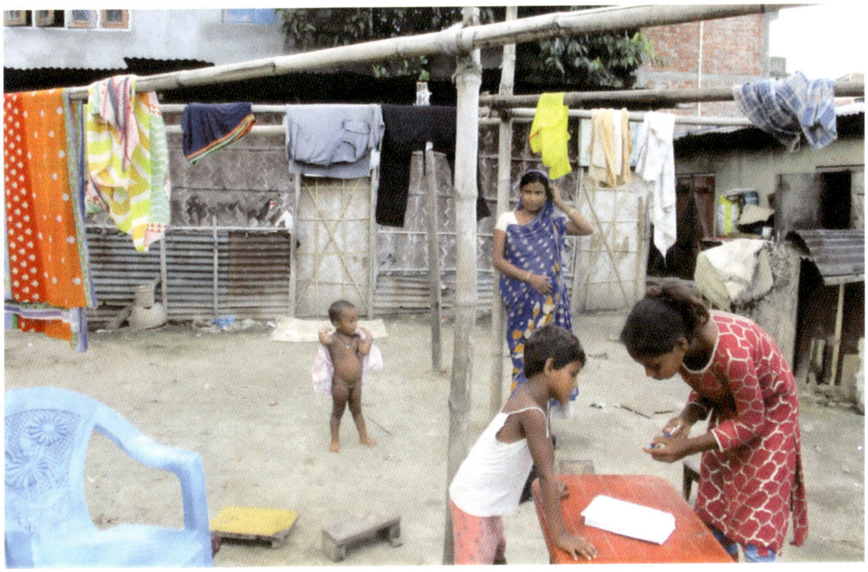

Children of migrants, Dhirenpara, Guwahati.

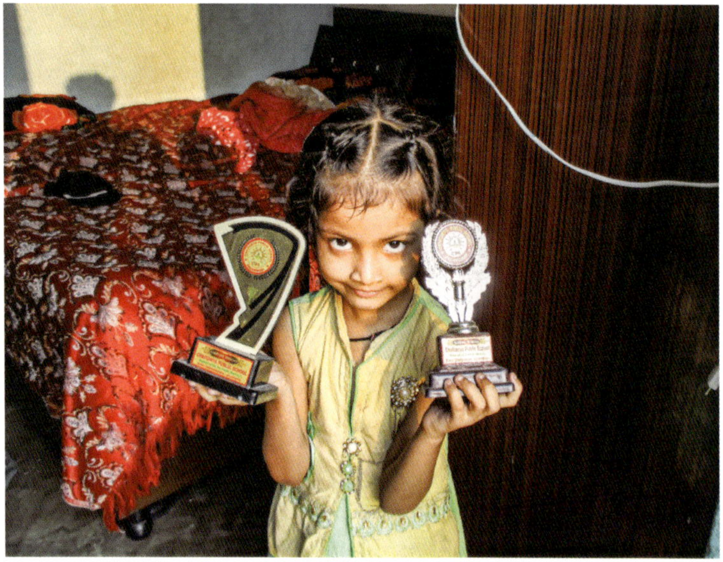

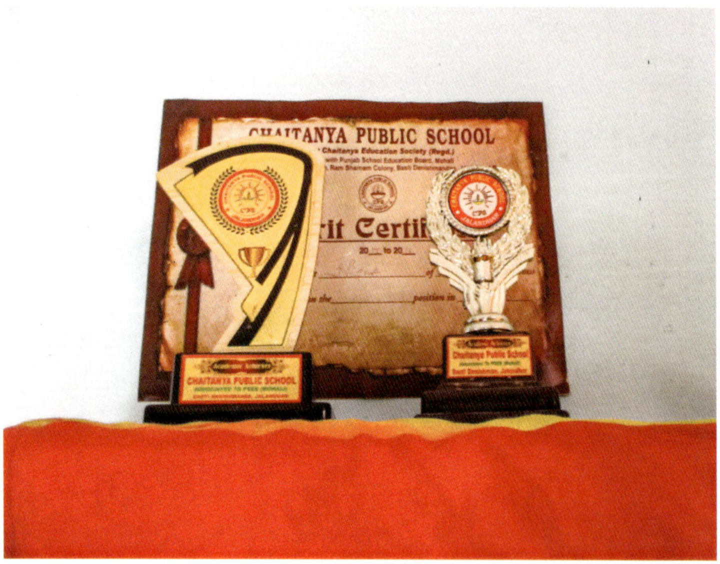

A child's achievements are prominently displayed in a migrant's home.

Welfare in the City
Injustice and Redressal

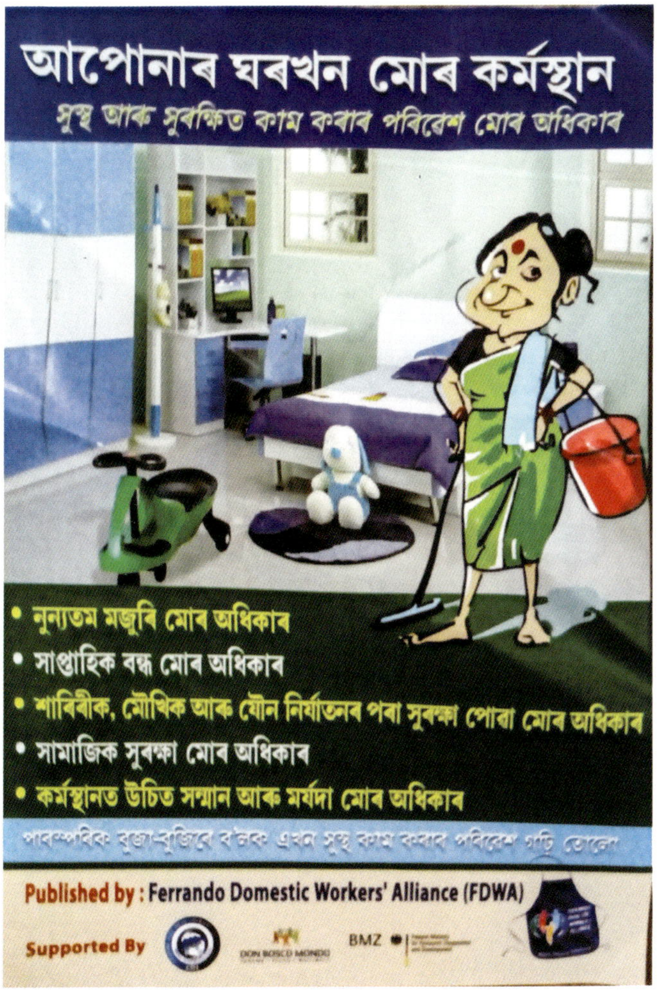

In the quantitative survey conducted as part of the Project, an overwhelming number of low-income migrants reported that they do not feel safe in the city. In Guwahati, 60 per cent migrants surveyed in detail and interviewed at length, said that they do not feel safe in the city. In Jalandhar, the numbers are lower; 42 per cent do not feel safe in the city. However, the instances of being robbed of mobile phones and money when walking or cycling back from work, often by motorbike riding snatchers, is high in Jalandhar. A surprisingly large number of low-income migrants said that they have been ill-treated in the city. Ill-treatment ranges from cuffs to more severe beating. In Guwahati, 89 out of 126 low-income migrants said that they have been ill-treated in the last year. In Jalandhar, 33 of the100 low-income migrants interviewed, reported ill-treatment.

Verbal abuse is rampant and vicious. A young male migrant in Jalandhar said that during the course of seeking work, he meets all kinds of people as potential employers in the city. He narrated an incident to illustrate the verbal abuse that employers use with impunity. It is his practice to ask the employer what kind of work is expected of him. One potential employer told him that his work was to get sodomized. For a minute, Manoj was silent when he narrated the incident. "What do you say to someone like that? I retorted, 'go, do it to yourself'."

Safety in the City

	Guwahati		Jalandhar	
	Female	**Male**	**Female**	**Male**
Yes	32.00%	42.11%	63.64%	85.90%
No	66.00%	56.58%	36.36%	14.10%
NA	2.00%	1.32%	0.00%	0.00%
Grand Total	**100.00%**	**100.00%**	**100.00%**	**100.00%**

Ill-treatment in the City

	Guwahati		Jalandhar	
	Female	**Male**	**Female**	**Male**
Yes	60.00%	77.63%	13.64%	38.46%
No	40.00%	22.37%	86.36%	61.54%
Grand Total	**100.00%**	**100.00%**	**100.00%**	**100.00%**

Extract from fieldnotes, 20 October 2019, Jalandhar

ST is from Munger, Bihar, and has been in Jalandhar since 1981. He emphatically stated that migrants are discriminated against, there is no *apana-pan*, inclusiveness. He said that verbal abuse and intimidation are general and widespread here. People in general behave differently toward Punjabis and *Bhaiyyeh* (migrants from eastern India; now a term used more widely for all migrants). Employers and particularly foreman acting on behalf of employers, are very rude and abuse him (*ashabd bolta hai*). He said that he tells no one about it, as he has to bear it himself (*kis se baat karenge? Sun ke reh jaate hain. Ye sab baat kaun sunta hai? Koi nahin sunta hai.*)

Given their precarious position, and weak bargaining power, low-income migrants habitually encounter injustice in the city. Frequently, employer's refuse to pay the agreed amounts, or delay payments for inordinate periods of time. Some refuse to acknowledge any agreement whatsoever.

Extract from fieldnotes, 27 January 2018, Jalandhar

In the course of an interview, in response to a question about wage payments, a migrant worker said that payments can often be delayed or reduced from what is actually due. He said, "*hota hai ki paise nahi dete hain. Kai malik hain aise. Dekhte hain ki jo nahin bol pata hai, uska paisa nahi dete hain. Ki kya bigaad lega?*" (Yes, it happens. Employers don't pay wages, or what is due. There are many employers like that. They notice the one who doesn't assert himself. Then they don't pay him, thinking what can he do?) In response to a question of whether other labourers would continue to work for that employer, SU replied, "*karte hain. Ek ke saath aisa hua, to baaki sau log kaam thode chhod denge. Malik ko pata hai ki ek ke baad doosra aa jayega. Bahut log hain kaam karne ke liye. Ek jayega, das aayenge.*" (They do keep working. It happens to one person, but that doesn't mean the other hundred labourers would quit working for that employer. The employer also knows that if one labourer goes, another one will come. There are many people who want to work. One goes, ten will come.) SU lamented, "*ekta nahi hai*" (there is no unity). I asked whether they talk to other people in the settlement about these issues. SU said, "*baat karte hain. ki usne aisa kiya hamare saath. Lekin aage kya karenge. Agla kaam dhundhne lagte hain.*" (We do discuss this, about what an employer did to us. But what more can we do? We start looking for new work.)

Extract from Fieldnotes – 2 August 2019 (7.30 am), Fatasil, Guwahati

We met S., a 25-year-old young man from Tripura waiting for work at a labour *chowk* in Guwahati. He works as a carpenter. He had been in Guwahati for two years before we met him. S. lives in the city with his wife and a two-month-old daughter while his older daughter stays with her grandmother (the man's mother) in Tripura.

A few months before we interviewed him, he and his cousin (with whom he shares the accommodation) were picked up from the labour *chowk* by a man to do some work in his house. The potential employer bargained with them, and then eventually agreed to pay INR 1200 for the *kaam*, to fix something. S. and his cousin initially wanted to do the job on a daily-wage (*haziri*) basis, but the employer wanted a fixed price for the job. Once they went to the employer's house, they completed the agreed work and then the employer asked them to do several additional *kaam*, jobs, including fixing windows for the same wage, which they refused. The employer got very angry and said he would not pay them until the additional work is done. S. and his cousin insisted on their payment, and kept asking for the money but the employer refused and asked them to 'go back'. The employer also threatened to beat them if they persisted in asking for their dues.

Extract from fieldnotes – October 2019, Jalandhar

Lives of single male migrants are extremely precarious, as they come to the city almost solely with the intent to earn and remit money. They have few savings and very little to fall back on. We met BalR. in the Labour Union office in Jalandhar, where the union leader D, who fights cases on a pro-bono basis under various state labour laws, was helping BalR with his case. BalR was probably around 35 years old. He was from Gorakhpur, UP. He had been working in a steel mill making ball bearings. At the beginning of February 2018, he had an accident while operating machinery during work. Two fingers as well as the thumb of his right hand were severely fractured. He was hospitalized and had to undergo surgery and prolonged medical treatment. BalR. did not get any compensation. He was fired from work, and the salary dues were not paid to him. He also had to ask for money (INR 30,000) from relatives in his village for his treatment. He contacted D. through someone he knew.

D. filed a case on BalR.'s behalf in the Labour Court. Though BalR had been working informally in the factory, his employer first filed a reply in the court saying that BalR. did not work for them. D. had to provide testimonies from enlisted workers of the factory, sometimes covertly gathered, to prove that BalR. was working in the factory. The employer offered INR 50,000 as compensation. D refused to accept this amount and wanted the worker's correct dues.

D. suggested that BalR. should get a medical certificate from the Civil Hospital, which would mention the extent of disability, to strengthen his case and enable him to negotiate with the employer from a better position. The doctor at Civil Hospital told BalR. to get the X-ray done privately, to verify the injury. After he got the X-Ray, the doctor refused to give a certificate because the address on BalR.'s Aadhaar Card was not a Jalandhar address. BalR. had to get his Aadhaar Card address changed, for which he had to get residence proof from the landlord as well. The process took weeks and by the time his Aadhaar Card got updated, the doctor at the hospital got transferred. The new doctor asked for a new X-Ray and said that if the old doctor didn't give a certificate, he would not do so either. With all the delays, BalR. did not get the medical certificate. The employer kept sending people to intimidate him for the settlement and put pressure on him not to go to the Labour Court. BalR. requested D.'s help to get his case settled before Diwali, so that he could send money home. Unfortunately this could not happen and BalR did not come back to meet D. or continue the case.

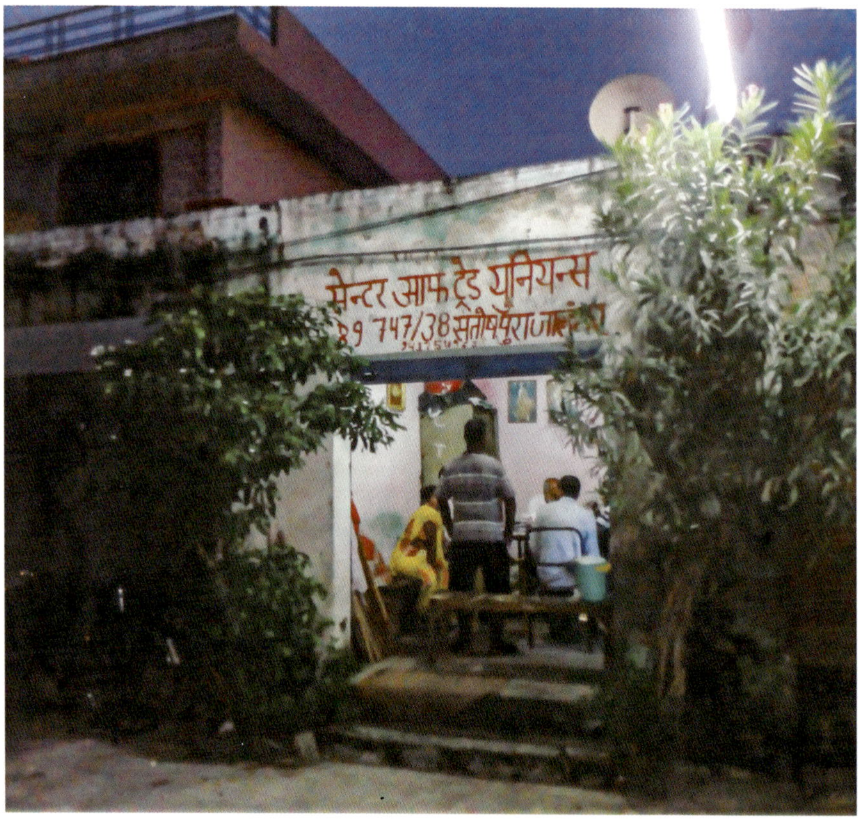

A late evening meeting at the Centre of Trade Unions, Santokpura, Jalandhar. The Devanagari script signals that those who need to know about the Centre might not be able to read the Gurmukhi script. The script reaches out to non-Punjabi workers.

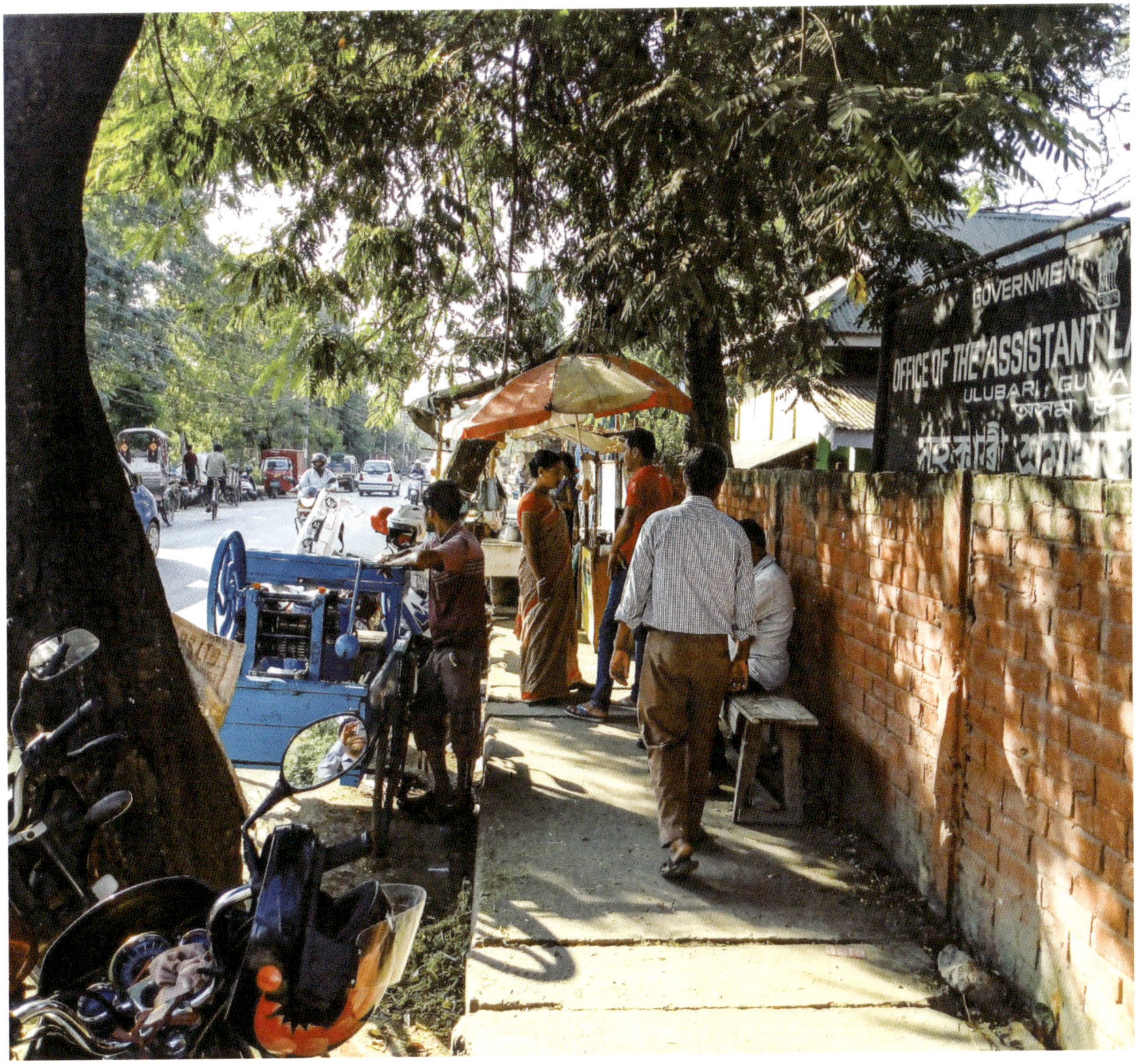

A migrant sugarcane juice street vendor, stands outside
the Office of the Assistant Labour Commissioner, Ulubari, Guwahati.

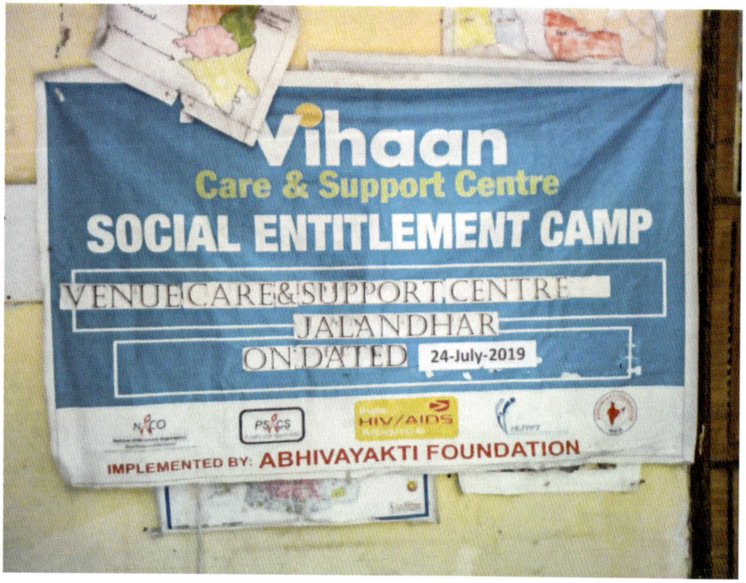

Abhivayakti Foundation, which helps patients with HIV/AIDS, advertised and held a Social Entitlement Camp, to inform workers about their rights and entitlements. The primarily disease control centre has become a focal point for workers to get information and acquire documents to access welfare.

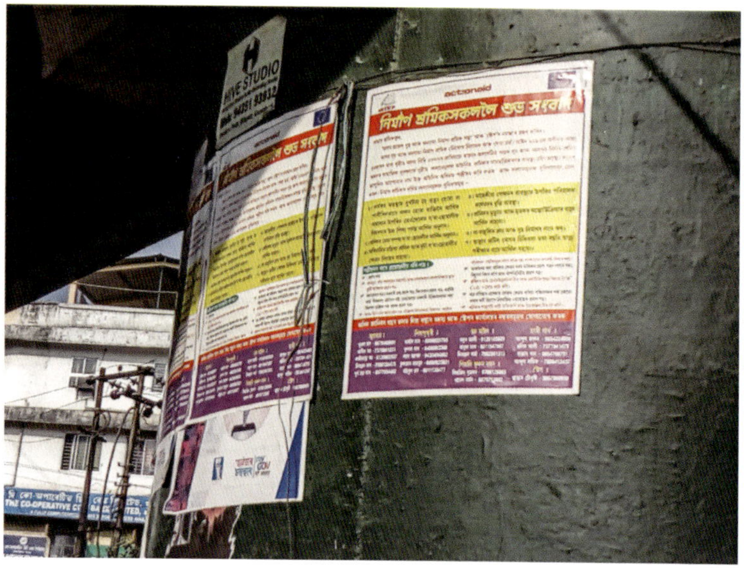

'Good news for construction workers'. Action Aid poster outlining new policy for workers. The construction sector employs a very large number of urban migrants.

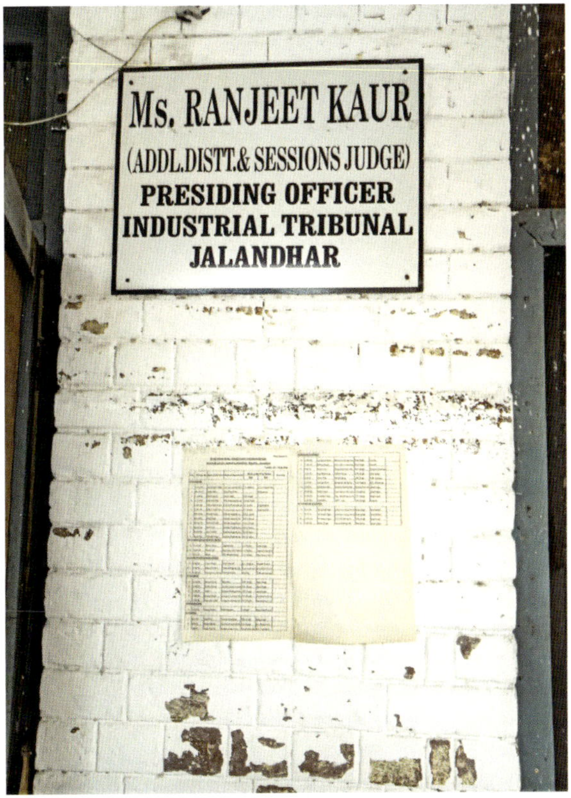

Office of the Industrial Tribunal Judge, Jalandhar. Urban factories employ significant numbers of migrants.

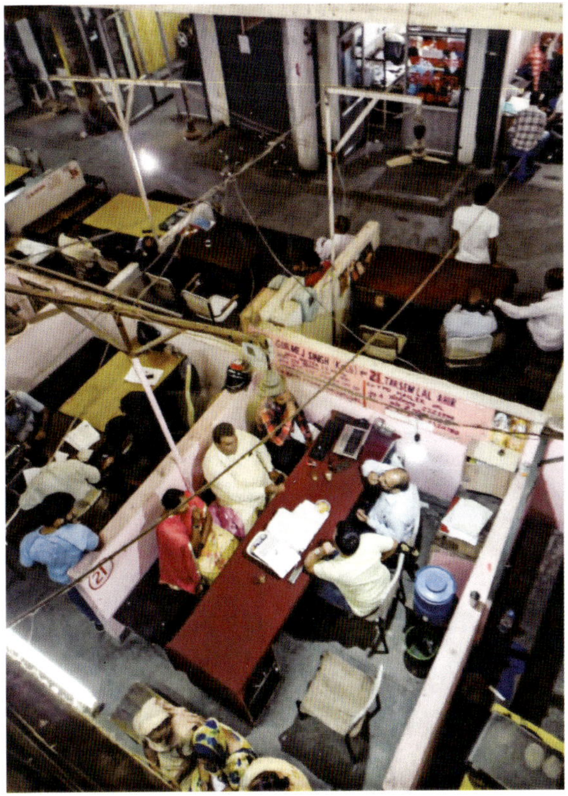

Arbitration.

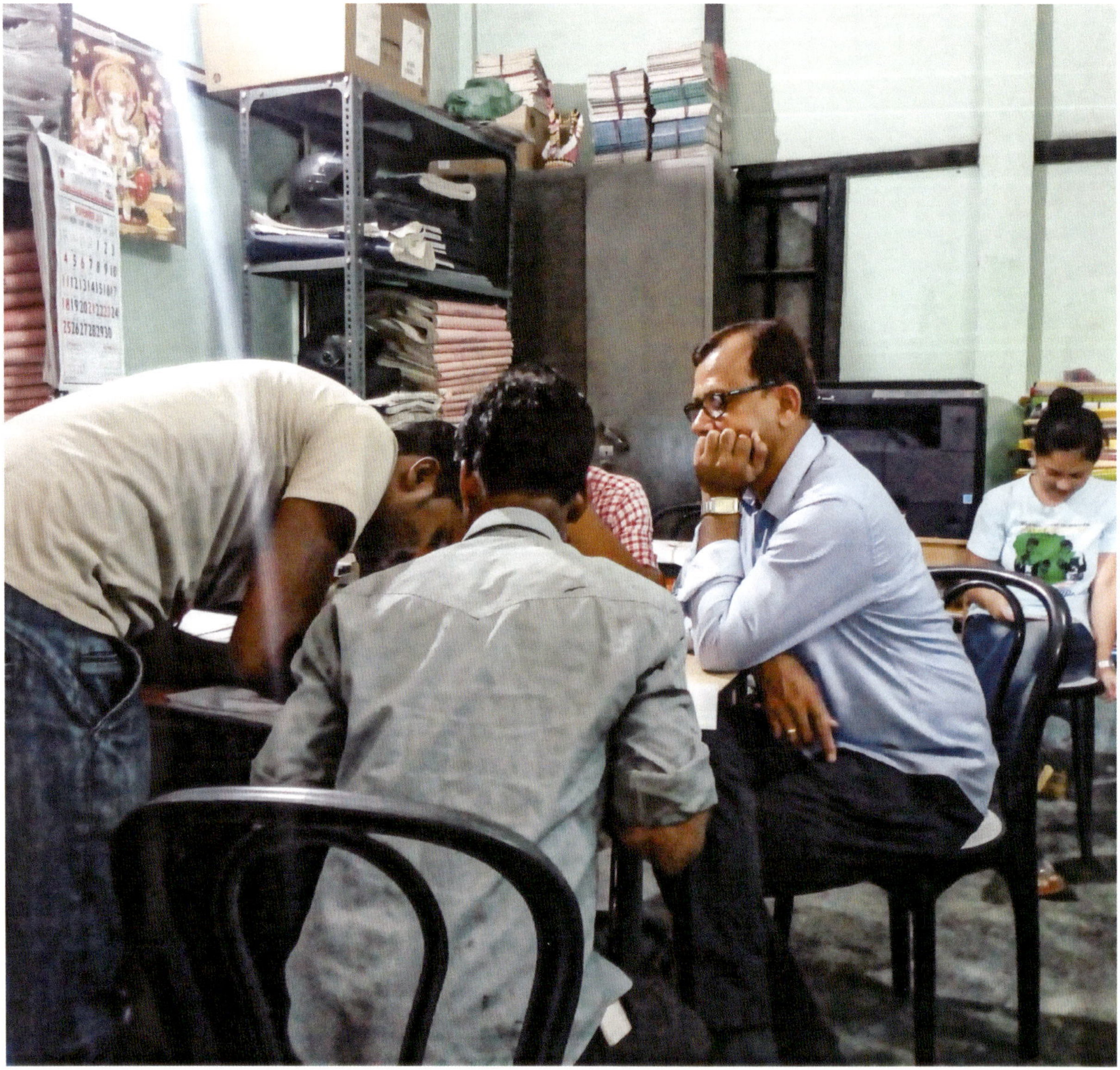

Filling arbitration forms.

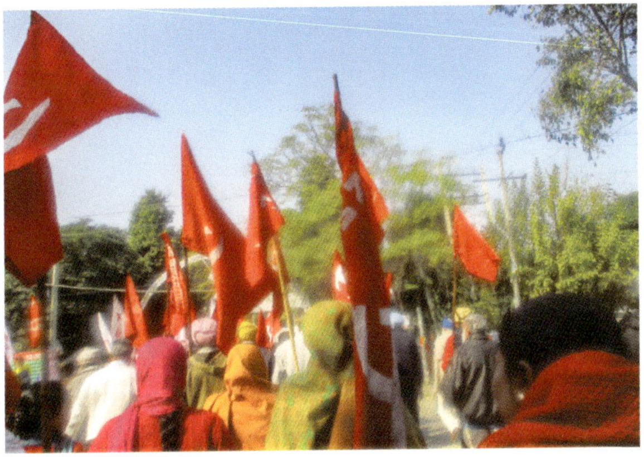

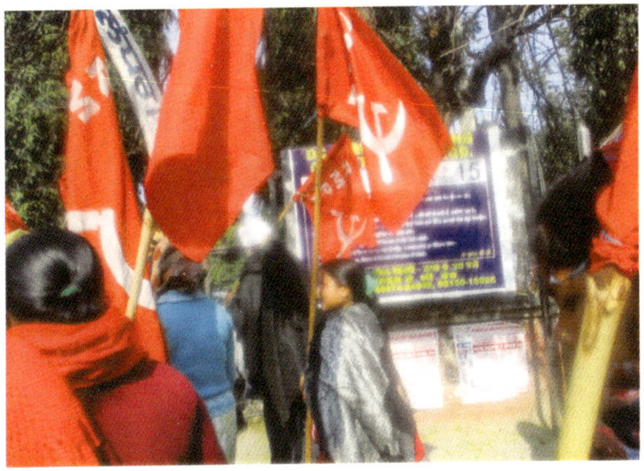

Migrant women workers in Jalandhar carrying red flags, march in protest to the court of the Sub-Divisional Magistrate, December 2019.

Protests

Protests are rarely resorted to. To speak about injustice, a woman migrant worker, R., decided to use her mobile phone camera, as part of a photovoice session, to record a protest march of women workers. The fuzzy images do not obscure the resolution of the women carrying their red banners nor blur their determined march to the Sub-Divisional Magistrate's court, despite the large police presence.

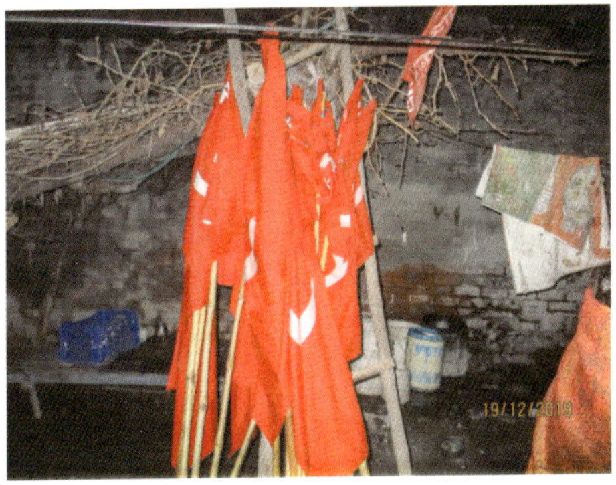

Red flags of protest propped up against a bamboo ladder, after the demonstration and march. December 2019.

Doing Research with Migrants
A Reflection on Methods

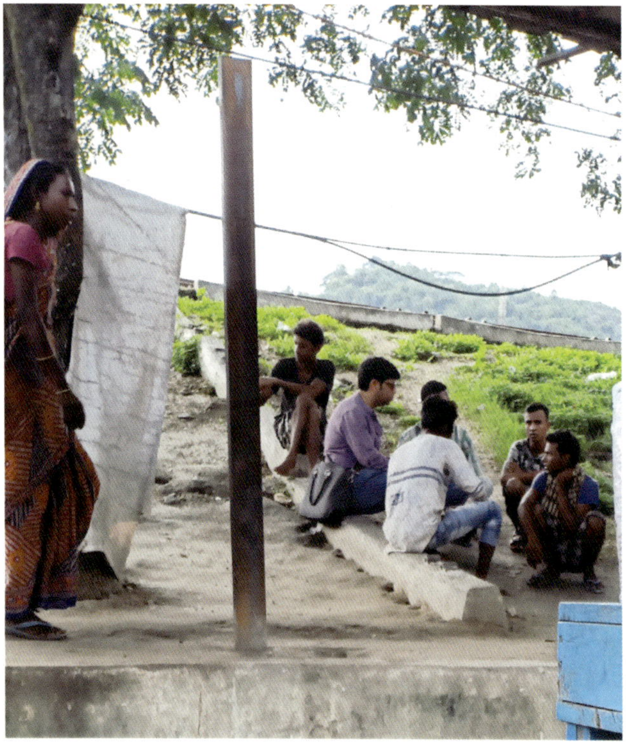

When we began conceiving of the project on trying to map the margins of urban spaces, the first choice we had to make was to choose a place. Not just 'which city' but where in the city. We decided to begin with the bazaar, an urban hub of the city, where we'd literally and metaphorically stub out toes against goods of the bazaar. The goods produced the questions: How did the goods get here? Who brought them and how will they leave? Displayed goods were the 'lead-in' into the lives of migrants who are unquestionably present but almost completely shadowed. Goods and commodities are the surface upon which migrant labour leaves a trace. We were enabled to 'see' labour through the good, and begin to understand the mobilities of urban migrant labour through the circulation of goods.

'Seeing' is a visual exercise and a social exercise; it demands from us the use of visual ethnography, but also shows us that visual is not 'innocent'. It shapes who can be seen; why we see certain people, and not others in specific spaces. It forced us to reflect on the method of the interview in relation to the mobile migrants and ask : what's 'an interview'? Is the interviewee the person who 'comes forward' to 'do' the interview? Who do we manage to 'interview' in the formal sense of the word? Would a disrupted conversation, interspersed by conversations with others seated around, be counted as an interview? If we don't interview the same person through successive days along the same route, does it count as an interview or do we consider it as fragments of information? Should we piece them together as a coherent whole?

The reflection on method taught us more about lives of low income migrants. The disrupted, sometimes incoherence interviews gave us pause, impelled us to ask – so why didn't I see the same person reporting for work day after day at that place in a predictable fashion? If I didn't see the predictable pattern, what does that mean about urban transformation and marginal lives?

Sometimes an interview took a number days because migrant workers had to continue working or complete a task. The interview transcript was not a single, coherent, perfectly structured document. Interruptions illuminated the pressure of work on migrant lives.

The second step in mapping urban migrants was to move from the question: where do migrants work, to where do migrants live. We know from patterns of displacement and urban reconstruction that low income migrants are frequently and easily shifted off from a location, with no recourse to appeal. But we also know from the work on urban transformations that displacement does not mean leaving the city. Displacement means a shift to an area not necessarily further off, but more legally precarious, reflecting in part the condition of social and legal precarity of migrants. Mapping migrant settlements revealed that poorer migrants usually occupied 'micro-encampments' on parapets, pavements, edges of by-lanes and so on, areas that are legally 'out of bounds'.

Frequent displacements have a direct bearing on how, and if, poor urban migrants will be able to access any government designated welfare schemes – many of which depend on a 'local' address of some specified duration. To acquire proof of length of stay in the city, an individual needs documents like utility bills, rent receipts, employment certificates or formal letters from an employer, a bank account in the city, an Income Certificate issued by the local District Commissioner's office among others. All these documents need to be verified and 'attested' by a local magistrate or a notary. An Aadhaar Card is not treated as a single window of access. For example, an Aadhaar Card does not guarantee access to schooling for a migrant child. Such migrant children often shuttle between homes of numerous relatives, employers and others, creating a new category among the labouring poor: shuttle children.

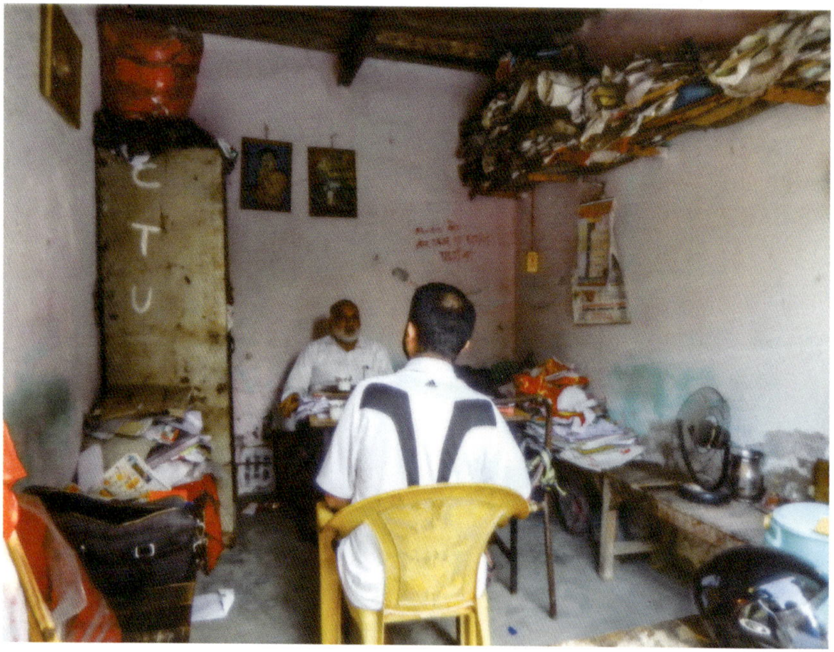

Anurag interviewing a labour union leader.

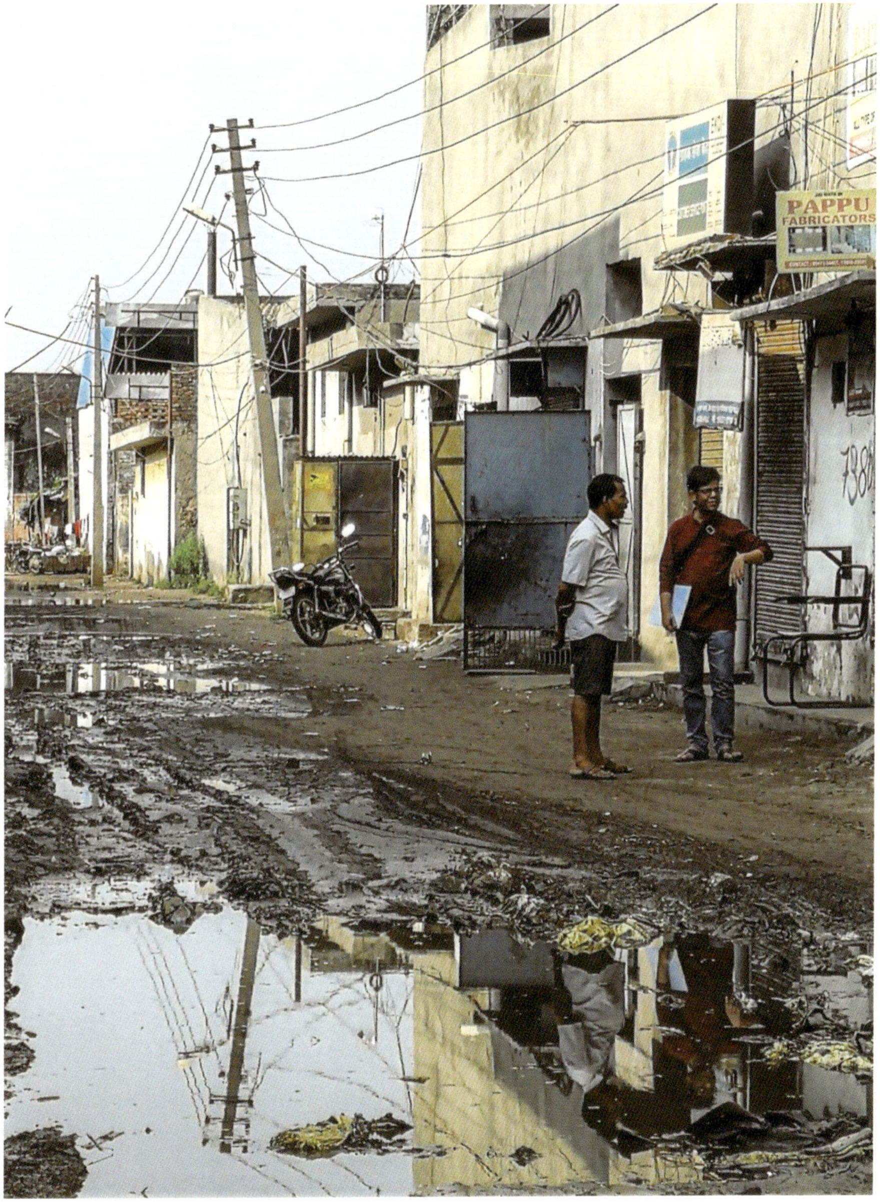

A factory worker talking to Jeevan.

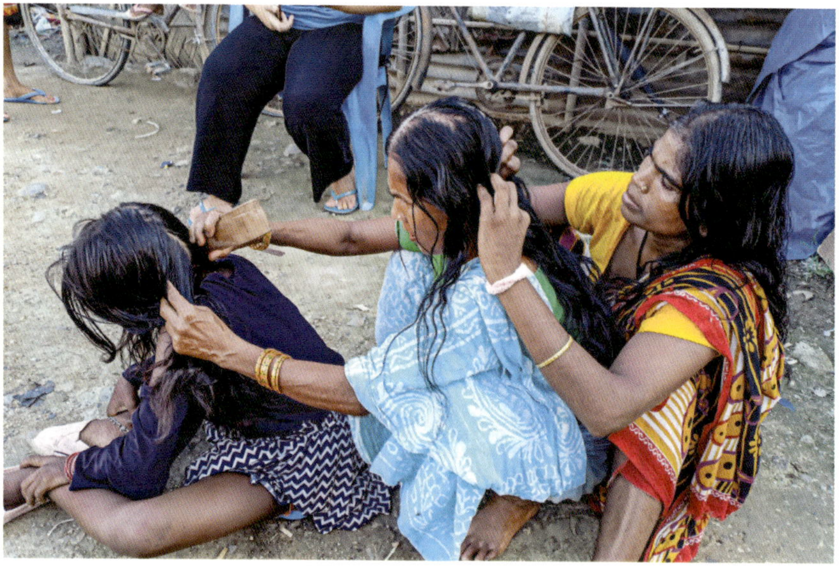

Anuprova talking to a group of women in Dhirenpada, Guwahati.

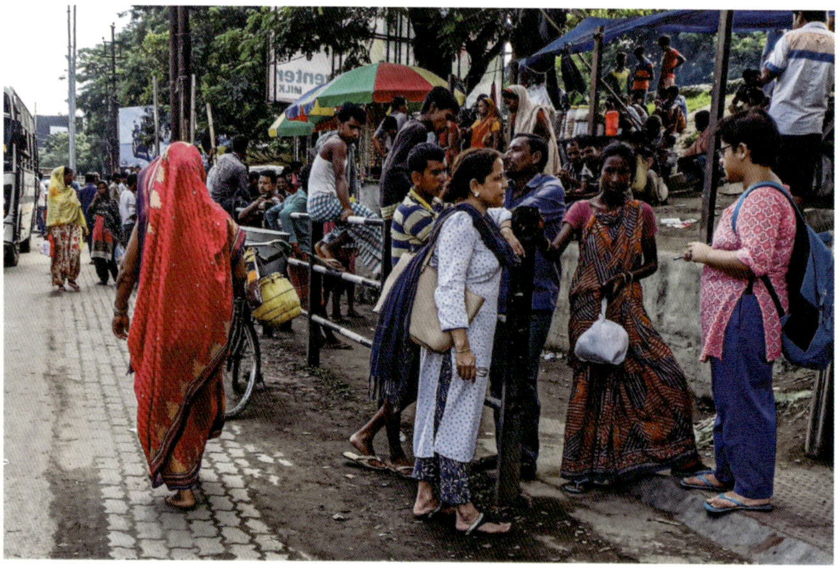

On their way to work, domestic workers at a Guwahati bus stop, converse with Anurita and Anuprova.

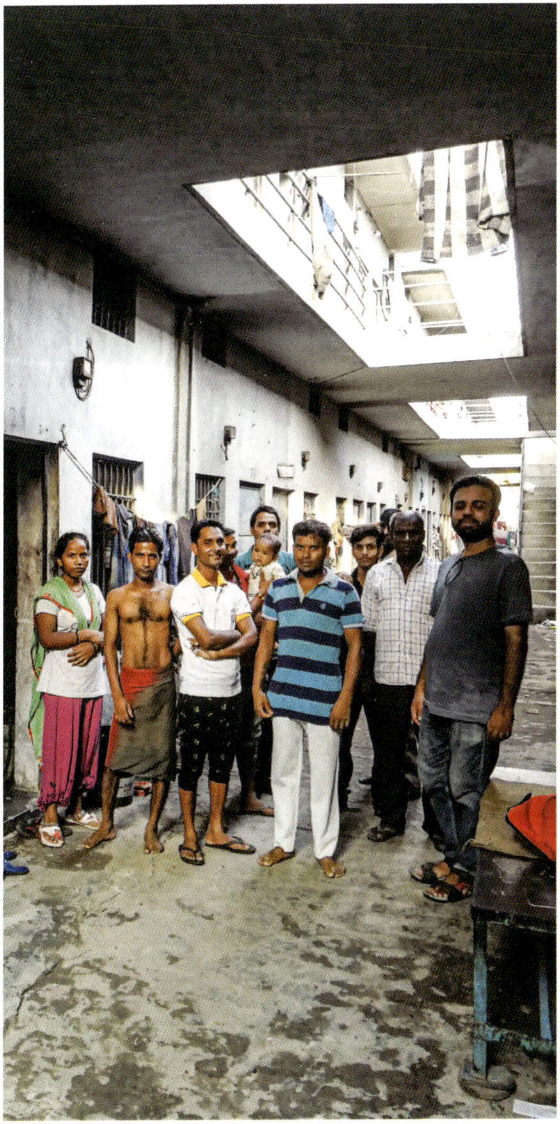

Anurag stands with a group of workers outside their rooming houses.

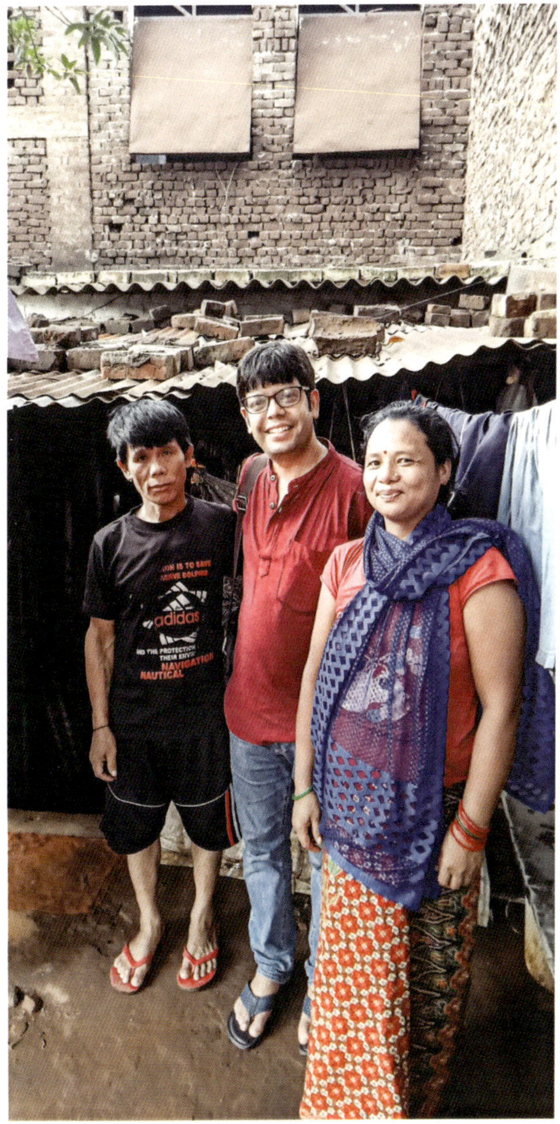

Jeevan with D. and her husband who told him about their migration from Nepal to Punjab.

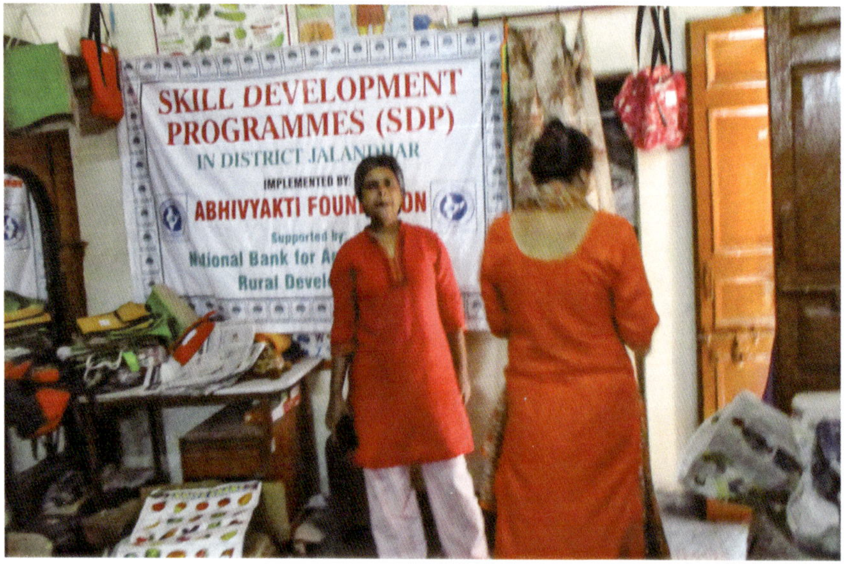

Bharti at the Abhivyakti Foundation office, Jalandhar, after a meeting with migrant workers.

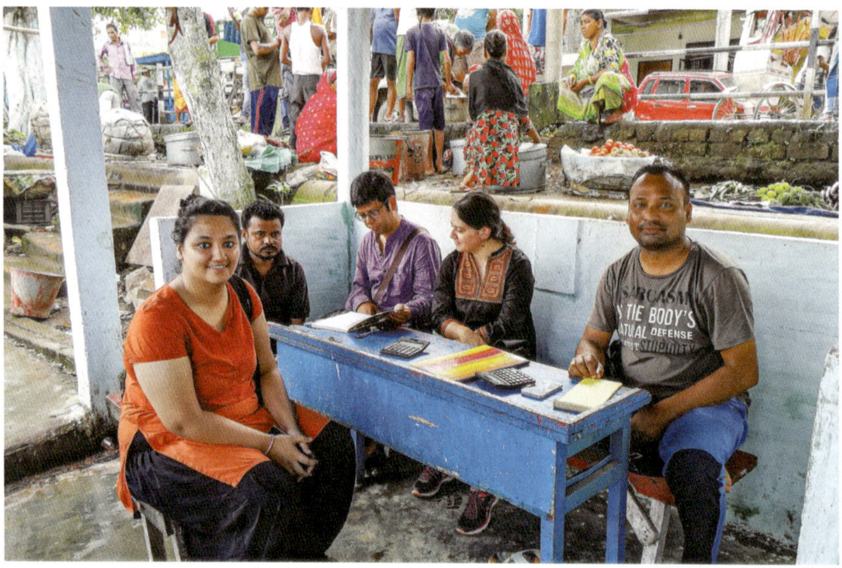

Interview with a fish wholesaler, *maas ghat*, Guwahati.

Nature of Work

	Guwahati		Jalandhar	
Work	**Female**	**Male**	**Female**	**Male**
Begging	14.00%	10.53%	0.00%	0.00%
Casual Labour	30.00%	38.16%	0.00%	8.97%
Vending	16.00%	19.74%	13.64%	33.33%
Factory/Shop Work	6.00%	3.95%	9.09%	47.44%
Construction	0.00%	14.47%	0.00%	2.56%
Domestic Work	20.00%	0.00%	27.27%	0.00%
Home-based Work	0.00%	1.32%	18.18%	0.00%
Homemaker/Household Work	2.00%	0.00%	13.64%	0.00%
Hotel/*Dhaba*	0.00%	1.32%	0.00%	2.56%
Riksha/Cart Puller	0.00%	2.63%	0.00%	2.56%
Security Guard	0.00%	2.63%	0.00%	0.00%
Multiple	12.00%	5.26%	13.64%	0.00%
NA	0.00%	0.00%	4.55%	2.56%
Grand Total	**100.00%**	**100.00%**	**100.00%**	**100.00%**

Nature of Employment

	Guwahati		Jalandhar	
Nature of Employment	**Female**	**Male**	**Female**	**Male**
Daily Wage	26.00%	48.68%	0.00%	12.82%
Piece Rate (Factory/ Shop)	2.00%	0.00%	0.00%	17.95%
Piece Rate(Home)	2.00%	0.00%	18.18%	0.00%
Salaried/Pay Roll	18.00%	2.63%	54.55%	29.49%
Self-Employed	22.00%	23.68%	13.64%	38.46%
Don't Know	28.00%	25.00%	0.00%	1.28%
NA	2.00%	0.00%	13.64%	0.00%
Grand Total	**100.00%**	**100.00%**	**100.00%**	**100.00%**

Doing Research with Migrants

Photovoice

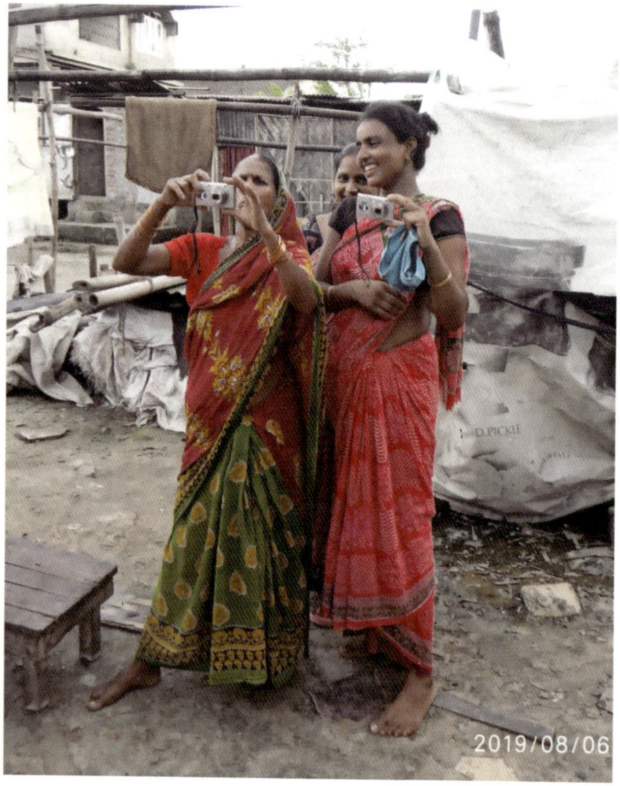

Photovoice is a visual, image-based method where participants are not merely research 'subjects' to be studied but engage in knowledge production from their respective standpoints. Embedded in the Participatory Action Research (PAR) tradition, photovoice can be understood as a process that involves researchers and participants in a collaborative and reflective approach to discuss issues that affect communities, and where participants "identify, represent and enhance their community" (Wang & Burris 1997). The process involves participants taking photographs that capture their lives, neighbourhoods and experiences, and use these images to share and make meaning of their personal struggles and reflect on community concerns (Kapilashrami & Marsden 2018).The logic of the method is to empower people through the medium of the visual and the use of technology, to express and talk about their experiences.

In photovoice, the camera is no longer a microscopic lens or an object that distances people from their own image. It allows the person in the photograph to depict themselves in ways they want to be seen. What is 'my' image of 'myself' creates the connection between two sets of participants speaking through the image – the person in the photograph and the person to whom the photograph is explained – the anthropologist, the field worker, the social activist. A photograph becomes the material object of discussion, and enables reflection. Just as the impulse of the oral history method was to hear and listen to the voices of participants in producing knowledge, photovoice enables individuals to identify and speak of what is meaningful to them, through the use of images and photographs taken by them.

The migrants in the study among low-income migrants, were a highly heterogenous group, engaged in diverse and precarious occupations, residing in dense settlements in varied locations in the city. For the purpose of photovoice, some homogeneity of the group was necessary. We felt it would allow for a more meaningful engagement over time, rather than short, one-off interactions with a large number of heterogenous individuals. Interested migrants with some shared characteristics were interviewed through the course of research. This process led to a group of migrant domestic workers being identified in each city, a migrant labourer group in Guwahati and in Jalandhar, migrants accessing HIV interventions via a non-governmental organization.

Participants were asked to use the camera, to depict aspects of their lives as migrants in the city. After an initial orientation meeting, each group was invited to at least two workshops to ensure that discussions based on their photographs, moved from descriptions to analysis of the problems. Through the images, participants raised a range of issues to highlight their aspirations, working and living conditions, household labour and work burden, freedoms in the city as well as domestic violence and abuse they experienced. Discussions were held in local organizations, expanding our understanding of the difficulties faced by migrants and of NGOs working with migrants.

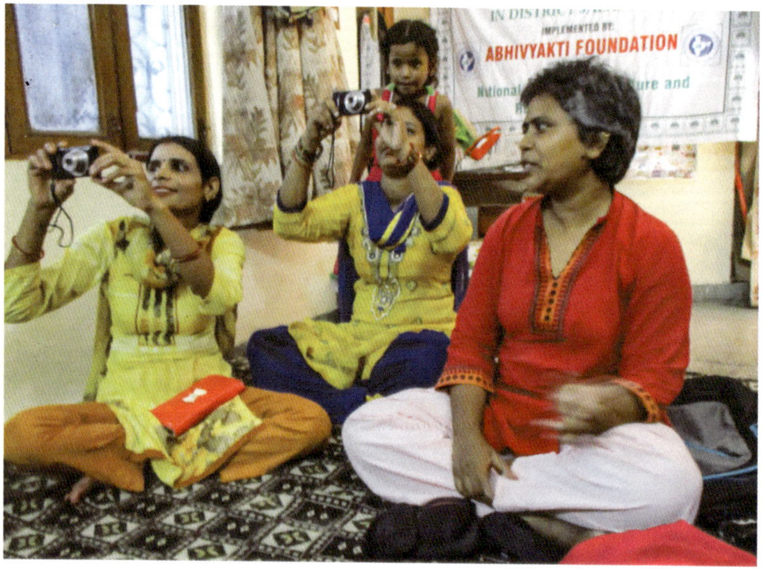

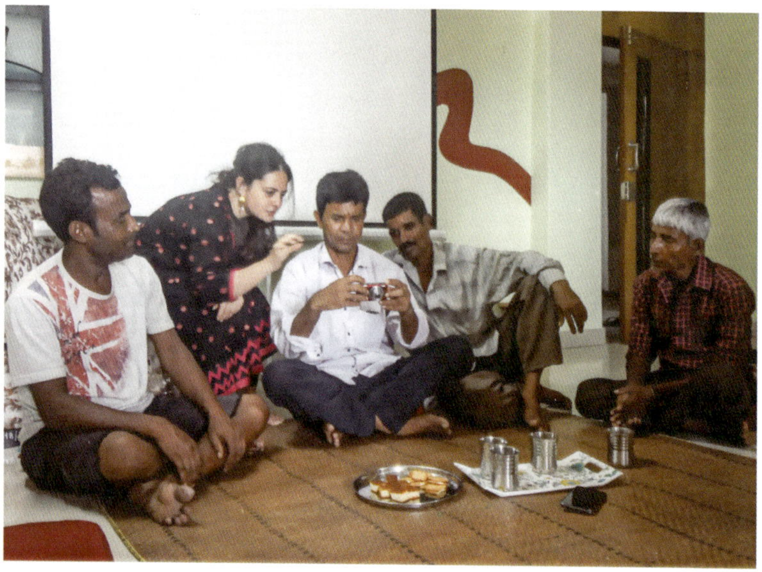

Project team members, Bharti and Anuj, conduct camera workshops for training migrant workers in Photovoice.

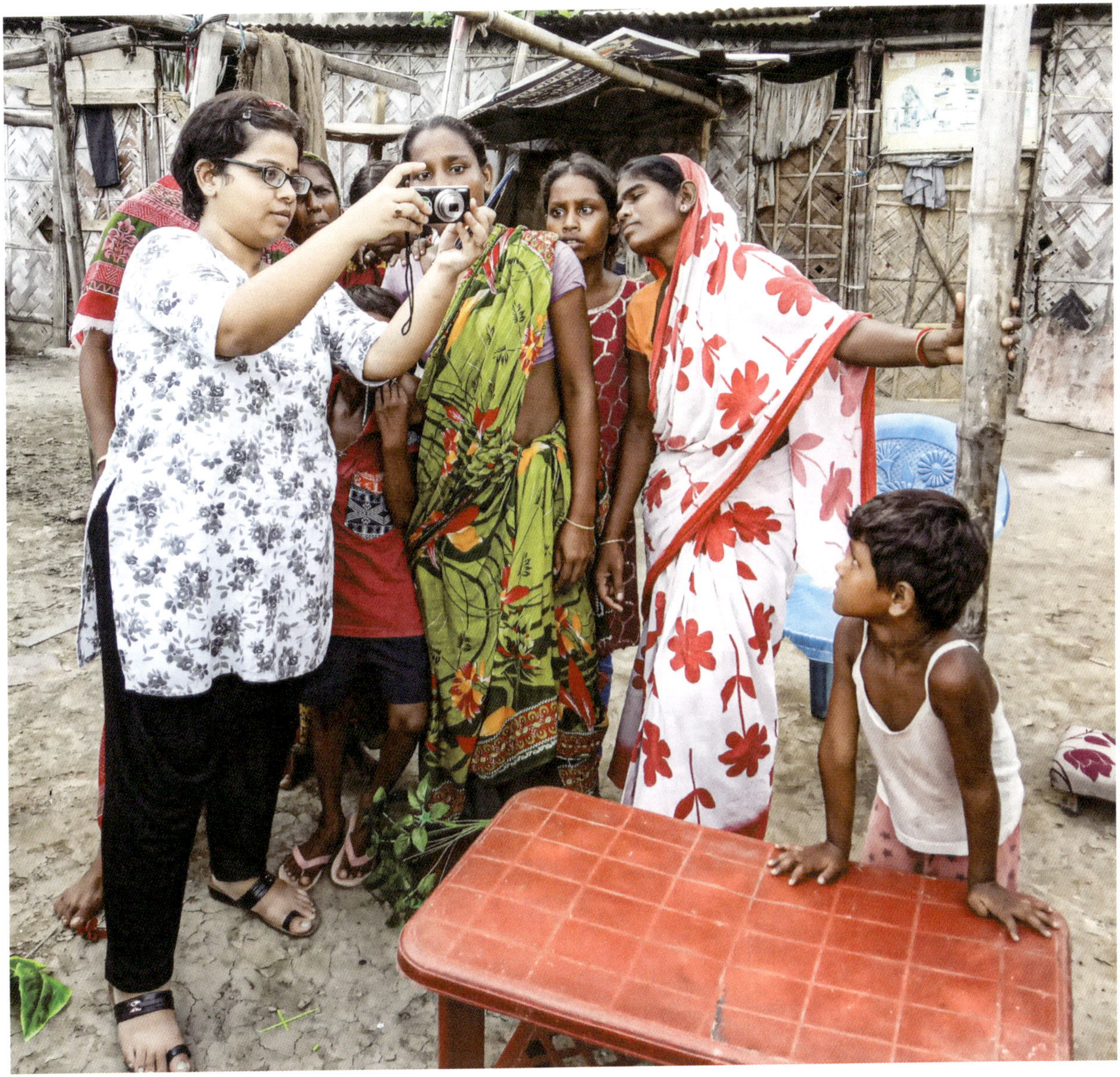

At Dhirenpara, Guwahati, Anuprova explains the camera, framing, and camera angles to women migrant workers.

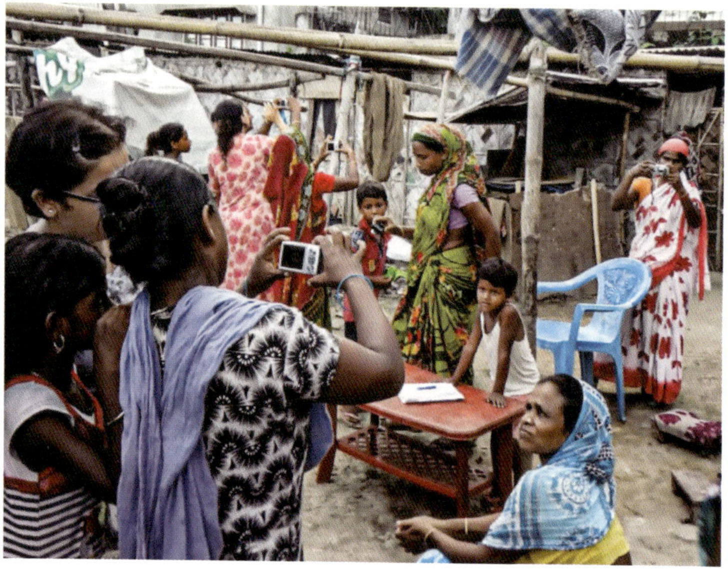

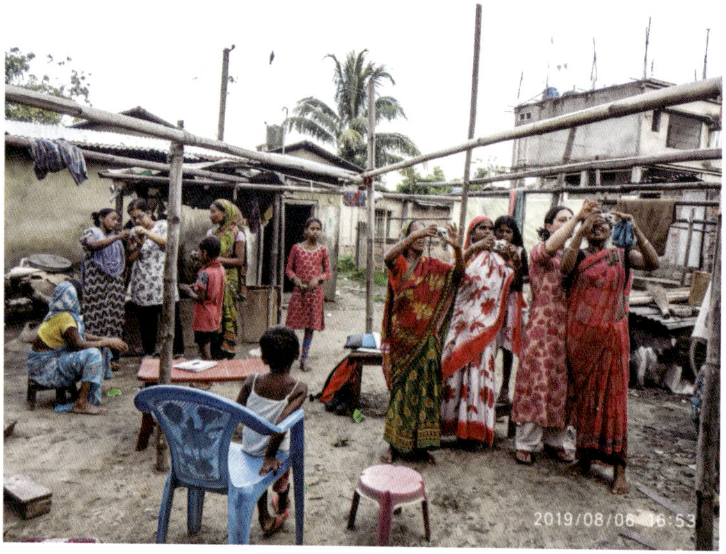

Camera angles explained during a photoshoot.

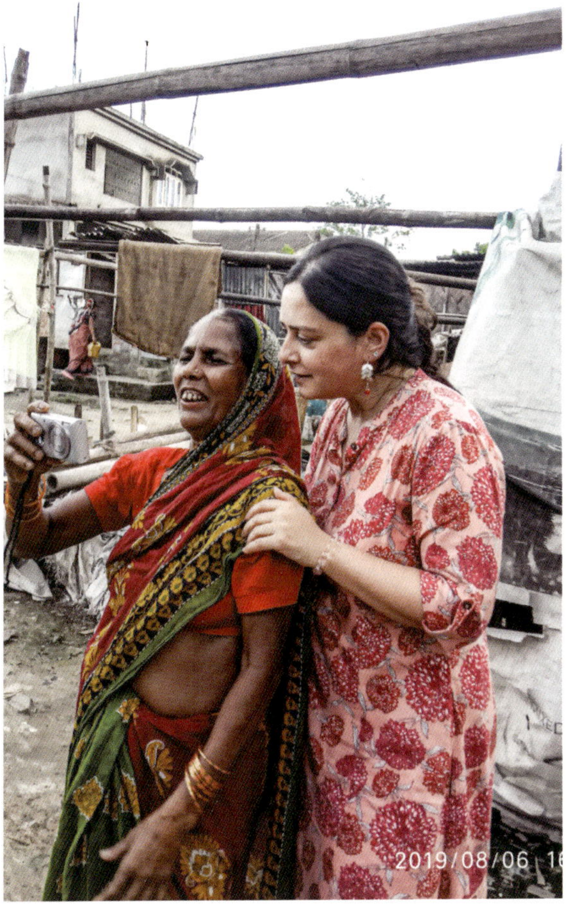

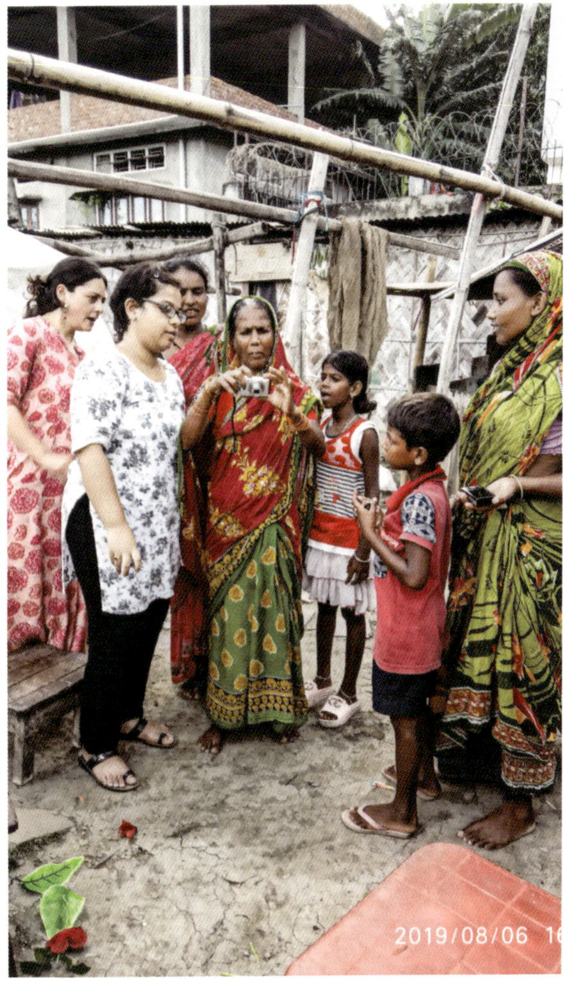

A woman shows the photographs
she has taken that are important to her.

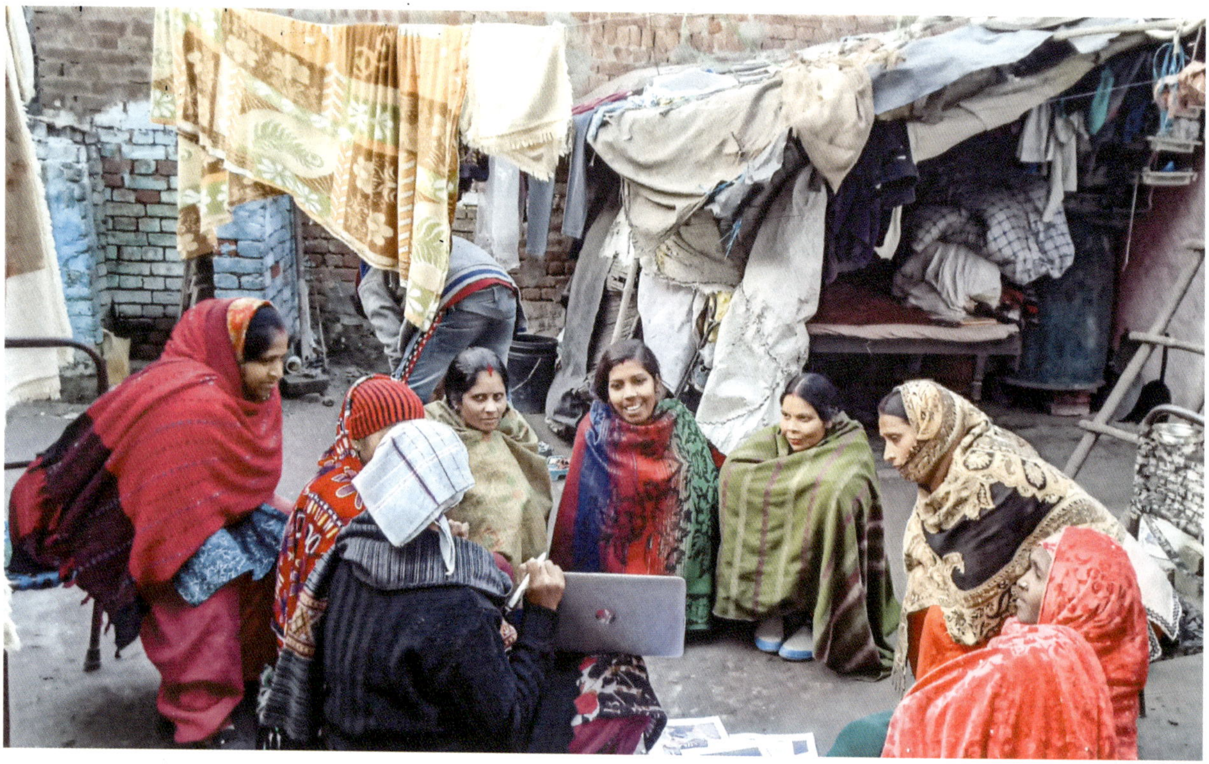

A photovoice session. After the photographs were taken, participants were asked to explain their images to the researchers.

References

Wang, C., & Burris, M. A. (1997). Photovoice: Concept, methodology, and use for participatory needs assessment. *Health education & behavior, 24*(3), 369-387.

Kapilashrami, A., & Marsden, S. (2018). Examining intersectional inequalities in access to health (enabling) resources in disadvantaged communities in Scotland: advancing the participatory paradigm. *International journal for equity in health, 17*(1), 1-14.

Contributors

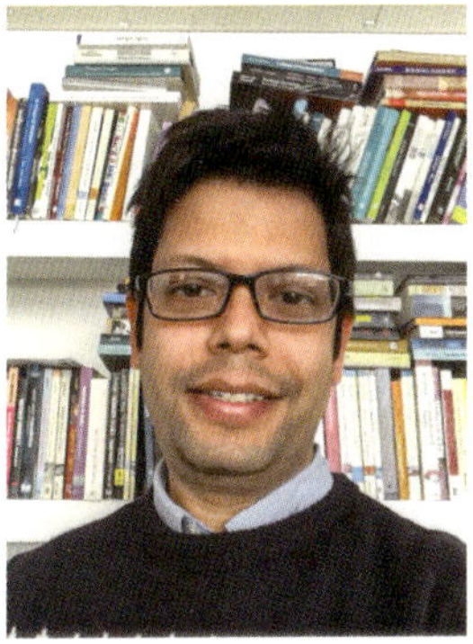

Jeevan R. Sharma is Senior Lecturer in South Asia and International Development at the University of Edinburgh. He is the author of *Crossing the Border to India: Youth, Migration and Masculinities in Nepal*, Temple University Press, 2018 (South Asian Edition published by Bloomsbury Academic India in 2019) and *Political Economy of Social Change and Development in Nepal, Bloomsbury Academic* (Forthcoming, 2021). He has carried out anthropological research on culture of migration, politics of aid funded interventions in Nepal, and on low-income migrants in Indian cities. His work has focused on labour migration in the context of social, economic and political transformations in Nepal Himalaya and South Asian region, especially culture of migration, border crossing, gendered, classed and racialized mobility of labour, ill-treatment, access to justice, and citizenship in South Asia. He is the Co-Editor of *Himalaya* and an Associate Editor of *South Asia: Journal of South Asian Studies*.

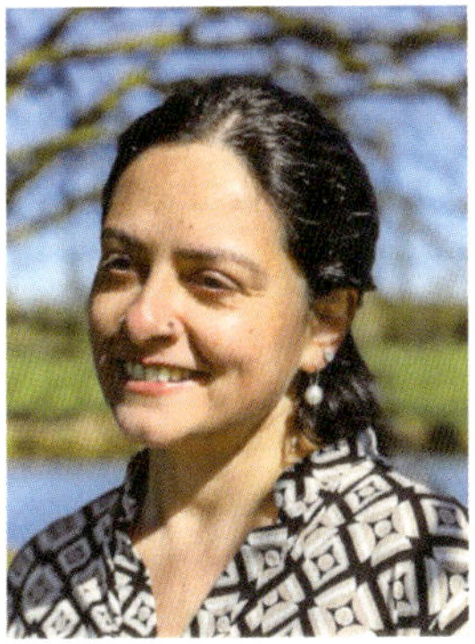

Anuj Kapilashrami is an interdisciplinary social scientist trained in Sociology and Public health working in the field of Health Policy and Systems research. She is a Professor in Global Health Policy and Equity in the School of Health and Social Care at the University of Essex. Her work lies at the intersections of health policy and development praxis, with particular interest in the social and structural determinants of health, and the rights and equity implications of public health policy and governance. She has longstanding research interest and experience that spreads over two decades and spans across both academia and civil society/development sector in South Asia and the UK. Her recent scholarship advances intersectionality – conceptually and methodologically – and its application in understanding health inequalities and structural determinants of health. Her current research focuses on migration as a structural determinant of health (in India, Central Asia and the UK) and examines how intersecting gender and other social inequalities (race/ethnicity, indigeneity, class) shape experiences of health, access to health and social protection, and gender violence. She is founding chair of the Migration Health South Asia network, a community of scholars and practitioners advancing regional evidence-base on migration health, and Gender Equity advisor to the SRHR programme of the World Health Organization.

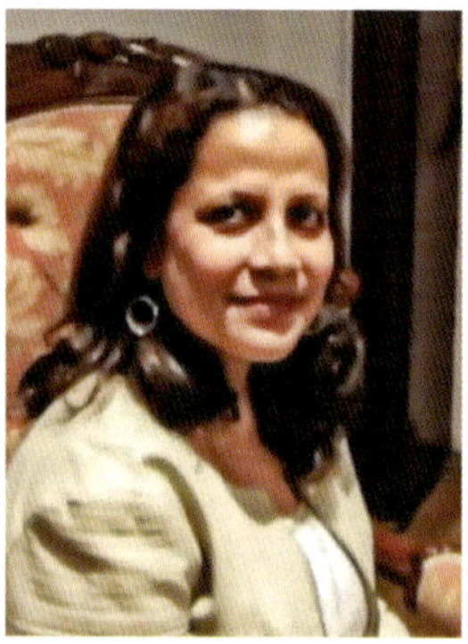

Anurita Hazarika has been associated with the North East Network (NEN) since 1998, beginning her stint with one of the earliest women's rights organizations of northeast India as a student volunteer and now is the State Coordinator of Assam. She has been vocal on women's issues by publishing fact sheets and reports to influence policy makers and also influence public opinion on issues of discrimination and abuse on women. At NEN, she has been instrumental in building women's leadership at grassroots level by setting up women's centre in villages called Gramin Mahila Kendras. She started connecting women survivors of violence to livelihood issues which is now popularly known as Saneki Weaves. Anurita has a Master's degree from Gauhati University and also attended a Women's Human Rights course at the University of Oxford. On the side she likes travelling and gardening.

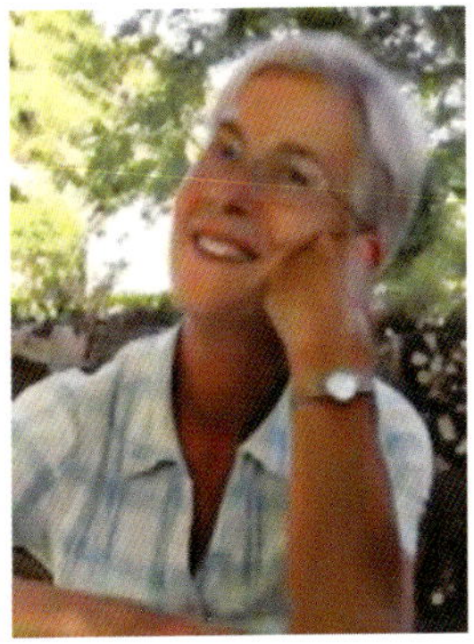

Patricia Jeffery is Emerita Professor of Sociology, University of Edinburgh, where her teaching included aspects of gender studies, especially Gender and Development, and race and ethnicity. Since 1970, she has conducted fieldwork in various parts of South Asia, focusing on gender politics, social demography, education and its links to women's status and demographic change, and childbearing (including pharmaceuticals and the [mis]use of oxytocin during childbirth). Her publications include *Migrants and Refugees: Muslim and Christian Pakistani Families in Bristol* (1976); *Frogs in a Well: Indian Women in Purdah* (1979); *Labour Pains and Labour Power: Women and Childbearing in India* (1989); *Don't Marry me to a Plowman: Women's Everyday Lives in Rural North India* (1996); and *Confronting Saffron Demography: Religion, fertility and women's status in India* (2006). In 2009-2010 she held a *British Academy/Leverhulme Trust Senior Research Fellowship* and Leverhulme Research Fellowship.

Her other activities have included membership of the Joint Committee on South Asia of the Social Science Research Council and American Council of Learned Societies (New York), of the Economic and Social Research Council Research Grants Board, of the Medical Research Council Global Health Faculty of Experts, of the British Academy South Asia Panel; consultancies on reproductive and child health projects in India and Pakistan; membership of the Technical Advisory Group for the PATH Oxytocin Initiative; and acting as expert witness on behalf of immigration and asylum appellants in UK. Until recently, she was Chair of the British Association for South Asian Studies.

She is preparing a book manuscript based on her long-term ethnographic work in a Muslim village in rural western Uttar Pradesh, contextualizing the demographic transition in relation communal politics and 'jobless growth'.

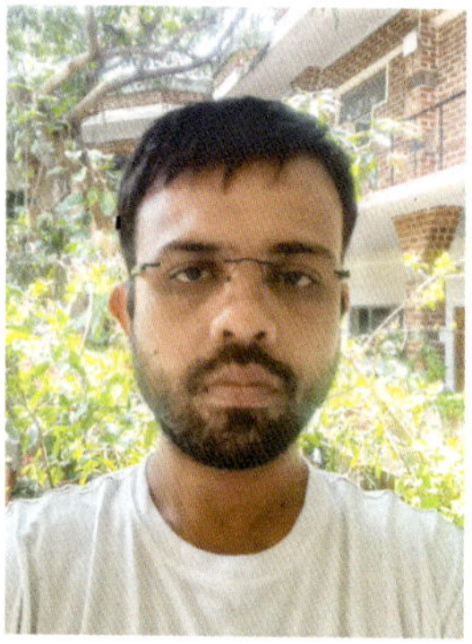

Anurag Sharma has studied Bachelors in Civil Engineering from Indian Institute of Technology Delhi and Masters in Development Studies from TISS Mumbai. In addition to his work on urban migrants in Jalandhar for collaborative ICSSR-ESRC research project, he has worked on grassroots organizations on issues around watershed management and MGNREGS. Currently he is working on community groundwater management with Gram Vikas, a non-profit that works in Adivasi area of Odisha on issues around health, sanitation, drinking water and livelihoods. His research interests include migration, labelling, masculinity, community groundwater practices and perspectives, and workplace politics and dynamics.

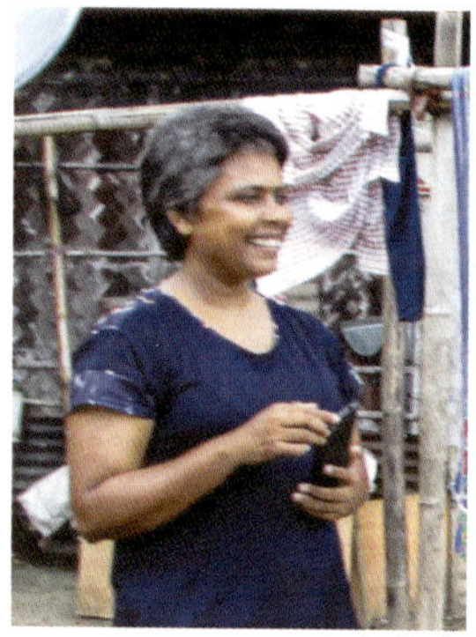

Bharti Kumari is a Social Work graduate and currently pursuing M.Phil. in Women's Studies from TISS, Mumbai. Her M.Phil. research topic is "*Presence of elected women representatives in rural local self-governance and women- friendly space in the gram panchayat- A study in the Kalahandi district of Odisha*". She has worked at the grassroots on the issues of women empowerment, child rights and strengthening of local democratic institutions. Her broader research interest area includes Gender, Migration, Interfaith disputes and Religious violence. She also intends to work on interfaith peace and harmony initiatives.

Anuprova Ghose is currently doing a Post Graduate Programme in Development Management at the Indian School of Development Management. Prior to this she used to work with Factchecker.in, a data journalism platform as a Factchecker. She has experience working with organizations like We.Log Trust, North East Network, The YP Foundation and North Eastern Social Research centre in various capacities.

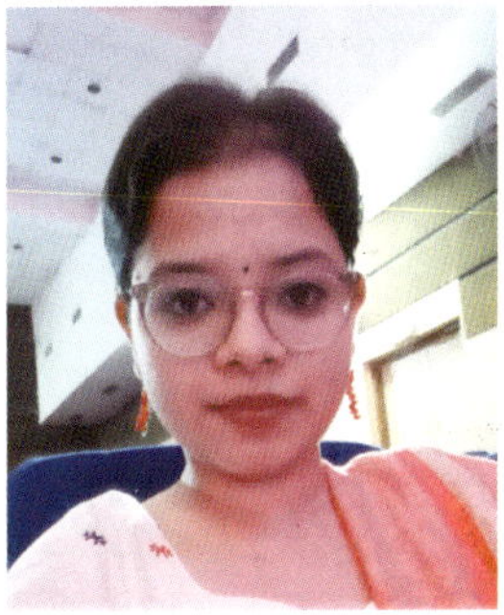

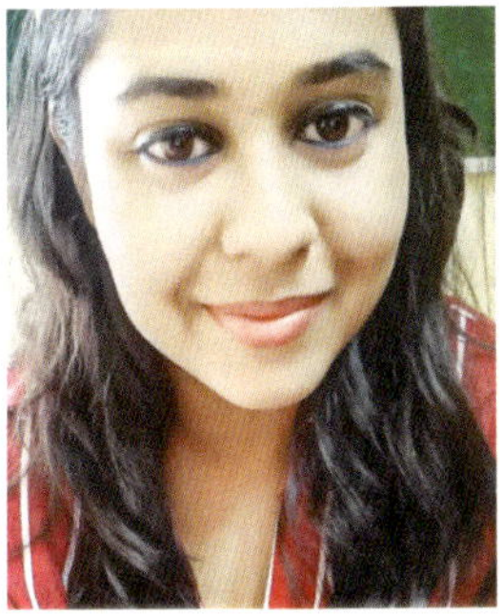

Ashapurnaa Dutta (uses pronouns – She/Her/They) is a full time Researcher and a Mental Health Professional (MHP) currently pursuing her M.Phil-Ph.D. from the Tata Institute of Social Sciences (TISS) Mumbai, with specialization in Health Systems Management. She's simultaneously working on a social innovation project titled 'Quality Health Rights and Decolonizing Generational Mental Health in the Global South' representing India. She has previously worked with organizations namely the World Wide Fund for Nature (WWF-India), Alzheimer's and Related Disorders Society of India (ARDSI), in Special Schools like Sevadaan (Mumbai) and Ashadeep (Assam) for Children with Austism, and engaged with grassroots movements such as Mission Birubala (on women empowerment and against witch hunting), Value-based Education (VBE in government-run schools) in India. She is a life skills' trainer by passion who consults for corporate organizations. She is currently writing her first book on Female Childhood Cancer in Indian Society stemming from her ten-years' long research on the decadal transformation of India's booming medical sector and the bio-psycho-political element of existence as survivors of Cancer in India. She was involved in an ESRC-ICSSR funded project with the University of Delhi and University of Edinburgh examining migrants' experiences on behalf of North East Network in Guwahati, Assam. She was part of the research team, on behalf of NEN, of the ESRC-ICSSR funded collaborative project between the University of Delhi and the University of Edinburgh examining the lives of low income migrants.